Wilderness Skiing and Winter Camping

796   Townsend, Chris.
.932   Wilderness skiing and winter camping / Chris
Tow   Townsend. -- Camden, Me. : Ragged Mountain Press,
        c1994.
          viii, 312 p. : ill.

        Includes bibliographical references (p. 283-285) and
        index.
        07104359   LC:93010902   ISBN:0877423970 (pbk.)

        1. Cross-country skiing. 2. Snow camping. I. Title

    1169   93OCT16   mu/ul   1-01018916

Wilderness Skiing and Winter Camping

Chris Townsend

RAGGED MOUNTAIN PRESS

Camden, Maine

Published by Ragged Mountain Press

10 9 8 7 6 5 4 3 2 1

Library of Congress Cataloging-in-Publication Data
Townsend, Chris.
Wilderness skiing and winter camping /Chris Townsend.
    p. cm.
Includes bibliographical references and index.
ISBN 0-87742-397-0
1. Cross-country skiing. 2. Snow camping. I. Title.
GV885.3.T68 1993
796.93'2--dc20   93-10902

Questions regarding the content of this book should be addressed
to:

    Ragged Mountain Press
    P.O. Box 220
    Camden, ME 04843

Questions regarding the ordering of this book should be addressed
to:

    TAB Books
    A Division of McGraw-Hill, Inc.
    Blue Ridge Summit, PA 17294
    1-800-233-1128

A portion of the profits from the sale of each Ragged Mountain Press
book is donated to an environmental cause.

Wilderness Skiing and Winter Camping is printed on 60-pound Renew
Opaque Vellum, an acid-free paper that contains 50 percent recycled
waste paper (preconsumer) and 10 percent postconsumer waste
paper.

Illustrations by Mike Walsh
Photographs by Chris Townsend
Printed by Arcata Fairfield, Fairfield, PA
Design by Joyce C. Weston
Production and page layout by Molly Mulhern
Edited by Dorcas Susan Miller, DeAnna B. Lunden, Pamela Benner,
and Annie Getchell

Contents

Acknowledgments

Too many people have contributed to this book and to my knowledge of skiing and winter camping for me to mention them all here. Some I must single out, however.

Mike Walsh drew the diagrams with great care and skill. Without them the book would be the poorer.

Cameron McNeish taught me how to ski in the Cairngorm Mountains of Scotland in the spring of 1983 and kindled a flame that has continued to grow.

Peter and Pat Lennon of Mountain and Wildlife Ventures, Ambleside, England, are two of the most experienced wilderness skiers around and have made many successful expeditions to Greenland and Svalbard. I've learned much from skiing with them and from our long discussions on techniques and equipment.

Brian Thomson of Highland Guides, Aviemore, Scotland, gave much advice and very generously loaned me equipment for trial use for this book. Over the years I have also learned much from other people involved with Highland Guides, especially Iain Hudson, Ian Maples, Ivan Trundle, Chris Hawson, John Eames, and Stevie and John Brown.

Information on gear was provided by Bill Wilson of Alpina Scotland, distributor of Tua skis; Gordon Ross, distributor of Karhu skis; Gary Richter of Merrell Footwear; Black Diamond; Snowsled; Alpina; Voilé; and Rainey Designs.

My thanks to Andy Smith, Dave Calder, and Johnny Walsh for solving computer-related problems during the preparation of this book.

I've also learned a great deal from those I've toured with, especially Chris and Janet Ainsworth, Scott Steiner, Todd Seniff, Clyde Soles, Denise Thorn, Rowena Thorn, Helen Charlton, and the members of Tyneside Loipers ski club.

Finally, thanks to all those who have been on tours and courses I have led for Mountain and Wildlife Ventures and Highland Guides. I hope they all learned as much as I did.

My views, of course, are my own, as are any errors. None of the persons mentioned should be assumed to agree with what I have to say. Indeed, I know that some of them will disagree strongly with some of my opinions!

Introduction

Snowflakes fall gently from a soft, gray sky, slowly blanketing the land. The scars of summer—eroded paths, flattened campsites, scraps of litter—disappear and the wounded mountains recover their wild glory. Winds whip the snow, swirling it high into the sky, filling in gullies, plastering cliffs, forming spectacular cornices. Eventually the blizzard abates and the sun shines on a pristine white world. At first this reborn mountain wilderness lies silent. But soon a soft, rhythmic sound can be heard, barely loud enough to disturb the peace. The first skier is venturing out into the winter hills.

Under snow the wilderness is transformed. It cannot be compared to its snow-free state. For a mountain range or a forest to be known completely, it has to be seen in all its guises, in the depth of snowy winter as well as in the heat of summer. A light covering of snow can be walked over without too much trouble, but as the snow builds, walking becomes progressively harder, until eventually the strenuous slog through knee-deep or deeper snow can hardly be called walking at all.

With skis you float on top of the snow, flying through the forest and over the meadows, climbing to the summits and swooping down to the valley. These are cross-country skis, not the heavy, cumbersome alpine gear many people think of, the skis that require chair lifts and tows and all the objectionable mountain-destroying paraphernalia of the modern downhill ski resort. All you need for cross-country skiing is snow. And, of course, the desire to explore the white world of winter. Forget the expensive, flashy clothing, the fashionable après-ski bars, the lift tickets, the lines, the summit café. These are for the alpine skier bound to mechanical lifts, remote from the real winter landscape.

Cross-country skiing is everything from a slow shuffle along a snow-covered forest road to a fast, effortless traverse of rolling hills or a wild rush down a steep mountainside. You can take it as far as you like. It is the original form of skiing, developed thousands of years ago in Scandinavia by people who wanted to move easily across land that is snow covered for eight months of the year. It can be thought of, therefore, as merely a convenient extension of foot travel, a way, in essence, of walking on snow. But it is more than a utilitarian means of transportation; it is a form of travel in its own right, a way of moving that fits perfectly with snow country. I am now so used to being on skis when the snow lies deep that walking on snow feels clumsy, inappropriate, wrong.

Moving on skis requires little skill, but if you want to do more than shuffle along on the flat, learning a few basic techniques can make a surprising difference in how far you can go and how much fun you have. It is quite possible to climb and, even more unlikely to the novice, descend hills in control within a few days of first attaching skis, especially if you take some expert instruction. I remember clearly the feeling of achievement I had on reaching the summit of Creag an Leth-choin in the Cairngorm Mountains in Scotland just five days after I first put skis on my feet. I remember, too, my surprised delight when I discovered I could ski back down with only a few falls on the way.

Since that first taste of real skiing I have skied every winter and in many places, from the Rocky Mountains in both the United States and Canada to Norway and the Alps. The memorable times are many. A sunny day of crisp snow and sharp, frosty views seized from a gray winter of rain and wind. Fifteen miles across a high mountain plateau alone on a day when the skiing was suddenly easy and I felt I could go on forever. A December sunset on a mountaintop with the sky turning from pale pink to deep red, then to a dark ice blue, followed by an eerie descent down abandoned alpine ski trails in the freezing night. Climbing Mount Gordon on the Wapta Icefield on a day of blue sky and bright sun, with the vast mountain wilderness of the Canadian Rockies spread out on all sides. Struggling through the Kyrkjedori pass on the Halingskarvet ridge in Norway in an exhilarating blizzard. These and many more days and hours of magic are evoked by the thought of cross-country skiing.

The joys of ski touring are many and varied. For me the appeal lay initially in making travel easier in deep snow. Plodding through the spring snow of the High Sierras during a walk along the Pacific Crest Trail, I watched two skiers swooping down wide snowfields and gliding rapidly across frozen meadows. I vowed then never again to exhaust myself struggling on foot through soft, deep snow when I could be skimming over the surface. After a few days on skis I realized that skiing offered far more than the solution to moving over snow-covered terrain. The pleasure of a new physical discipline, a new physical sensation overwhelmed me.

If you enjoy snow and like to wander the hills in winter, you could well enhance your pleasure by learning to ski. Whether you like exploring the mysterious silent world of the winter forest or

A magnificent lunch stop on the summit of Norway's second-highest mountain, Glittertind, in the Jotunheimen Mountains.

climbing high into the mountains to top some winter summits, you can go faster and more easily on skis.

Much cross-country skiing takes place on prepared tracks in valley bottoms. Although such machine-cut trails can be fun to ski and are good for practicing techniques, if you want to get into the winter wilderness you have to leave them behind. The most exciting places to ski are high above the cut tracks.

Once you leave the tracks and the valley bottom and climb through the forest to the mountains, skiing becomes more akin to hiking, and many of the skills required are the same. And when you stay out for more than one day, sleeping in tent or snow-hole, it becomes ski backpacking. The techniques and equipment needed to undertake such ski tours safely and comfortably are the subject of this book.

I've been ski touring and winter camping for over a decade and have taught skiing and winter skills and led tours for several years. I hope this book will pass on some of what I have learned and encourage others to seek the freedom of the winter hills.

Note 1: Winter is not the time for beginners to start camping or traveling in mountain wildernesses. I have assumed a basic knowledge of backpacking and navigation skills in the chapters that follow. For those who would like more detailed information on these topics, I suggest looking at my *Backpacker's Handbook*.

Note 2: I have adopted two approaches to the problem of weights and measures. Where metric measurements have always been the norm, as with ski and pole lengths, I have not added English versions. Elsewhere I have followed the example of many gearmakers and used English units as the main system, giving the metric units in parentheses.

Starting Out

Ski: one of pair of long narrow pieces of wood etc., usually
pointed and turned up at the front, fastened under foot for
traveling over snow.

—The Concise Oxford Dictionary

A Brief Schuss Through the History of Skiing

Skiing started as a means of traveling over snow at least 5,000 years
ago. Cave drawings of skiers have been discovered in Norway and
Russia, and a fragment of an actual ski between 4,000 and 5,000
years old has been found in Sweden. Scandinavians have used skis
for travel and hunting throughout northern Europe and Asia from
those early days to the present day. *Ski* is a Scandinavian word, being
derived from the Old Norse *skith,* one translation of which is "snowshoe." Arguments are made that skis were first used in China and
taken west by migrating tribes, but most historians think that
Scandinavia is the origin. Not being an expert, I won't comment on
this debate. What is indisputable is that in Scandinavia skiing
remained important over the years both as a sport and for travel, and
at the end of the last century it began to spread around the world as
a major form of winter recreation.

Early skis were of basic design and made of wood. Upturned
tips were developed early, but otherwise skis were simply boards.
Often one long ski was used for gliding, a shorter one with fur underneath for gripping. One long pole was used for balance, propulsion,
and braking. Bindings were simple toe straps or loops of cord.

Modern skiing can be dated from 1868, when Sondre Norheim,

a 42-year-old tenant farmer from Morgedal in the Telemark region of Norway, won a major competition in Christiania (as Oslo was then known), the capital of Norway. This competition involved jumping, cross-country, and slalom (as downhill running was called, from *sla*, a smooth hillside, and *lam*, a track).

Sondre Norheim's superb skiing skills were only part of the reason for his success; just as important were his innovations in equipment and techniques. To the simple toe strap he added a cable of twisted birch roots that encircled the heel to give a much better linkage between foot and ski, which facilitated turning. He also made the first skis with side-cut, which also made turning easier. His skis were shorter than average, 240cm rather than the normal 300, and he used a shorter pole. But Norheim is most famous for introducing the telemark turn, which he used both as a stable finish to a ski jump and as a way of controlling his speed on downhill runs. He also developed the parallel turn, incorrectly known as the "christie," after Christiania, despite its origins in Telemark. Because the skiers raced uphill as well as down, Norheim developed a new technique for climbing, the herringbone.

After retiring from skiing at the age of 59, Sondre Norheim emigrated to the United States, settling in North Dakota, where he died in 1897. The renaissance of Norheim's telemark technique came about in his adopted country some hundred years after he invented it.

Another Norwegian, Fridtjof Nansen, demonstrated the usefulness of skis for exploring the remote polar regions of the world with his pioneering 40-day, 320-mile crossing of Greenland in 1888, a major breakthrough in Arctic exploration. And the superiority of skis for snow travel was brutally made evident in 1911 when yet another Norwegian, Roald Amundsen, led the first successful expedition to the South Pole: his party, on skis, had few difficulties, while at the same time Captain Robert Scott and his British party, who reached the Pole shortly after Amundsen, perished in the snows of Antarctica as they attempted to return from the Pole. They had been on foot. (Scott's party had set out with ponies and motor vehicles, but the ponies perished quickly from the cold and by falling into crevasses, and the vehicles broke down within hours, leaving the men to haul their sledges.)

Others had made long expeditions on skis before Nansen and Amundsen. In the United States, where skiing had been introduced by Norwegian immigrants in the 1840s, Jon Thorensen, better known as Snowshoe Thompson, made his first journey over the

Sierras from California to Nevada in 1856—carrying a mailbag weighing 42 pounds—on 270cm-long skis he had made himself. The 80-mile journey took just three days. He was paid $200 a month and made the journey again and again every winter for 20 years.

In the late nineteenth century the center for the growing sports of competition and recreational skiing moved to the Alps. With this move came the adoption of different techniques and the development of equipment specifically for skiing down steep slopes. Skis had been introduced in the Alps in the late 1870s, but it was 20 years later that Austrian Mathias Zdarsky started using much shorter skis for the steep terrain of the Alps, descending the slopes in an endless series of short turns and thus initiating the split between the two styles of skiing that have come to be known as nordic and alpine.

Zdarsky, known as the father of alpine skiing, seems to have been an eccentric, even downright unpleasant and vindictive, character. He insulted Norwegian skiing and ski equipment, starting a feud that echoes to the present day. While Zdarsky may have started the move toward modern alpine technique, it was another Austrian, ski instructor Hannes Schneider from Arlberg, who developed it. Schneider's Arlberg system of progressive instruction, popularized by Englishman Sir Arnold Lunn, became the standard form of skiing instruction in the 1920s and 1930s. The new alpine style took over, leaving telemarking to tourers in undulating terrain.

Mass downhill skiing and modern alpine ski resorts flourished following the appearance of the first fixed-heel bindings in 1950. Touring on free-heel gear continued in many areas, especially Scandinavia, but as cross-country skis became skinnier and footwear lighter in order to be more suitable for racing on cut tracks on the flat, they came to be regarded as unsuitable for mountain or wilderness use. It was assumed that ski mountaineering could be done only on alpine skis, a belief that hasn't totally died. The telemark turn was rapidly receding into skiing history.

Then in the early 1970s, probably the point of greatest divergence between the two styles, the telemark turn was rediscovered in Colorado by skiers who wanted to escape the alpine resorts and venture into the backcountry. New equipment was developed to meet the new demands, a process that is still continuing. The result is equipment and techniques suitable for wilderness touring anywhere in the world. Many major journeys have been made using nordic gear in the last 20 years, including the first expedition to the North Pole without dogsleds or air support, by two Norwegians, and a circumnavigation of Mount Everest by American skiers Ned Gillette and Jan Reynolds.

Defining Terms

The term *skiing* has come to mean alpine skiing to the majority of people, while the original style usually has "cross-country" or "nordic" attached to it, implying it is a secondary version. However, as befits its position in this book, I have used *skiing* as the general term for cross-country skiing, only using qualifying words when necessary for clarity. It is alpine skiing that is the more specialized modification.

In addition to the terms *nordic* and *cross-country*, a variety of other names, such as langlauf, classical, freestyle, telemark, cross-country downhill (XCD), free-heel, and backcountry are given to different aspects of skiing. Randonnee, slalom, and downhill refer to types of alpine skiing.

These various names are often used interchangeably, which can lead to confusion. Rough definitions have evolved in recent years, but there is still some crossover. *Nordic* is a general term that embraces all the others. *Cross-country* is often used as a general term too, but, confusingly, it is also used to mean skiing only in machine-cut tracks. *Langlauf* refers to valley and forest skiing in tracks as well. Track skiing itself splits into two disciplines: classical, which uses the traditional diagonal stride, and freestyle, which uses various skating techniques first introduced in the early 1980s. *Telemark* refers not only to skiing downhill using the telemark turn on groomed pistes at alpine ski resorts or in the mountains but sometimes also to mountain touring or any skiing on metal-edged skis. Free-heel skiing, cross-country downhill, and nordic downhill also mean downhill skiing but include all turns, not just telemarks. Wilderness skiing means skiing in remote country away from cut tracks and prepared pistes. It is sometimes called ski touring, the European term, or when peaks are climbed, ski mountaineering, and it can be done on either alpine or nordic skis. When nordic skis are used, both track and cross-country downhill techniques may be used. Other names for wilderness skiing are backcountry skiing and, when camping is involved, ski backpacking.

Why Not Alpine?

A few ski tourers (more in Europe than North America), especially those who climb high mountains, prefer to use alpine skis, arguing that skinny free-heel skis are too unstable and difficult to use on steep terrain. This is a valid viewpoint, but it is not mine, so if you want to learn about alpine ski touring you will have to look elsewhere. My choice of free-heel gear for touring is based on having tried alpine ski mountaineering on several occasions. I found the rigid plastic boots painful and restrictive and the skis and bindings (which can be released at the heel for travel on the flat) heavy and tiring. I will admit that it is much easier and faster to descend steep icy slopes on alpine gear than it is on free-heel equipment, but it is far easier to travel on the flat and uphill on the latter. Further, I know on nordic gear I would have reached earlier in the day—when the snow was still soft—many of the icy descents I have made on alpine skis. And modern telemark skis and techniques bring even the steeper slopes within the province of the skilled free-heel skier. For the person who wants to explore the hills on skis, traveling through them as well as up and down, lightweight, flexible free-heel skis are ideal. For myself, I decided after a final week of alpine ski mountaineering in the Algäu Alps that in the future I would ski only terrain I could handle on free-heel gear.

Ways to Learn

You don't need to be a highly proficient technical skier to go touring. The more skillful you are, however, the easier you will find skiing and the farther you will be able to go. You will also be able to explore more rugged terrain and feel comfortable on difficult types of snow.

Once you have some basic skills you can start touring, refining your style and picking up new techniques as you go. While you can teach yourself by trial and error, it is usually a very slow process and can lead to the development of bad habits that may prove hard to shed. It is far better to have proper instruction when you start, at a specialist ski school or with a professional mountain guide. The American Mountain Guides Association (see Appendix C for the address) can provide a list of guides and outfitters.

A less effective way to learn is from a book. This may sound strange in a book on skiing, but my own experience is that books are best used as adjuncts to instruction and practice. Written descriptions of techniques are more useful after I have grasped what I am meant to do. However, books provide good general information on ski equipment and on touring gear and techniques.

Nordic skiing is rarely covered in ski magazines, which usually focus on alpine skiing. But *Cross-Country Skier* covers all aspects of skiing, from track to telemarking, and appears monthly from October to February. A useful column always worth reading is Alan Bard's "Backcountry." *Backpacker, Couloir,* and *Outside* magazines occasionally run reviews of ski gear.

Fitness and Training

Lack of fitness is a problem common to many ski tourers, particularly novices. I have been on tours with fairly experienced skiers who have found what should have been an enjoyable experience turned into an ordeal because of inadequate training. Wilderness skiing is a strenuous activity, particularly if long camping tours are undertaken or high mountains climbed. Good aerobic fitness is essential, so if you don't exercise regularly it is worth doing so several months before a ski tour. Cycling, running, swimming, and walking, especially hill walking with ski poles, are all worthwhile. Wilderness skiing also requires flexibility, so stretching exercises are good preparation. Steve Ilg's *The Outdoor Athlete* contains skiing exercises that will be helpful if you like to structure your exercise routine.

Regular wilderness walkers and backpackers will probably find they are fit enough for skiing, though they may find their arms ache the first few days of each season. That happens to me, and each autumn I vow that the next summer I will work hard at maintaining my arm and shoulder strength. I haven't gotten around to it yet. Maybe this year! Mountaineers and climbers are better off, since upper-body and arm strength is part of their game.

For off-season training you can use roller skis or roller blades (on parking lots and other hard surfaces). I have tried them and have to say that I hate them. Skiing is about traveling in the wilderness, about the freedom of the mountains, and I find imitation skiing on artificial surfaces a travesty. I would much rather keep fit by going for long walks in the hills and woods.

Ways to Go

Day tours are fun and a good way to explore easily accessible country close to lodges and trailheads. Once you head for remoter areas and go deeper into the wilderness, some form of overnight accommodation is needed. It is, anyway, far more satisfying to spend your nights as well as your days in the wild, to fully experience what the winter wilderness has to offer. Staying out also allows you to undertake long tours. There are a number of overnight options, depending on the area you are touring in and your own preferences.

A few mountain areas have networks of huts or lodges, some with good facilities, such as meal services and hot water. Others merely provide a roof over your head, with perhaps a wood-burning stove and bunks to sleep on. Hut systems are most common in the Alps and the mountains of Norway and Sweden, though there are

Getting ready for a day tour outside a hut in Norway.

some in parts of the Appalachians and the Canadian Rockies and along the Tenth Mountain Trail and in other areas of the Colorado Rockies. The big advantage of hut networks is that you can tour with a relatively light pack and know that there is secure accommodation at the end of each day. The best routes between huts are often marked with sticks or poles, making navigation easy.

In most North American wilderness areas and mountain ranges, however, camping or building snow shelters is often the only option. Heavy loads are then the norm. Multiday or even multiweek tours in remote regions are serious expeditions and are only for those who have a fair degree of experience or go with an experienced tour leader.

Solo Skiing

Most people ski as part of a group, whether with an organized tour or a small, informal party of friends. Apart from the pleasure in sharing the mountain experience, skiing in a group is good safety. Some people, however—and I am one of them—relish the freedom of being alone in the wilderness. Being able to make snap decisions about when and where to go, about whether to make camp early or climb that delectable-looking slope in the distance for the excitement of the descent heightens greatly the intensity of being in the mountains. My awareness of the wilderness, my contact with it, is immeasurably greater when I am alone. But solo skiing is potentially dangerous, and I have done most of my skiing with other people. Skiing in the wilderness should always be done conservatively, but when I go alone I am even more careful, constantly aware of where I am and what the risks are.

Planning a Tour

There are a number of factors to consider when planning a ski tour. The first is that it probably won't turn out as intended! There are two variables you cannot plan for: the weather and the nature of the snow. Either can cause you to change your plans totally. So, however detailed a plan you have put together, it is always wise to be prepared to ditch it if you have to and accept a less ambitious alternative. Rarely—but it does happen—conditions are such that you do far more than you intended. Whichever is the case, it is advisable to revise the next day's plan the night before in light of the weather and snow conditions and the state of the party. In some cases it is necessary to revise again the next morning because of worsening or unexpectedly improved conditions.

You still need an overall plan, and a number of questions need answering. What are your goals for the trip? To climb peaks or do a through-tour from A to B? Everyone should understand and agree on the aims of the trip if disputes aren't to arise later. All tour participants should look at the map too, so they know what to expect. The size and experience of the party is very important; larger parties will usually take longer to cover a distance than small ones, and any trip must be within the capabilities of the least-experienced skier.

Will decisions be made democratically, or will an experienced skier be the leader, having the final word if necessary? People have different skills, so it may be that one person does most of the navigating, another the cooking. Decide this before you go.

Prior to planning a route you need to know how many days you have for the tour and how far you expect to travel each day. Twelve to 15 miles (20 to 25km) a day is a good average for a fit and experienced party to aim for in reasonable snow conditions in mountain areas. Are there any huts or cabins in your chosen area? Even if you intend to camp you should note their position, as they may be needed in an emergency. Are you going to move on every day, or do you want to spend a few days at each camp while you climb nearby peaks? If you want to climb, will ice axes and crampons be needed? Are there lodges or stores near your route where you can resupply, or must all the food for the tour be taken with you? Which routes look as though they might be feasible in bad weather? Are there cut tracks or marked trails in the area that could be used as escape routes? What is the weather usually like at that time of year? What overnight temperatures can be expected? If you are flying to your destination, what stove fuel will you be able to buy on arrival (fuel cannot be carried on aircraft)?

Good topographic maps are essential for planning, and guidebooks are useful if they are available for the area. Up-to-date information can be obtained from national park and national forest offices and from local ski shops, and it is always worth seeking out.

When and Where to Go

Although winter is usually thought of as the season for snow, spring is actually the best time for ski touring. The stormiest weather normally occurs in winter, and it is the time of the longest, coldest nights and the shortest days. Which is not to say that winter isn't a time for ski touring—just that it is wise to pick where you go carefully and not to be too ambitious in your planning. Go for lower and more sheltered areas early in the season. Lodges or huts are preferable to camping at this time too. March and April are often the best months for high-level touring. There is plenty of daylight and the weather is usually calmer and sunnier than earlier in the year. In the highest regions and after snowy winters, touring may continue well into May. In some areas you can ski throughout the summer, though you may have to carry your skis much of the time. Late-autumn skiing is sometimes possible too. Where to go? Well, where there are mountains there is snow, and where there is snow you can ski, so the choices are many.

Getting to the Snow

Traveling to the start of your adventure may seem simple, but there are a few points worth considering before you set out. The way in to remote roadheads may not be well plowed or even plowed at all, so off-road tires or snow chains might be essential. I use chains and have found them very useful at times. Cold temperatures while you are away may mean you need a lock deicer to get back into your car; the need for antifreeze in the radiator should be obvious.

Travel by train, bus, or, especially, air means you need to protect your gear. Ski bags are standard, but check that you can leave them somewhere while you are in the wilderness; they are rather heavy to carry around. If carrying them is unavoidable, try to get the lightest bag you can, or maybe make one from ultralight material. Airports usually have sturdy plastic bags. Take some duct tape to seal them with. The most vulnerable parts of your skis are the tips. They can be wrapped in foam padding (your sleeping mat is excellent if it will fit in the ski bag) or even socks. Some people also wrap foam around the tails and the bindings, but I have never done so, and so far haven't had any damage.

Ski Equipment

*Never ski the high fells without a piece of string; in
emergency it can secure broken goggles, rucksack, binding,
ski-stick basket or even trousers.*
—*A. H. Griffin*, Adventuring in Lakeland

Walk into a good ski store and the sheer amount and variety of equipment on display can be overwhelming. Even if you know roughly what you are looking for, making a final choice can be difficult. Just because equipment is described as being for the backcountry or the mountains doesn't mean it is. Knowing what features to look for will help ensure that you end up with the right gear for your sort of skiing. You also need to consider the details of materials and construction. In this chapter I have summed up what features to look for and the purpose of different types of gear. Equipment is changing rapidly, however, so I have also tried to indicate the direction of ski-gear development.

In places I have described specific items of brand-name gear in detail because I believe that is the best way to show the ideal features to look for or because the item is unique. I have used the gear I recommend, but my recommendation doesn't mean there is nothing else that works as well. There is good gear that I have never seen, let alone tried. Like every skier, I have preferences. I don't claim to be objective, and I'm wary of authors who do. Here you will find my views and opinions, all based on many years of ski-tour leading and instructing, but subjective for all that. Many skiers, especially experienced ones, will disagree with some of what I say. That's fine. These are simply recommendations and suggestions that I think will be helpful.

If you rush into buying gear you will probably find yourself replacing most of it within a few years. I speak, unfortunately, from experience. Fired up by my newfound enthusiasm and convinced it was best to learn on the gear I would be using later, I rushed out and bought a "mountain-touring" package a few weeks before I started learning to ski. Because I knew nothing about ski equipment, I didn't know I was buying mediocre skis, inadequate poles, and, most disastrous of all for a beginner, appallingly sloppy, unsupportive boots. The bindings, mind you, weren't bad. The poles broke the second week I used them; I replaced the boots in my second season after I had borrowed a friend's pair and discovered that it wasn't only my lack of skill that was making descents so difficult, and I bought new skis in my third season. All in all it was an expensive error.

A second mistake I made was to buy from an outdoor shop whose staff, while they knew all about backpacking and mountaineering gear, knew nothing whatsoever about ski touring, though they assured me glibly that the gear they were recommending was "ideal." Buy from people who use the gear themselves and know what they are talking about. If in doubt, ask. If you are still not convinced, go elsewhere.

If you already have some experience and are replacing items, trying out gear before you buy is a good idea. Total beginners won't be able to distinguish between different skis or boots, so this method isn't much help to them. Specialist retailers, ski centers, cross-country ski areas, and ski schools usually have demonstration or rental skis you can try, and specialist centers have expert staff who can point you in the right direction. They usually offer mail-order service too, so it is worth contacting them for advice and information.

If you are taking a course, it is better to rent gear from the ski school rather than buy in advance. Your instructor will be able to advise you on what is worth buying, and by the end of the course you will have some idea what to look for and what you like. I wish I had done this.

Before buying you also need to know what type of touring you intend to do—something that is easier to decide once you have done a little skiing.

There are roughly three levels of touring and touring gear, though all of them overlap, and equipment is interchangeable to some degree. The lightest gear is for the easiest terrain, so it is best to buy for the steepest, most rugged country you expect to encounter, not the gentlest. If you intend to stay away from steep slopes and icy terrain and prefer the idea of zipping through forests and speeding over undulating uplands and gentle hills, then general touring gear is the stuff to buy. If you want to head higher and tackle rugged mountain terrain, look for gear designed for mountain touring. Finally, skiers whose ambitions are for the longest, steepest descents they can find need heavy-duty telemark gear.

Whichever you choose, it is important that skis, bindings, and boots are compatible. Mismatched gear will be very difficult to use, and something will probably fail in time. Don't make the mistake of thinking that all gear that isn't compatible simply won't work—it can work, but not well. Some combinations just won't work. I have seen people trying to turn heavyweight skis with lightweight, sloppy boots or fitting heavy boots into lightweight bindings that then rip out under the strain. Compatibility means that items are designed to work well together.

Skis

Modern nordic skis are complex creations; there are a number of different designs, which I will discuss later. If you understand what each type is for and how they are put together, then it is easier to make the right choice. First, there are two types to exclude, one lying at each end of the spectrum of nordic skis. The first type is set-track and racing skis, which are too thin and light for touring out of prepared tracks; the second is the heaviest, widest telemark skis, which are designed for lift-served downhilling on groomed trails or for off-trail skiing on steep mountains, with ascents being done using climbing skins and with little or no flat or undulating terrain to traverse. Expert skiers can, and do, use skis from these categories for touring at times, but overall it is not a good idea for the novice or intermediate skier.

Design

Outlined below are a number of characteristics to consider when choosing a ski. They should not be taken in isolation; it is the combination that determines how well a ski will perform.

SIDE-CUT. To aid turning, skis need to be narrower at the waist than at the tip or tail so they form an elongated hourglass shape (see Figure 2-1). When a ski is put on its edge, this side-cut, as it is called, forms a curve, and the tip then leads the ski around the turn, the pressure of your foot causing the rest of the ski to pivot sideways. In general, more side-cut means easier turning, but touring skis have to do more than just downhill turns, so the ski with the greatest side-cut isn't necessarily the best. Other features also affect how easily a ski turns, but skis that will be used for downhill turns should have at least 7 to 8mm of side-cut.

CAMBER. One of the main functions of a nordic touring ski is to glide quickly and easily over flat and gently undulating terrain. The camber stiffness of a ski determines to a great extent how well it does this. The camber is the arch in the middle of a ski (see Figure 2-1). A classic cross-country ski rises high off the snow in the middle when there is no weight on it. This arched midsection, called the wax pocket, is in contact with the snow only when the skier applies pressure, kicks down on it. The rebound from the kick then speeds the ski along on tip and tail over the snow. On waxable skis, grip wax is applied to this area to prevent the ski from slipping backward when pressured onto the snow, hence the name wax pocket. On waxless skis this section is where the grip pattern is found. The type of camber that creates a wax pocket is called nordic camber, sometimes double

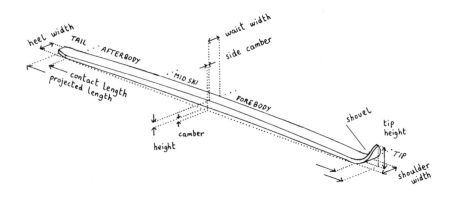

Figure 2-1. The cross-country ski.

camber (a confusing term, since skis can have only one camber). The stiffness of the nordic camber varies from ski to ski, with track-racing skis having the stiffest camber and telemark touring skis the softest.

There is a trade-off between gliding and turning. A ski with a very stiff camber that requires a forceful kick to press it into the snow will be much harder to turn than a ski with a softer camber; conversely, the softer-cambered ski will be slower on the flat. It also won't hold wax as well. Very soft-cambered skis turn more easily because they form an evenly curved arc, known as reverse camber, when weighted. Nordic-cambered skis bend at the tip and tail, leaving a long flat section in the middle. This can be seen by grasping a ski at the tip with the tail firmly on the floor and then pushing hard in the center. If you want a ski that will turn easily, look for one with a base that forms a smooth arc with no sharp corners or flat sections.

Because they are designed purely for downhill turning, alpine

Types of camber: nordic (left); alpine (right).

It's hard to squeeze the bases of nordic-cambered skis together.

Alpine-cambered skis can be squeezed together easily with one hand.

skis have a very soft camber so the skier's weight is distributed equally along their length. Many telemark skis come with alpine camber. This doesn't necessarily mean they are unsuitable for touring; you just have to work harder on the flats.

To test for camber, put the skis base to base and squeeze them together in the middle. With stiff-cambered skis it will be difficult to get the bases to touch, with soft-cambered ones it will be easy.

Which is best for touring? It depends mainly on your aims. Stiff-cambered skis are good for long tours over undulating terrain, softer ones (though still with a nordic camber) or even alpine-cambered ones for steeper, mountain terrain. If you go for stiff-cambered skis, make sure they aren't too stiff; if they are you will find them constantly slipping backward. Overall, the trend is toward softer nordic-cambered skis (ones that enable diagonal striding) for mountain touring and alpine-cambered skis for steep downhills and tours where there isn't much travel on the flat.

The paper test is a rough way to check that the camber isn't too stiff. While you stand on the skis at the point where your boots would go, have someone slide a large sheet of paper under the mid-section of the skis. With your weight applied equally to both skis, the paper should be relatively easy to slide out, but when you apply all your weight to just one ski, the paper should be impossible to remove. If it can still be pulled out, then the skis will require a dynamic kick to get them to glide and are too stiff for touring. If the paper can't be moved when your weight is on both skis, then the skis are very soft—fine for downhill turning but not so good for gliding on the flat.

For touring I prefer a soft nordic-cambered ski to a stiff one. When you are breaking trail through soft snow with a heavy pack on your back a fast glide isn't possible anyway. A shuffling slide is more likely. As well as being easier to turn, soft skis are easier on uphills because they require less effort to press the grip section into the snow. Of course, a ski that is too stiff for one person may be just right for someone heavier, so there is no "best" ski.

OVERALL FLEX. How much pressure is needed for a ski to go into reverse camber (or as close as you can get in nordic-cambered skis) is determined by its longitudinal stiffness, or flex. For soft snow a soft flex is best, for hard-packed snow a stiff ski. Telemark competition

This lineup demonstrates the variety of equipment available to cross-country skiers.

skis are stiff-flexing for more stability and better edging on packed runs. They are best avoided by tourers unless you know that most of the snow you ski will be hard and icy. Very soft skis, however, are often a bit unstable on hard snow, especially at faster speeds. A compromise is best for touring, leaning toward a softer- rather than a stiffer-flexing ski unless you usually ski on hard, icy snow.

TIP FLEX. The flexibility of the ski tip, here meaning the front quarter of the ski, is less important than the side-cut or camber, but it does play a part in how a ski turns. Stiff tips are good for hard snow or ice, as they edge well, but they tend to bury themselves in soft snow rather than ride over it, making for slow turning and hard work. Skis designed for lift-served telemarking usually have a stiff tip, those designed for powder snow a soft one.

Tip flex can be gauged by pulling the tip toward you with the ski tail on the ground and the base facing away from you. A soft tip will curve easily, a stiff one with difficulty. A medium to soft tip flex is best for most touring. A tip that flexes gradually well down into the body of the ski will track and turn better than a stiff tip that bends abruptly.

TORSION. If it is torsionally soft, a ski won't hold an edge well during turns on hard snow, so a good touring ski should resist twisting along its length. With your hands well apart along its length and with the tail on the ground, try twisting the ski. Reject any ski you can twist easily.

LENGTH. The old method of finding the right length of ski was by raising your arm in the air and choosing a ski that reached your palm. While this may be fine for track skiing (though even here shorter lengths are becoming popular), it produces too long a ski for easy turning. A better way is to select a ski that is your height plus 10 inches (25cm). This is only approximate, and 2 inches (5cm) one way or the other make very little difference, though it is better to err on the shorter rather than the longer side if you are doing much downhilling. I am 5 feet 8 inches tall (173cm), and I use 195cm skis. If you want more stable skis, go for wider rather than longer ones.

CENTRAL GROOVE. The shallow groove running down the center of the ski helps it glide in a straight line. All nordic-cambered skis have this groove. There is a belief, however, that the groove can hinder turning, and it has been dispensed with in many alpine-cambered telemark skis. Whether this matters or not I can't say, but I suspect it doesn't. I can't perceive any difference in tracking in a straight line or downhill turning. Not having a groove does make base waxing much easier.

CONSTRUCTION. How skis are built contributes greatly to their performance, and makers go into great detail in catalogs about their construction methods. Skiers often spend hours debating the merits of various methods, but the quality of manufacture and materials and selecting the right design features for your type of skiing are much more important than whether your skis have a beechwood, poplar, or fiberglass and polyurethane-foam torsion-box core or ABS plastic side walls or Titanal top decks. Nonetheless, for those interested, here is some information on ski construction.

Traditional wood skis (still available from companies such as Asnes and Tua) are made from solid blocks of wood. Modern synthetic skis are much more complex; they have outer walls and a core incorporating half a dozen or more different materials. Despite the name, synthetic skis may have wood cores, but they will be laminated layers rather than solid blocks of wood.

Skis need structural layers for load bearing and cores to give them shape. There are two common constructions: sandwich and box. In sandwich construction, layers of material are laminated together, with structural layers on the top and bottom and side walls added to protect the core. A typical heavy but tough sandwich construction for telemark skis consists of an upper structural layer of a durable ABS plastic top sheet over a Titanal aluminum sheet for even flex and torsional rigidity, a laminated wood core, a P-tex polyethylene base with carbon steel edges, and ABS plastic side walls. Lighter mountain-touring skis often replace the aluminum sheet with fiberglass and sometimes the wood core with polyurethane foam. Both types of ski may also contain other materials such as fiberglass, Kevlar nylon, and rubber to enhance strength and rigidity or to help in dampening vibrations.

In box construction the structural layer is wrapped around the core. Because the flex and stiffness of a box-construction ski cannot be precisely controlled, it isn't as good as sandwich construction for mountain-touring or telemark skis, but it is often used in general touring skis. The main disadvantage of sandwich construction is delamination, something I have seen happen on a number of occasions, usually at the tip.

Types of Skis

GENERAL TOURING SKIS. The lightest skis suitable for off-track touring, general touring skis don't differ that much in their dimensions from the heavier mountain-touring skis. The big difference is that they don't have metal edges and so aren't suited to steep slopes or terrain where ice and hard-packed snow may be encountered. Not having metal edges does make them lighter and faster on undulating terrain. General touring skis should be stiff-cambered for fast glide on flat terrain and have at least 7 or 8mm of side-cut for turning. They also need to be reasonably wide at the waist, not much below 50mm, so they won't sink in soft snow.

A typical example is the Asnes Skarven, which has tip-waist-tail dimensions of 63-54-58, giving a side-cut of 9mm and a weight (in a 210mm length) of 3¾ pounds (1,700 grams).

Still in this category but verging on the next are skis such as the

Karhu Kodiak (side-cut 60-52-57, weight 4¾ pounds/2,170 grams), which has metal edges just in the middle third, and skis that, although narrow and lightweight, have full-length metal edges, such as the Asnes Viking MT (side-cut 56-49-53, weight 4½ pounds/2,100 grams). These could be the skis to choose if you intend skiing mostly on undulating terrain and in soft snow but want to know you can cope with the occasional steep slope or spot of ice.

MOUNTAIN-TOURING SKIS. This category encompasses the skis most suitable for backcountry skiing in all its aspects. Mountain skis should have nordic camber for glide, at least 8mm of side-cut for turning, plus metal edges for icy terrain. Although slower than general touring skis, they will glide with relative ease along the flat; and while not as stable as pure telemark skis, they will handle most descents other than the steepest and iciest gullies. Good all-arounders in other words. They can even be used on the piste or in tracks. Compared with general touring skis, they have the weight and width to support heavily laden skiers heading into the wilderness with several days' supplies. Typical dimensions are 63-54-58, typical weights 5 to 5½ pounds/2,300 to 2,500 grams.

There are many skis in this category, each with different characteristics. Which you choose depends on your weight, where you will ski, and once you have skied enough to know, what type of ski you prefer. Most mountain skis used to have stiff nordic cambers and were basically beefed-up general touring skis. These days virtually all mountain skis have a soft camber to make them turn more easily, manufacturers having realized that turning ability is more important for wilderness skiers than being fast on the flat.

A good example of a well-established ski that used to have a very stiff camber but has become much softer with successive models over the years is the Fischer Europa 99 (side-cut 65-55-60, weight 5¼ pounds/2,400 grams). They turn easily and glide reasonably well. They have a soft flex that makes them a bit bouncy on hard snow but easy to turn in soft snow.

I prefer skis with a medium flex and a medium camber, my favorites being the long-established Karhu XCD GTs (side-cut 62-54-59, weight 5½ pounds/2,400 grams), which turn more quickly and easily than any other nordic-cambered ski I have used but are stiff enough to handle most types of snow. When I first tried the XCD

GTs after years of skiing on stiffer skis (Asnes Sondre Telemarks), I kept over-turning and had to learn to apply much less pressure than I was used to (this was before the camber of the Sondre was softened—current models, especially the MT2 Soft, turn very easily). Overall the XCD GTs feel almost as though they turn themselves. They glide reasonably well, but they are a bit slower and require slightly more effort than stiffer-cambered skis.

Mountain-touring skis being the most popular category, a large number of models are available, all with a choice of waxable or waxless bases. When buying new skis, try to get the latest information, as specifications and names of models may change. For example, the Sondre was previously known by the rather less snappy name of MT54.

TELEMARK SKIS. If you find yourself eyeing the steepest slopes longingly and peering down icy gullies wondering what it is like in there, or even just intend skiing regularly in mountainous regions with lots of steep climbs and long descents and not much flat work, then you will probably be better off with telemark skis. Designed to turn easily, they have alpine rather than nordic camber and lots of side-cut, from 12 to 20mm. They are also wide, 68 to 80cm at the tip, and heavy, 5¾ to 7 pounds/2,700 to 3,200 grams, which makes them stable at high speeds and in cruddy snow. Those with a very stiff flex are designed for telemark racing and lift-served skiing and should be avoided for touring use. The softer ones are good for mountain touring, though, and will even glide a little, but the lack of nordic camber may result

The author's favorite ski gear: Karhu XCD GT skis and Riva cable bindings.

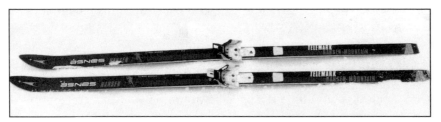

A wide ski suitable for long descents.

in wax stripping off fairly quickly. (This is the standard wisdom. Since I wrote it in the first draft of this book, I ascended a peak on icy snow on my Tua Wilderness telemark skis using klister. The party with me were all using nordic-cambered mountain-touring skis. On the summit I was the only person who had to scrape off the klister before the descent. And it wasn't because I had put more on my skis; I had waxed several of the other pairs with identical amounts. It is hardly conclusive, but it makes me wonder whether wax really does strip off alpine-cambered skis more quickly.) If you use skins (which I discuss later) on long steep ascents, you don't have to keep rewaxing or scrape off the wax at the top.

The telemark ski I have used most often is the Asnes Nansen Mountain (side-cut 73-56-66, weight 5¾ pounds/2,700 grams), which has a soft flex and a near-alpine camber. I bought them for high mountain touring with a heavy pack and took them on the six-week tour of the Canadian Rockies described in Chapter 10. They are very supportive in soft snow when carrying a heavy load and are stable on downhills too, especially on long-radius faster turns.

There are increasing numbers of telemark skis, many makers offering several models for general backcountry, off-piste telemarking, lift-served telemarking, and racing. The Tua models look exceptionally well made and designed (by Paul Parker, author of *Free-Heel Skiing,* the definitive work on nordic downhill techniques), with the Wilderness (side-cut 72-60-65) probably the best for touring. Needing a replacement for my worn-out Nansens, I bought a pair of Wilderness skis while writing this book. Initial use has shown they turn very easily on wind-blasted, rippled, icy snow and in shallow powder and they glide surprisingly well for an alpine-cambered ski. The stability, especially on steep slopes, is excellent. The extra width at the shovel also makes them good for bushwhacking in deep, soft snow. I have yet to take them on a multiday mountain tour, but so far I am very pleased.

Final Points to Look For

Once you have decided on a specific model of ski, it is worth renting a pair, if possible, to try them out and make sure they really are what you want. A day's skiing will tell you far more about a pair of skis than any amount of technical information will.

However good the reputation of the brand, there is always the possibility that a specific pair of skis will have faults, so you should check carefully the ones you are buying. While you can always exchange new skis that are faulty, it is best to minimize the possibility. A problem with a ski can ruin a tour, and a guarantee is no consolation at the time. Not that you can always spot potential flaws. I once took a new pair of skis on a two-week mountain tour in a remote area of northern Norway. By the end of the trip the tips were starting to delaminate. Another few days and I would have had a serious problem, yet there had been no sign of their splitting before the tour.

Apart from looking for signs of delamination, you should check that the top plate, base, and side walls aren't damaged in any way. Even if a ski passes this visual examination it may still have defects that lead to difficult skiing. Unless skis are straight they won't run straight. You can check them by looking along the length of the skis with the bases held together to see if they touch right across the ski at the tail and shovel. If there are any gaps, at least one of the skis is twisted. When squeezed together in the middle the ski bases should match exactly from tip to tail. Offset bases mean a warped ski that won't track properly. By running a flat edge along each base—a ski scraper will do—you can look for spots of light. If these exist the base isn't smooth, which can cause poor glide and, in a waxable ski, uneven wear of the wax.

Nothing can be done for warped or twisted skis, but uneven bases can be smoothed out. See the section on ski preparation and care (page 36) for how to do this. Note, too, that imperfections won't affect wilderness-skiing performance as much as they will skiing on the smooth, hard surfaces of set tracks or prepared downhill runs.

To Wax or Not to Wax

A far bigger problem for most people than choosing skis is deciding whether those skis should have a waxable or waxless base. Generally novices go for waxless bases, feeling, with some justification, that they have quite enough to learn without having to delve into the mysteries of waxing as well. Many skiers, as I did myself, then move on to waxable skis when they buy a second pair. Both bases, by the way, will glide better if glide wax is applied to the tips and tails.

A waxless base has a pattern cut into it that grips when pressed onto the snow, while a waxable base is smooth and needs wax applied to it to make it grip. In both cases the section that grips is the midsection of the ski. In skis with nordic camber this wax pocket is only in contact with the snow when under pressure, allowing the tips and tails to glide over the snow when the pressure is released. The difference between the two types of base is that while you can select a particular wax for a particular type of snow and a particular temperature, a waxless pattern has to cope with all conditions. Consequently, a well-waxed ski will always outperform a waxless ski. On the flat it will glide faster and farther with the same effort; on descents it will be easier to turn.

WAXLESS SKIS

Most waxless patterns are variations on the original Fishscale configuration introduced to nordic skiing by Trak (though it was first designed for alpine skiing with the intention of improving glide and stability). Some grip better than others, some glide better, but overall there is not much difference between them, and I suggest making the other characteristics of a ski the basis of your choice. Avoid positive waxless bases; their pattern is raised above the base and catches and drags on the snow. Thankfully, they are now quite rare. Most waxless bases are negative, the pattern being cut into them. Most skis with nordic camber are available in both waxable and waxless versions. A few skis come only with waxless bases, while telemark skis usually come only with waxable bases. Most makers have their own waxless-base design, such as Kinetic (Karhu), Crown (Fischer), and Quickstep (Asnes).

If you ski only occasionally or primarily in temperatures around freezing point, then waxless skis are certainly worth considering, for that is when waxing is most difficult. Indeed, waxless patterns work best on just such transitional snow. There is also a place for waxless skis on long tours when you don't want to bother with waxing and rewaxing or carry the weight of a wax kit. I can't wholeheartedly recommend them, however; when I occasionally try a pair now I usually notice the drop in performance over a waxable ski, especially when gliding on the flat. I also don't like the noise—ranging from chattering to squeaking—that waxless skis make on hard snow or ice. I am prepared to put up with the hassle of finding the right wax and waxing in return for easier skiing. Sometimes, usually in cold conditions, even waxless skis slip. The solution? Apply some wax!

WHAT IS WAX?

Modern waxes consist mostly of petroleum distillates, such as paraffin wax, rather than natural ingredients. In the past all sorts of odd things were used for wax, including tar and spermaceti and beeswax, the first commercial wax, now long gone.

HOW WAXES WORK

Enabling a ski to both grip and glide by rubbing wax on it seems like magic. It *is* a little mysterious. When a grip-waxed ski is pressed into the snow, the tiny points of the snow crystals penetrate the wax and hold the ski in place. Once the weight is taken off the ski this bond is broken and the ski can glide. Exactly why the ski glides is a debatable point, and there are a number of theories, the most common being that whether through friction or pressure a gliding ski melts the very top surface of the snow and slides on the thin film of water thus produced. Whatever the reason, a shiny layer of glide wax on the tip and tails provides additional glide.

As snow changes with temperature, age, and weather, a range of grip waxes is needed. Too hard a wax and the snow won't bite into it, leaving you slipping backward when you pressure the ski. Getting up even gentle slopes will be very difficult, though you will shoot down the other side. Too soft a wax will allow you to walk straight up steep slopes, but you will have to walk down again as well—you won't get any glide. The key to successful waxing is to find the compromise between these two extremes.

CHOOSING AND USING WAX

How easy or difficult waxing is depends on the state of the snow, which in turn depends on the temperature both at the moment and since the snow fell. In steady cold temperatures, below 25°F/–4°C, snow is stable and waxing easy. Around the freezing point snow can change quickly, just half a degree having an effect, and waxing appropriately can be challenging and frustrating. You may find your skis slipping in the shade and sticking in the sun.

Most of the time waxing need not be difficult. Neither need you carry a large variety of wax for every minuscule change in temperature. Such kits are for track skiing and racing and are unnecessary for touring, where the simpler you can keep it the better. Half a dozen grip waxes is the most you need, and that only if you are keen on waxing. You can usually get by with just two wide-range waxes.

The following discussion is based on Swix waxes—the ones I use—the biggest and arguably the best name in waxes. There are many other brands: Rex, Start, Briko, Maxi-Glide, Toko, Holmenkolen, Ski-Go, and Solda. They all perform slightly differently, and the key to successful waxing is to get to know well one selection of waxes (not necessarily all of the same brand).

THE TWO-WAX SYSTEM. Most wax companies offer a two-wax system. Swix labels theirs red and blue, the first being for snow at above freezing, the second for snow below freezing. How do you know which to use? Most of the time it is obvious, but if you are unsure just pick up a handful of snow and squeeze it. If it compresses into a snowball and leaves your hand wet, use the red wax; if it crumbles into powder and feels dry, use the blue.

HARD WAXES. The full color-coded system is more sophisticated than the two-wax system. Swix offers fourteen hard waxes for fresh and finely grained snow, covering temperatures from 5°F/15°C and below to 41°F/5°C. (The company also offers nine tubes of soft klister wax, to be discussed later in this chapter, for changed and wet snow.) The tourer needs to carry only a few waxes to cope with all conditions.

The color scheme for hard waxes, starting at the warmer end, is red, violet, blue, and green, with yellow klister and white polar wax at the ends of the range. The four main colors each have three variations, the standard version plus an Extra and a Special. Special is for temperatures slightly lower than the standard is suitable for; Extra is for temperatures slightly above. Of these three types, I use Extras most often. The higher the temperature the wax is designed for, the stickier it is, with Red Extra being very sticky indeed.

Blue Extra (32 to 20°F/0 to −7°C) and Red Extra (37 to 41°F/3 to 5°C) cover most conditions except extreme cold, and they are often the only hard waxes I carry. If it looks like the temperature will stay below freezing I take Green Extra (21 to 14°F/−6°C to −10°C) instead of Red Extra. On long tours I carry all three. By applying layers of different thickness, depending on the conditions, these waxes can be extended beyond their range if necessary. Only rarely do I carry waxes for colder temperatures. The Green Special (16 to 5°F/−9 to −15°C) I have had for several years remains unused, but I have been on a tour when the temperatures dipped to −17°F/−27°C and never rose above 5°F/−15°C, and I used polar wax (below 5°F/−15°C) every day.

When the temperature is around freezing, standard Violet (32°F/0°C) applied on top of Blue Extra works very well if the Blue alone slips. I now carry both if such conditions are likely.

In total I usually carry just three hard waxes, and rarely more than four. I use a snow thermometer rather than handfuls of snow to tell me which wax to use. I often place it in the snow at the start of a day, when the air and snow temperatures can be very different, but for most touring the air temperature is a good enough guide. If you find your skis slipping or sticking during the day, check the temperature. If it is much the same, you probably need only to scrape off or add to the wax you are already using. If it has changed, you probably need a different wax or, in the case of the two-wax system, perhaps a thicker layer. When temperatures stay below freezing, you can often ski for days on end without rewaxing at all. I have often used just one coating of Blue Extra, the wax I use far more than any other, for four days at a time.

Hard waxes come in little foil tubs about the same size and shape as a 35mm-film carton. To apply the wax, peel back a strip of the metal foil from around the top edge of the tub, then simply crayon the wax onto the midsection of the ski for a length of maybe 15 to 18 inches (40 to 45cm). Several thin layers are better than one thick one, and you should be careful to keep wax out of the central

Waxing a ski on the trail.

groove. Cold waxes should then be smoothed with a wax cork. Warm, sticky waxes like Red Extra are better smoothed in with the heel of your hand. Otherwise they make a mess of your cork. Smoothed-in wax stays on the skis longer but doesn't grip quite as well; wax left rough grips better but is rubbed off faster. For better grip you can also wax a longer section of the ski.

If you wax your skis indoors, put them outside to cool for a few minutes before you use them, otherwise the snow will stick to the wax. Then, to find out if your wax is right, you need to ski a few hundred yards or so to try it out. If the skis slip, apply extra layers of wax and extend the waxed area. If they are still slipping after another few hundred yards, you need a softer wax. Too much or too soft a wax will make the skis stick. Then you will just have to scrape some wax off with a plastic ski scraper, available wherever wax is sold. (I have seen credit cards used for scraping, which is fine if you don't want to use them again!) Metal scrapers are available and perhaps are more effective than plastic, but I prefer not to risk damaging my skis.

KLISTER. Hard waxes are for unchanged snow—snow that hasn't been through a freeze-thaw cycle. For changed snow, ice, or very wet snow a much stickier wax is needed because the snow crystals are rounder and smoother and therefore less able to penetrate wax. Even when hard waxes work on such snow they are usually stripped off quickly because the snow is also abrasive. The wax needed is klister, the name coming from the Swedish word for glue, which tells you what it is like and how carefully it needs to be handled. Klister comes in tubes, and it is wise to keep them in plastic bags. Once opened it will stick to everything, and even if you can get it off it usually leaves a stain. Klister needs to be warm before it can be used, so it should be applied inside. If you need it on the trail or during a camping trip it can be warmed close to your body (make sure it is well protected!), between your legs or under your armpit, or, with care, over a stove.

Of the many available, three klisters cover most of the tourer's needs. Universal klister, as the name suggests, has the widest range and is the one to choose if you want to carry only one klister. Blue klister is designed for cold temperatures and is very durable, ideal when you have to ski on ice for any distance. Klister is used most in spring when wet, warm snow that has thawed and

Applying klister.

frozen many times is common. Red klister is the stuff for this.

Klister needs to be applied with care—it sticks to everything and is hard to remove. To apply klister hold the nozzle against the ski and squeeze gently. As soon as the klister begins to flow, slide the tube in a zigzag pattern down one side of the ski without lifting it off. This minimizes the number of strands of klister. Repeat on the other side of the central groove. A thin smear of klister is enough, so don't squeeze the tube too hard. Often I don't smooth the klister in, but if I do I use the heel of my hand. To keep the klister off your skin you could put your hand in a plastic bag, but I have found the klister sticks to plastic more than to skin. The same happens with gloves. Klister on your skin isn't a problem, it just helps your gloves stay in place.

The biggest problem with klister is removing it if the snow changes. If you don't remove it you will be able to climb anything, but you won't have any glide, even downhill, and your skis will ball up badly. A change in the snow may be due to a fresh snowfall or because you climbed into colder temperatures. If you expect to move into colder temperature, use climbing skins (described later) rather than klister to get you there. To remove klister, cool the skis by placing them in the shade, then use a scraper to peel off the wax. This isn't as easy as it sounds, and if I think I'm likely to use klister I often carry a rag soaked in wax remover in a plastic bag to aid removal. If you are carrying white gas (a solvent) for your stove you can also use that to remove klister (or any other wax) by dripping a little onto the ski, waiting for thirty seconds or so, then scraping off the wax. If you don't have any wax remover and can't scrape all the klister off, an alternative is to rub it in until it is really polished and then simply apply a harder wax on top.

I have to say that I don't use klister very often, but when I do it is essential. I have skied for days in a row when klister is all that would work, so I never tour without at least a tube of universal in my pack.

There is a wax halfway between hard wax and klister called yellow klister. It comes in a tub and is intended for moist, wet, new snow and icy tracks. It has quite a wide range, and I often use it instead of a tube klister. It is easier to apply and a little easier to remove. Like klister it should be applied in very small amounts.

In ski shops you will find other waxes, most of them aimed at increasing glide for skaters and track skiers. These aren't necessary for touring, though it is worth applying a layer of glide wax (discussed farther on) once or twice a season and perhaps carrying a universal glider for touch-up on long tours.

WAXLESS WAXING. Waxes for waxless skis—or perhaps they should be called minimum-wax skis—are not the same as those for waxable skis, as the composition of the ski base is different. The two kinds, glide and grip waxes, come in tubs and as sprays. I have found the sprays to be fairly ineffective, so I recommend the wax that comes in a tub, which you rub onto the ski. Glide waxes are intended for just the tip and tails, but if your skis start balling up—that is, collecting lumps of snow underfoot that slow you down and make progress very hard work—applying a little glide wax can help. Make sure it is only a little though, or you may find that instead of sticking you are slipping backward. Grip wax for waxless skis is for those times, often on gentle uphills, when your waxless pattern fails to work. It helps a little, but usually you end up having to take a gentler traverse or else herringbone or side-step up—which can be very annoying when those on waxable skis are happily heading straight uphill. Beware of using grip wax intended for waxable skis unless you are prepared to spend a very long time cleaning it out of the indentations in the waxless pattern.

Ski Preparation and Care

You don't need to do anything to your skis other than wax them (waxless skis need no treatment at all), but a little bit of extra work can increase their performance and extend their life. Modern synthetic skis, whether waxable or waxless, come with a porous base that needs hot-waxing if they are not to stick on the snow because of suction. A layer of base wax will both seal the base and aid glide.

A workshop, or at least a shed with a floor you don't mind getting messy, is useful for working on skis, and a workbench with a vise to hold the skis makes life easier. Place newspapers on the floor under the workbench to soak up dripping wax.

BASE WAXING. There are a number of waxes that can be used as a base. Nordic Uniglider base wax is best, but a universal glider, alpine base wax, or even a skating glider intended for cold temperatures will work. An iron is required to heat the wax and bond it to the ski. Special waxing irons are available, but an electric household iron on a "wool" setting is just as good—just don't plan on using it ever again to iron your woollies, because it will have wax on it forevermore. With the ski held in a vise or laid level, drip the base wax onto the surface by pressing it against the iron. If it smokes, the iron is too hot. Try to get as little wax as possible in the central groove to make the next stage easier. Many experts say that you should wax only the tip and tails of a ski, leaving the wax pocket alone, as otherwise wax won't stick to it. Removing wax from the base pattern of a waxless ski is extremely difficult, and this section is sealed anyway, so I agree there is no need to add a base wax. But I always hot-wax the whole base of waxable skis, and I have never yet had problems with grip wax afterward.

Once you have dripped wax along the whole ski, smooth it out by skimming the iron over the wax. Beware of pressing too hard, and keep the iron moving. Ski bases can melt! Once the wax is smooth, leave the skis to cool.

Next scrape the wax off. This may sound perverse, but you

Base waxing: Melt the wax onto the ski with a hot iron.

Iron the wax onto the ski, keeping the iron moving.

After the wax is dry, scrape it off, taking special care to clean the central groove.

need only a very thin layer of wax to aid glide. Use a plastic rather than a metal scraper so there is no chance of scratching the base or digging holes in it. In particular make sure that the central groove is cleared of wax. The rounded corner of the scraper is ideal for this. Wax that has strayed onto the metal edges should be removed too. When you finish, the skis should look as though there is no wax on them.

How often should you hot-wax your skis? When they are new, certainly. After that maybe two or three times a season if you ski regularly. You can tell if skis need rewaxing by looking closely at the tips. If they look dull and slightly hairy, with pale spots in places, they could do with some more wax. I always (at least intend to) hot-wax my skis at the end of the season and then put them away without scraping them to protect them for the summer. If you cover metal edges with wax, it will prevent rusting. On long tours I carry a universal glider to rub into the tips and tails, then buff with a cloth every so often. It is not the same as hot-waxing, but it does make a difference. A polar or green grip wax will serve the same purpose, unless you are expecting bitterly cold temperatures.

CLEANING SKIS. Before you apply base wax and whenever your skis are particularly dirty they should be cleaned. Scraping will remove most wax, but it may not be enough if there are many layers and the bottom ones are ground in. Special wax removers are available, but some contain hazardous chemical solvents, and care should be taken with their use. (Some of the newest aren't harmful and are probably worth seeking out.) In particular, plenty of ventilation is needed. An alternative method of cleaning ski bases is to use hot wax. A soft wax (Swix suggests Orange Racing Glider) melted onto the ski base will draw out the old wax. It should be scraped off while it is still molten or only partly hardened. Special cleaning cloths are available, but I just use whatever old cloth (clean, not oily) comes to hand. Wax that has crept up the side walls should be wiped off too. While you're at it, you might as well do the top plate.

Railed skis (edges are higher than the base) can adversely affect the way a ski turns. To check ski bases for flatness, run a scraper down them and sight for light showing through gaps. A metal scraper can be used to flatten out high spots on the base. Don't press too hard, and keep the action smooth so you don't gouge chunks out of your ski base. The ski should be held in a vise while you work on it.

If the ski is railed, the expert advice is to use a long file. Hold it at an angle across the ski with both hands and stroke it down the ski carefully until the base is flat, cleaning filings off both the file and the ski frequently. I can't say I have ever done this myself, and unless you have experience with hand tools, my advice is to take your skis to a ski store with a tuning shop to have them examined and if necessary run through a grinder by experts. I would rather pay for this service than risk ruining my skis.

Metal edges can be squared off and sharpened either with a special edge sharpener or—carefully—with a file. Finish off with sandpaper to ensure smoothness. Burrs, formed when the edge hits a rock, can be removed with a stone. Only the central section of the edge needs to be sharp. In fact, sharp tips and tails can catch during turns, so they should be dulled a little. Edges don't need to be sharpened very often unless you do a lot of steep downhilling. Indeed, many people never sharpen them at all.

Climbing Skins

If you wax your skis so you can take steep climbs head-on, you will probably have to scrape most of the wax off at the top or else walk down the other side. Therefore people usually wax only enough to enable them to get up a slope in a series of long gradual traverses and then descend without sticking. With waxless skis you will find upward progress almost impossible in some types of snow. The solution for long climbs is to use climbing skins. These strips of brushed nylon or mohair (the name comes from the days when real sealskin was used) will slide forward but, like cat's fur, resist movement in the other direction. Their grip is phenomenal and has to be experienced to be believed. Because you can take a steeper or even direct line you save both time and energy by using skins. On a number of occasions I have timed skiers climbing a slope, some with skins, some without. Each time it took at least twice as long for those without skins to finish the climb—even in the case when a skier was using skins because he was tired and lagging behind.

Most skins fix to skis by means of glue on their inner surface. This glue lasts a long time but does eventually wear off. The skins can then be treated with replacement glue. The instructions say that

Putting on climbing skins.

you should use a special solvent to dissolve all the glue and then reglue the whole skin, but I have found that regluing just those parts that aren't sticky anymore works fine. It is quicker and easier. To keep the skins sticky for as long as possible and to avoid getting glue on the rest of your gear, they should be stored by folding them in half with the sticky sides together. Because they stick less well when wet they need to be aired and dried after use. On warm days draping them over your skis or poles during rest stops may be enough. An alternative is to put them inside your clothes so your body warmth can dry them out. If your skis are wet, wipe them down with a cloth or dry clothing before putting the skins on. It is a good idea on long tours to carry a tube of spray-on glue such as Black Diamond's Glue Renew.

Stick-on skins need to be put on carefully. If you have waxable skis, try to remove as much wax as possible or buff it in very hard.

Then slip the front loop of the skin over the tip of the ski and unroll it down the length, pressing down firmly to make sure it is stuck well and smoothing out any creases. Failure to do this carefully can result in the skins peeling off. Some skins come with a stretchy adjustable loop that fits over the tail of the ski, other more simple designs just have a square end. Directions are to trim the ends to a length a few centimeters shorter than your skis. Having said that—my current skins have been about 5cm longer than my skis since I bought them in 1984, and it has never been a problem.

To remove stick-on skins start at the tail. Make sure they don't touch the snow. In a wind it is easiest to remove half the skin and fold it back on itself and then the other half. Skins folded like this are easier to put on in a wind too. Any glue remaining on your skis can be removed with something like Black Diamond's Skin Wax, which can also be rubbed onto the skins to increase glide or even used to touch up the glide wax on your skis.

There are several makes of stick-on skins that come in different widths—35, 38, 45, 50, 62, and 64mm. If they are to work well, skins

If you have no skins and your wax just won't grip, straps wound around the skis may help.

should be at least half the waist width of your skis. Some people prefer full width. The skins I use are 38mm wide, my skis being 54mm
at the waist, and they grip well. On the occasions when I have to
take a traversing line it is usually because the slope is too steep to put
one ski comfortably in front of the other rather than because my
skins are slipping. Depending on width, skins weigh 7 to 12
ounces/200 to 300 grams a pair.

Before stick-on skins appeared, skins had to be strapped onto
the skis, a time-consuming and inefficient system. I have toured with
people using old-fashioned strap-on skins and wasn't impressed.
They took much longer to put on than stick-ons and didn't stay on
very well. However, Voilé has an updated version called Snake skins,
which have straps heat-welded to the skins. Voilé says they are easy
to put on and take off, there are no maintenance hassles because
there is no glue to wear off, and they can be put on over waxes without problem.

Skins have other uses than for climbing steep slopes. I often
keep mine on in order to slow down on a mountain or ridge top that
is icy and dotted with rocks, especially if the visibility is poor. In very
soft snow, particularly deep powder, skins prevent backward slippage
and make trail breaking much easier. They can be used for keeping on
your feet in very windy weather too. I have even seen them used by
exhausted skiers without the energy to slide their skis forward; with
skins on at least, they could slowly plod on without fear of falling
over. All in all they are so useful that I never tour without them.

Bindings

The Rat Trap

Standard since it was first developed in 1927, the three-pin binding
was named by the then king of Norway for its resemblance to a rat
trap, in Norwegian, *rottefella*. Although superseded for track skiing by
the systems bindings (the Salomon SNS and the Rottefella NNN), the
three-pin is still the norm for wilderness touring and telemarking.
This isn't surprising, since it is both simple and effective. The three
pins, which jut out of a metal plate that is screwed to the ski, mate
with three holes in the boot sole at the toe. An adjustable bail, which
should be flat to avoid damage to the welt of the boot, clamps down

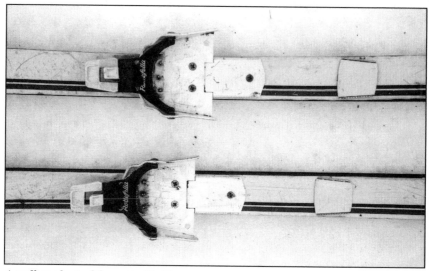

A well-used set of three-pin bindings.

over the front welt to keep the boot in place. Side walls help prevent the boot from twisting in the binding. There used to be a wide variety of sizes of three-pin bindings, all measured in millimeters, but for many years now only one has been produced, the 75mm Nordic Norm. The old sizes, ranging from 38mm to 79mm, are really no more than historic curiosities now. I suggest avoiding them if you come across a set, unless you want them for decorations.

During the 1980s, with the rise of piste telemarking and racing and the increasing use of wider, heavier skis, manufacturers beefed up the three-pin binding to produce the tough, virtually unbreakable aircraft-aluminum models available today. Most are still made by Rottefella (including some with other brand names), with the Rottefella Super Telemark being a popular model. I used the Super Telemark for many years and found it tough, secure, and supportive. Of the alternatives, Voilé makes a standard-weight three-pin binding called the Telemark, plus a tougher one called the Heavy Duty Mountaineer; Black Diamond and Asolo are two other brands.

Lighter-weight three-pin bindings are still available, but they aren't strong enough to use with mountain-touring and telemark boots and skis. They are gradually being replaced by the better NNNBC system.

The modern heavy-duty three-pin binding is tougher than a lot of boots: ripped-out boot pinholes are the most common cause of failure of this system. The three-pin telemark binding offers very good control as long as your boots are laterally stiff. For most tourers it is perfectly adequate. I used three-pin bindings happily for years with no problems, but I have since changed to cable bindings because of the number of damaged boots I have seen—enough to cause me to worry about when it might happen to me.

Ice and packed snow can build up around binding pins when skis are left out overnight or taken off during the day, possibly causing difficulty in getting your boots into the bindings. Trying to force them isn't a good idea. The ice just has to be scraped off, a process that can be difficult and frustrating in cold, stormy weather (the tip of a ski pole may be helpful). Spraying with silicone minimizes the chance of ice buildup, or you could rub your bindings with glide wax or even candle wax.

Cable Bindings

Cable bindings, not so long ago regarded by many as old-fashioned, have become popular again, with modern designs giving better control for telemarking than three-pin bindings do. Cables predate the three-pin by three-quarters of a century. Early ones were fairly crude, which is why the three-pin took over. Modern versions have much to offer the tourer, however, not least the fact that they obviate the possibility of damage to your boots, making them particularly useful for tourers who head deep into the wilderness for long periods. When cranked up tight, cable bindings reinforce torsional stiffness and so are good for downhilling and for extending the life of old boots that have gone soft. And since there are no pins, icing up isn't a problem.

The standard cable binding has a spring at the back that fits into the groove cut into the heel of all three-pin-boot soles, side walls that the toe of the boot fits into, and a front adjustment lever or throw for tensioning the cable. These bindings are usually adjustable for different thicknesses of boot soles (if not, make sure your boots fit) and are available with three different cable sizes for different-size boots.

Better, however, is a new design of cable binding first brought on the market by Black Diamond in the form of the Riva cable binding. The throw is incorporated into the cable and situated at the side

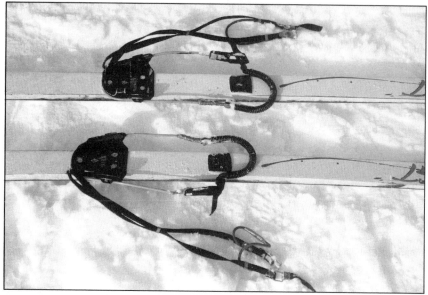

Cable bindings with safety straps.

of the boot rather than out at the front and linked to the cable by a hook, making the binding, when tightened up hard, superb for downhill use because it adds substantially to the torsional stiffness of your boots. For touring it is advisable to loosen the cable a little to allow free heel lift for diagonal striding. I have found the Rivas excellent and now use them all the time.

Since the appearance of the Riva binding, other cable bindings have appeared with the throw on the side of the heel. Two with good reputations, though I have not used them myself, are Voilé's Classic cable and Rainey Designs' Super Loop cable. The Voilé has a spring-steel cable that can be easily unhooked for transportation, while the Rainey has a continuous-compression cable with an internal spring. Both of these bindings are lighter than the Riva—not that the weight seems significant.

Besides protecting boots, the new cable bindings give greater control on downhills, moving the point of pressure on the ski from in front of your toes to under the ball of your foot. Breakages are unlikely, but even so I carry a spare cable on long tours.

Combination Three-Pin and Cable

Combined cable and three-pin bindings, such as the Rottefella Super Telemark cable and the Voilé Three-Pin cable, are designed for heavy-duty expedition use and have the advantage of providing a built-in backup in case of failure. If the pinholes of your boots rip out or the cable snaps you can still ski. The cables are removable, so you can use just the three-pin binding for short tours. Voilé uses their Classic cable, while Rottefella uses a traditional cable system. For most touring, however, I think the new-style cables, like the Riva or Voilé Classic, have all the advantages—if you carry spare cables—of the cable and three-pin combination while being simpler and lighter. This is especially true in less remote areas where backup is not essential.

Voilé Plate

The Voilé plate is a wide strip of flexible nylon that fixes to the ski under a three-pin binding and clips onto the back welt of the boot. Its purpose is to add stiffness to a sloppy boot and to help protect the boot toes by taking some of the stress off them. When an old, extremely comfortable pair of touring boots of mine became so flexi-

Voilé plate with three-pin binding.

ble that the heels were twisting off the skis during turns I put Voilé plates on my skis rather than give up using the boots. I found the plates effective at stiffening up the boots and giving me greater control, but I also found that when skiing in soft snow there was often a buildup of snow between the plate and the boot sole. However, they work, and they are certainly worth considering.

Releasable Bindings

The purpose of a release system is to snap the binding open in a fall to prevent injury. The tension needs to be adjustable as on an alpine release binding. Releasable bindings are sophisticated pieces of gear, designed originally for lift-served skiing, particularly telemark racing, where skiers can catch ski tips in the gates. I have seen releasable bindings in use in the mountains only a couple of times. One of the skiers was a doctor who was using them because he had seen too many knee and ankle injuries to skiers. There may well be a use for releasable bindings for touring, but such injuries are unlikely unless you are a fairly reckless skier, and I think they are too complicated and heavy for all but the steepest mountain touring.

Voilé is the only maker of releasable bindings. Their first model, designed for telemark racing, fits under a three-pin binding. Of more interest to tourers is the newer Voilé Complete Releasable Bindings (CRB) system, which comes as a complete unit with either a three-pin, a cable, or a three-pin and cable combination binding. This makes for a simpler, lighter, and less bulky system.

New Nordic Norm Back Country

Totally different is the Rottefella New Nordic Norm Back Country binding (NNNBC). This is the first of the modern systems bindings designed for serious touring use. It can only be used with an NNNBC boot, so you have to buy the two together, and if you want to change to a different boot or binding you have to change the whole system.

Basically a beefed-up version of the standard NNN binding, the NNNBC is lightweight and simple to use. The boot has a bar embedded in the sole under the toe that fits into a slot in the binding. The slot is then closed over the bar with a curved hinge and locked into position with a jointed lever. Unlike static three-pin or cable bindings, it is the NNNBC binding that flexes rather than the boot. When

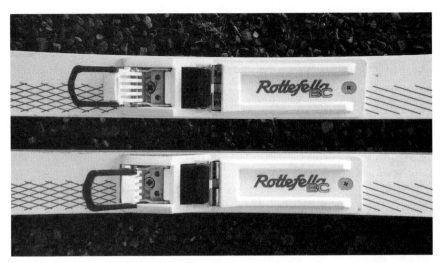

NNNBC binding in the open position.

you lift your heel the bar pivots in its slot and the boot toe pushes forward against a rubber "flex-bit."

When Salomon first introduced this type of binding to track skiing and racing with their Salomon Nordic System (SNS) in the early 1980s, it proved so superior to three-pin bindings that it soon took over for serious use. Rottefella, until then the undisputed leader in nordic bindings, responded with the NNN system. There are two big advantages to systems bindings: First, because it is the binding rather than the boot that flexes, boots can have very stiff soles. Consequently,

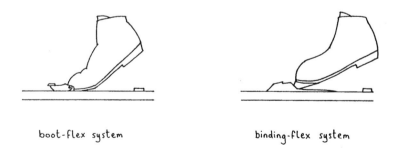

boot-flex system   binding-flex system

Figure 2-2. The binding-flex versus the boot-flex system.

the kick or push during diagonal striding or skating is much more powerful, because all the force is transmitted to the ski. Second, the foot and ski contact point is under the toes rather than in front of them, so that force applied to the ski is transmitted more directly to it.

How useful is the NNN system for touring? To find out I spent four weeks skiing in Norway over varied terrain with NNNBC bindings fitted to Asnes Sondre Telemark mountain-touring skis and using Artex ATC 30 boots. Overall I was impressed with the system, especially for skiing over undulating terrain and in tracks. My diagonal stride was more dynamic and faster, while I noticed no lack of control despite the light weight and narrowness of the bindings. Alpine turns (wedges, stems, parallels) on downhills were quite easy. The longitudinal grooves in the boot sole mate with raised plastic ridges on the binding, ensuring that when your foot is flat on the ski it can't twist off. Telemark turns were slightly more difficult. Having to go right up onto the toes of the rear foot due to the lack of sole flex made the rear ski wander a little, giving an unstable feeling. This test, however, was done with the original plastic NNNBC sole, which is very rigid and doesn't flex easily. The latest version has a rubber sole that is more flexible and should allow the rear ski to be weighted properly when telemarking.

The NNNBC system does have disadvantages. The main one I found is that the bindings ice up easily, there being many small crevices for snow to get into. On a couple of occasions I couldn't get the boots out of the bindings and had to remove the boot and the skis together and take them inside to thaw. This would be OK if you are staying in a heated lodge but could be a problem when camping. On another occasion, after I had removed my skis to walk the last few hundred snowless yards to a mountaintop, I had to spend a long time scraping snow out of the bindings in a bitterly cold wind before I could get my boots back in. Spraying the bindings with silicone would probably help, and I wouldn't go far with them in the future without carrying a can of silicone spray, but this icing problem would still stop me from using NNNBC bindings for long tours in remote country.

Although the bindings seem durable and well made, the possibility of breakage is a concern because they couldn't be easily jury-rigged. If I were to use them on a long tour I would carry a spare binding and screws in case of failure.

The NNNBC is an ideal match for general touring skis or light-weight, narrow, metal-edged skis, and can also be used with moun-tain-touring skis. For tourers who aren't aiming to do a lot of down-hill skiing and who aren't heading off into the mountains laden with heavy packs, NNNBC bindings are a good idea. If you like to mix track skiing with light touring, they are ideal. Unlike cables or three-pins they don't have side walls to catch the edges of tracks, and they speed you along faster.

For more serious mountain touring with heavier loads and in steeper terrain I still prefer cable or three-pin bindings, which I find give more support and control and which, frankly, I trust more, a subjective view that may have more to do with familiarity than actual performance. Certainly the systems binding is the area of interest at present and the one where new developments are most likely.

Safety Straps

Whatever type of bindings you choose, it is a good idea to fit them with safety straps of some sort in case a ski comes off, so you won't have the heartbreak of watching a ski zoom back down the steep slope you have just spent a morning climbing or, even worse, vanish from view into deep powder or a stream gully, possibly never to be found again. Most downhill ski areas insist on safety straps on tele-mark skis to prevent runaway skis from injuring people, so if you plan on practicing on the pistes you must have them.

Retaining straps can be quite simple, just a length of cord or webbing clipped or tied onto your boot or gaiter and your binding (most bindings come with holes drilled for such straps). Black Diamond makes some nice tough-looking ones from plastic-coated cable called Ski Leashes. Because my supergaiters have no attachment for straps, I used to fasten long straps around my calf. But after I caught the tip of a rear ski in one of them while telemarking and tripped myself, I sewed webbing loops on my gaiters.

Boots

Skis are exciting, and skiers spend much time discussing the merits of different models. Boots, on the other hand, are just boots, and they are paid far less attention. But your boots are far more important to your skiing than your skis. You control your skis with your boots. I know from bitter experience that a pair of sloppy boots makes turns very difficult. If it is a choice between top-quality boots and average skis, or the best skis but mediocre boots, go for the boots every time.

The choice in styles of boots for touring is limited. Lightweight track boots and shoes can be discounted immediately, which just leaves boots that fit 75mm three-pin bindings (the majority) and the few but growing numbers compatible with the New Nordic Norm Back Country (NNNBC) systems binding (discussed above).

Fit

The fit of your boots is crucial, much more important than the make or model. A nordic ski-touring boot should fit like a hiking boot. Check in particular that your heels are held firmly in place. If they aren't, you will have less control over your skis, and you will probably develop sore heels and blisters. A boot that is too short will be very painful; your toes should not be pressed up against the end. There should be just enough room to slide a finger between the back of the boot and your ankle when the boot is unlaced. Look for a snug-fitting boot with room to move your toes—a tight boot will be painful and could cause cold feet and frostbite. The width is important as well as the length. Few models (the Merrell Legend is one) come in different widths, though some brands (Artex in particular) are fairly wide.

Try on boots with the socks you intend wearing, and try several models until you find a good fit. Your normal shoe size should be taken as a starting point but no more. Sizes vary from maker to maker and even from model to model in the same range. Take your time. Ill-fitting boots can ruin your skiing and turn what should be a fun excursion into purgatory. Walk around the store to see how the boots feel. Mimic a few ski positions, going down into a telemark stance, rolling your ankles sideways to put the boots on their edges.

Materials and Construction

The type of materials a boot is made from and the quality of construction are very important for performance, water resistance, comfort, and durability. Inferior materials and poor construction will result in a boot that will soon lose its shape and possibly fall apart.

UPPER MATERIALS. With the exception of the new all-plastic tele-mark racing boots that are starting to appear (described a little far-ther on), mountain-touring and telemark boots are made from leather. Lightweight synthetic materials, used for the uppers of set-track and light-touring boots, are not waterproof and are not warm or stiff enough for wilderness touring.

A quality full-grain leather such as Anfibio or Del Pozzo will be more water resistant and will hold its shape longer than will lower-quality, split-grain leather. Top- or full-grain leather is the outside of a cowhide and is tougher and more naturally water resistant than the inner (split-grain) layer. Sometimes split-grain leather is coated with polyurethane or PVC to make it waterproof. This doesn't last and isn't adequate for long-term wilderness use.

The thickness of the leather is important too: good boots are made from leather that is at least 2.5mm thick; some are 3mm.

HEEL AND TOE COUNTERS. A heel counter is an extra layer of stiff material, usually synthetic, that supports the heel and helps hold it in place. In most boots it is inside, between the lining and the outer; it can't be seen, but it can be felt. Some of the newer buckled tele-mark boots have external plastic counters. I have not come across a mountain-touring or telemark boot without a heel counter, but if you do, put it back on the shelf.

Toe counters, essentially standard, keep the boot toe rigid and prevent bruising.

ANKLE AND CUFF REINFORCEMENTS. Telemark touring boots often have stiffeners, usually made from a nylon like Flexan, built into the ankle for greater support when turning. Some have removable rein-forcements that you can take out for striding on the flat, when stiff supports can rub ankles. Telemark racing boots and some of the heavier touring boots have external plastic cuffs for maximum con-trol at high speeds and on steep slopes. Scarpa boots have resin-impregnated leather stiffeners rather than plastics, which, says dis-tributor Black Diamond, "eliminate the hot spots and hinges common in plastic-reinforced boots."

Recently, external plastic reinforcements have started appearing on touring boots, even NNNBC ones such as the Alpina BC 2000, which is described as being for "the on- and off-track ski tourer as well as for backcountry and light telemark skiing."

LININGS AND INSULATION. To keep weight down, synthetic inner linings such as Cambrelle or Tesivel are commonly used instead of leather. They dry quicker too. Linings of fur or wool fleece, once the norm, are still found occasionally. I have an old pair of Meindl boots with wool fleece linings. They are warm and comfortable but not quite as quick-drying as the synthetics. Fleece linings pack down in time, making the boots slightly looser, but I have not found this to be a problem. You just lace a little tighter.

Insulation of some form is essential. In modern boots it usually consists of a layer of EVA foam, usually around 2.5mm thick, between the inner and outer. A less common alternative is Thinsulate microfiber. Neither seems better than the other.

THE TONGUE. Most boots have bellows tongues with gussets sewn down each side to keep out snow. They are often padded with foam for warmth and in heavy-duty boots may have nylon reinforcements for extra stability. The material is usually leather, though flexible plastics are sometimes used in telemarking boots, and Cordura nylon may be used for the gussets. Heavier boots usually have double tongues: a reinforced padded inner tongue sewn only at the base, for extra support for the front of the ankle, and an outer tongue either of the bellows type or with foldover flaps. The two tongues can usually be attached to each other with a Velcro tab. This style keeps out snow better than the single bellows tongue. Snow can creep into the folds of the latter and then soak into the boot. Supergaiters (described later) are an even better way to keep snow out of your boots.

LACES AND BUCKLES. D-rings low down and hooks at the ankle are the best combination for easy lacing. They also allow you to vary the tension of the laces over different parts of the foot for the best fit.

Ratchet-fastened buckles of the type found on alpine boots are needed on telemark boots with external plastic-reinforced uppers. They are mostly overkill on boots intended for wilderness touring, but they are starting to appear on backcountry boots, including NNBC ones. The idea is to add ankle control. I haven't used ratchet-fastened buckles, but I'm told they are great for tightening boots that have become very cold—it is hard to lace cold boots.

SEAMS. Seams are weak points in the structure of a boot and good entry points for water and melted snow, so the fewer there are the better. Good boots are made from one piece of leather with seams only at the heel and around the tongue.

INNERSOLES. These removable foot-shaped foam boot liners are now found in many ski boots. They add a little insulation and comfort but aren't essential, and they often don't stay in place. They can creep slowly up the back of the boot and cause discomfort. This happened to me so often on one tour that I removed the innersoles and replaced them with the ones from my running shoes. They stayed in place, so I have left them in the boots ever since—and the original innersoles work well in my running shoes!

MIDSOLES AND INSOLES. The materials the midsole and insole are made from affect how long a boot will remain torsionally stiff. Traditional leather midsoles lead to sloppy boots much more quickly than do modern stiff synthetic midsoles—as I know from experience. I wouldn't buy a boot now without a polyurethane (PU), nylon, or thermoplastic midsole. Carbon fiber or steel shanks further add to stiffness and are found in many three-pin telemark boots but not in lighter touring models.

OUTSOLES. Outsoles must be suitable for walking on rough terrain and for use with crampons as well as for skiing. Vibram Ferret rubber lug soles are standard on three-pin telemark boots. They grip well and are durable. General touring boots may have lighter soles. They need to have a deep tread if they are to be used in the mountains.

NNNBC boots have Rottefella's NNNBC sole, which has a deep tread. It is laterally very stiff and now comes in two flexes, the softer one being better for telemarking, though either is adequate for touring.

SOLE THICKNESS. A thick sole is needed both for warmth and for lateral rigidity. The total thickness of the midsole and the outsole should be at least 12mm and preferably more.

CONSTRUCTION METHODS. How the boot sole is put together is important. All good three-pin telemark boots are welt-sewn, which is to say that the upper is turned outward around the lower edge and then stitched to one or more midsoles. Three rows of stitching at the toe is better than two, and single-stitched boots should be avoided. The outsole is then glued to the midsole. This construction is very strong and can be repaired, and the soles can be replaced when worn. (But check that this is done well. I once had the sole of a boot come completely unstuck at the toe just as I was about to set off on a ski tour.) Glued or cemented soles that aren't welt-sewn aren't strong enough for wilderness skiing and are generally found only on light-weight touring boots.

Backcountry boots with glued molded soles did appear in the early 1980s at the time when this construction first became popular for lightweight hiking boots. However, while this construction has proved adequate for hiking boots, it wasn't up to the much tougher treatment meted out to mountain-touring boots. Secondhand boots with such soles should be avoided.

NNNBC soles can't be welt-sewn. Instead, the lower edge of the upper is turned inward and stitched to a midsole (called Blake stitching) to which the outsole is bonded.

LATERAL STIFFNESS. Whichever of the boot styles outlined below is for you, one factor is very important: lateral stiffness. While a boot must bend fairly easily under the ball of the foot for diagonal striding, it must also be rigid from side to side for easy turning. The first thing I do with any boot is grasp it by the toe and heel and see if I can twist it. If I can I reject it immediately; such a boot will tend to twist off the ski when you try to make a turn.

Three-Pin Boots

Good three-pin boots are tough and durable, but eventually the soles start to lose their lateral stiffness. It is worth resoling to solve this problem if the uppers are in good condition, as they usually are. (You can also extend their life by using Voilé plates or cable bindings—which I discuss in the section on bindings, beginning on page 43.)

A bigger problem lies with the pinholes, which are easily damaged. The only link between boot and binding, they absorb all the stresses and strains of your skiing. To help them survive, virtually all boots come with a metal plate embedded in the sole or fastened on the outside as a reinforcement. Even so, durability isn't ensured. I have seen many boots with split pinholes, and all of them had such plates. Once the boot sole splits across the pinholes there is little you can do but have it resoled—not practical in the middle of a long tour. I have known people to limp out of the mountains wearing a boot crudely stitched with wire, hitchhike to a town, buy new boots, then return to continue a tour. While falling on your face frequently is more likely to rip out pinholes than anything else, soles split on the boots of cautious skiers too. It is not a frequent problem, but you should check the pinholes regularly and have the boots resoled if they start to crack or wear—unless, that is, you stop using three-pin bindings and use cables or change to an NNNBC system.

Even if the boot doesn't split across the pinholes, after a lot of wear the holes often start to widen, causing the boot to wobble in the binding and compromising control. Eventually you will find you keep kicking off the ski. If this occurs, resoling is the only recourse. One cause of pinhole widening is fitting the boot improperly into the binding—something I have seen many people do, usually when the binding has iced up and the weather is such that they don't want to spend time cleaning it out. Cable bindings are one solution. But if you do use three-pin bindings, then proper fitting is worthwhile, however nasty the conditions, if you want your boots to last.

PISTE TELEMARKING BOOTS. Boots for lift-served telemark skiing have very high ankles with alpine-ski-boot-style plastic clips. Most are made from leather with high plastic side cuffs, but all-plastic boots became available in the early 1990s (initially from Scarpa/Black Diamond and Vendramini) and will probably quickly become the norm now that the problem of forward flex has been solved (via cut-aways in the shell and the use of multidensity plastics). Trickle-down may be a dubious economic theory, but it works in design, and I expect general touring boots to be made from plastic before too long. The advantages of plastic, as alpine mountaineers and skiers long ago discovered, are total waterproofness, better torsional rigidity, lighter weight, and ease of care. At present plastic boots are for lift-served skiing only (as are all piste telemarking boots), though I have, to my great surprise, seen some in use for touring. I wouldn't recommend them for this unless your aim is to skin up steep mountains, then ski back down. Leather is still by far the most comfortable and suitable material for touring.

TOURING TELEMARKING BOOTS. Next down in weight are touring telemark models. They are very stiff and have high ankles reinforced with plastic inserts for greater downhill control. A few have plastic ratchets as well. Weights are around 5¼ to 6½ pounds/2,400 to 3,000 grams. They are a good match for telemark skis, though they can be used with mountain-touring skis for greater turning power and are ideal for mountain tours with much ascent and descent. I have a pair of Artex ATK 30 Super Pros in this style that I use primarily for tours in steep mountains. They definitely give good ankle support on descents, but they are more tiring on the feet than more flexible boots when skiing long distances on flatish terrain. This type of boot is a good choice if you intend doing a lot of descents.

MOUNTAIN-TOURING BOOTS. Boots with relatively soft uppers are best for most wilderness tourers. They are far more comfortable for travel on the flat and over undulating terrain yet still give good con-

Vibram three-pin sole.

trol on downhill sections. Compared with the heavy-duty telemark models, mountain-touring boots have lower ankles without stiffening but are still laterally very rigid. They weigh around 4 to 4½ pounds/1,850 to 2,050 grams and require little breaking in. I have worn new Merrell Legends, my favorite touring boots, for three weeks of skiing with no break-in period at all and had no problems whatsoever, finding the boots very comfortable from the first day. These boots go well with mountain-touring skis.

DOUBLE BOOTS. All the above are single boots. In extreme cold double boots will be warmer. They have removable insulated inner booties that can also be used as hut slippers. They weigh around 5¼ to 6¾ pounds/2,400 to 3,200 grams a pair. They are specialist boots that are worth buying (they are not cheap) only if you intend doing a lot of skiing in very cold conditions. For the record, I have skied in temperatures down to –13°F/–25°C in single boots (with supergaiters) and have had no more than chilly feet—but it wasn't for days at a time.

New Nordic Norm Back Country Boots

The boots described above are all designed for use with heavy-duty three-pin or cable bindings. There are lighter, softer leather touring boots available suitable for use with lightweight three-pin bindings and general touring skis. However, the new NNNBC boot and binding system is so superior to these even for low-level touring that I wouldn't consider them. Others seem to agree, as these lightweight touring boots are getting harder to find.

The three-pin system is one in which the boot flexes and the binding remains fixed. With the New Nordic Norm system it is the binding that flexes, which means the boot can have a much stiffer sole fore and aft. Originally the NNN system was designed for track skiing, but the New Nordic Norm Back Country version, as the name suggests, is meant for touring.

At first there were only lightweight NNNBC boots available, which weren't really suitable for wilderness use. Now there are a number of heavier boots around that perform as well in the mountains as any three-pin model, and more are appearing all the time. Like the three-pin type, NNNBC boots are made of leather. Some even have plastic cuffs and buckles. The sole, however, is completely

NNNBC sole.

different. Instead of the traditional welt-sewn leather-and-rubber midsole and Vibram outsole there is a thick synthetic midsole, with the bar that links it to the binding embedded in the toe, plus a lugged outsole. This sole unit is very rigid and, unlike a three-pin sole, shouldn't lose rigidity with use.

Only companies licensed by Rottefella, the makers of the NNN system, can use the NNNBC sole. These, at the time of writing, are Alfa, Alpina, Artex, Asolo, and Rossignol. I have used the Artex ATC 30 and been surprised by the amount of control it gives. I used it with mountain-touring skis, though it is perhaps an even better match for a general touring ski. The boots are very waterproof, mainly because there is no stitching at the toe through which water can seep.

The only problem I can see with NNNBC boots is that they can only be used with an NNNBC binding. But the system is a good one and will undoubtedly see more developments in the near future. (For more on this see the section on bindings, beginning on page 43.)

Boot Care

Leather needs looking after, and boots should be treated regularly with a waterproofing wax such as Sno-Seal, Biwell, Nikwax, or similar. If boots get wet, dry them out slowly. Heat can damage the leather. If you put them in a heated drying room, don't leave them there for long. I keep my boots out of such hot places even if it means skiing in them while they are damp. To minimize the chance of wet feet it is worth applying a welt seal such as Sno-Seal's to the stitching on welt-sewn, three-pin boots, especially around the toe, since the constant flexing can pump water through the stitch holes there.

Gaiters

Perhaps the best way to keep your feet dry and warm while protecting your boots from abrasion and nicks from ski edges is to use supergaiters. They have close-fitting rubber rands that form a seal around the lower edge of the boot.

Fitting supergaiters to your boots can be a tough chore, as the rubber rands are quite hard to stretch, but once they are in place you can leave them on. I put mine on at the start of the season and remove them only after the last tour, though I do flip the rands off the toes of the boots when they are not in use to prevent the tension from causing the boot soles to curl up. Using such gaiters means I need to wax my boots only once a year, when I put them away for the summer. Weights are around 12 to 18 ounces/350 to 525 grams a pair.

The fit of supergaiters is important, and they usually come in a number of sizes. Originally designed for double mountaineering boots, some of them have a baggy fit around the uppers on lighter touring boots. Checking the fit in the store is a good idea.

Unless you have long pants or bibs with built-in gaiters that fit well over your boots (most don't, being designed for alpine ski boots), some form of knee-high gaiter is essential when skiing in soft snow. If you don't fancy supergaiters, you need some standard ones (weights around 7 to 14 ounces/200 to 400 grams). They half cover the boots, keeping snow out and providing a windproof, snowproof covering for the lower leg. Many varieties are available. Those with front zippers, if you can find them, are easier to use than those with rear or side zippers because you can adjust your boot laces without having to remove the gaiters. Velcro-fastened gaiters are available, too, but you need to keep the Velcro clear of snow and ice or else the two halves won't stick together properly. Overall I prefer zippers. The cords or straps that run under the instep and hold the gaiter down on the boot wear out surprisingly quickly, so carry some spare cord or nylon webbing. These laces are also prone to icing up, sometimes accumulating balls of ice and snow large enough to interfere with your skiing.

Nylon is the standard material for gaiters, usually heavy-duty at the bottom, lighter for the uppers. Although more expensive, uppers made from waterproof breathable fabrics like Gore-Tex or Ultrex are far more comfortable than nonbreathable ones. Cotton canvas gaiters, hard to find now, are usually tougher and longer lasting than synthetic fabrics. They can be re-proofed too. Insulated versions, usually filled with Thinsulate, are available for extreme cold. Gaiters should be stiff enough to stay up without needing to be fastened tightly below the knee. Such fastenings can be uncomfortable and usually slip anyway. You should need to pull in the top of the gaiter only enough to keep snow out, not to keep it up. Short lengths of cord tied to the zippers can make zipping and unzipping much easier in bad weather.

Heel Lifts

On long climbs, especially direct ascents using skins, your unsupported ankles and Achilles tendons come under a great deal of strain, which heel lifts are designed to prevent. Several different styles are available. Black Diamond's Tele-Vates and Rainey Designs's UpHeel are heel plates with flip-up metal lifts. Voilé's Climbing Post is a triangular block that is attached to the boot by means of a bungee cord and cinch strap and can be flipped out of the way when not needed. I have never used a heel lift, but they look useful and I intend to. I have a pair of Tele-Vates—all I have to do is get around to fixing them to some skis.

Poles

Compared with the intricacies of skis, boots, and bindings, poles are a relatively simple item. Their purpose is to help push you along when on the flat and uphill and to aid balance and timing when turning downhill. Features to look for are length, strength, tip design, basket size and shape, and handle shape.

Length

For general touring use, the traditional method of choosing a pole that fits under your armpit with the point on the ground is still valid. Calculating your height less 14 inches (35cm) will yield about the same. A shorter pole whose basket is on the snow when you hold it with your forearm parallel to the ground is better for downhilling.

You can avoid choosing between these two if you buy adjustable poles, first developed for alpine ski mountaineering but nowadays often called telemark poles. You can shorten the pole for downhills, bring it up to armpit height for diagonal striding, fully extend it for skating, and even have one pole short and one long for traversing steep slopes. That is the theory. However, after five years of using adjustable poles I have realized that I rarely actually alter their length, for reasons of time and bother. When wet or snow-covered, the poles can be hard to grip firmly and the adjustment threads very difficult to move. I have seen them frozen solid. I now prefer non-adjustable poles. It is often said that downhilling is difficult with long poles, but it need not be so. (See the section on downhill techniques in chapter 3 for details.) If you are tall, by the way, note that most adjustable poles extend to a maximum of 145cm, which may not be long enough. The longest I have come across is the Leki Rainier, which extends to 160cm. Nonadjustable poles are available in lengths up to 160cm at 5cm intervals. Some adjustable poles, like the Leki Lawisond, can be joined together to form an avalanche probe, an advantage worth considering if you ski in avalanche-prone terrain. Two-section poles are stronger than three-section ones, though both are surprisingly tough.

Strength

Strength is important. Skiing with a single pole is difficult, to say the least. To minimize the chance of breakage the shaft should be made of aluminum alloy rather than fiberglass: aluminum is stronger, and if it does break it tends to do so cleanly, making it easier to mend. Fiberglass shatters and splinters along its length, making repair difficult, and the cracks in the pole tend to extend beyond the repair quite quickly. The best alloys, such as 7075 T6, bend rather than break in all but the most severe fall. To lessen the chance of breakage, poles shouldn't be used as levers to heave yourself up after a fall. I have often seen heavily laden skiers doing this, their poles bending alarmingly under the strain. Even with care the strongest poles can break, so I always carry repair items with me. On long tours in remote country it is worth carrying an adjustable pole as a spare. The ones with three sections collapse small enough to carry easily strapped to a pack.

Tips

Poles should have sharp tips for security on hard snow and ice. Many don't, especially some of the adjustable ones. Wide flat alloy tips are fine in soft snow but tend to skid off ice. The tungsten carbide steel points on Swix poles are the sharpest I have come across. Leki adjustable poles have carbide tips that are rounded rather than pointed, but they work on ice. Tungsten tips are also hard wearing and remain sharp a long time.

Baskets

Baskets should be fairly large, around 4 to 5 inches (10 to 12cm) in diameter, for use in soft snow. If they are flexible they work fine on hard snow too, but stiff ones can catch. Big baskets can catch on brush in trees, but I have never found this a problem. Most track and alpine baskets, designed for packed snow, aren't really suitable for touring. Track baskets, in particular, are often made from fairly rigid plastic that skates on icy snow. I have seen a few resulting falls on steep slopes of hard-packed snow. Adjustable poles usually come with alpine baskets, but wider touring baskets are available for most models and are worth getting. Baskets can and do break, so carrying a spare is worthwhile. They are usually interchangeable, so you needn't worry about the make. When a basket on my Leki poles snapped I replaced it with a Swix one that was more flexible and worked better than the original.

Grips

Traditional nordic grips are simple tubes of leather or plastic that are comfortable and allow for an easy pole swing. Adjustable poles usually have alpine grips with finger grooves and, sometimes, guards at top and bottom that can hamper pole handling a little. Overall I prefer the simple nordic grip. Some grips, such as those found on Leki adjustable poles, are a compromise between the two. They are comfortable and worth considering.

If you venture into really steep mountain terrain where a slip could be serious, the self-arrest grips made by Black Diamond or Leki could be worth having. They have two sharp spikes protruding from a curved pick that fits into the top of the grip. The picks can be removed when not needed. Although designed for the maker's poles, they will fit other models.

Wrist Loops

Wrist loops should be adjustable for different thicknesses of gloves and mitts. Breakaway loops are a good safety feature. I don't use wrist loops when descending through forests, brush, or anywhere that I think I might snag a basket, which could lead to a dislocated shoulder. It is also a good idea not to use wrist loops in avalanche terrain or on steep icy snow where you might need to attempt to self-arrest with your poles.

Models

My favorite poles are the nonadjustable Swix Mountain poles. They are extremely strong, have wide floating baskets, nordic grips, and lethally sharp tungsten steel tips. They also balance very well and swing easily in my hands, making them less tiring to use than other poles. For downhill use, when shorter poles are in theory an advantage, I find that by cocking my wrist I can plant the pole farther away from my body and thus keep my position low. Of the adjustable poles, I like the two-section Leki Lawisonds, which have tungsten tips and modified alpine grips without guards and can be used as avalanche probes. I have used my Lekis a great deal and have found them tough and efficient, but they don't balance quite as well as the Swix poles. Leki also makes a popular three-section pole, the Makalu, that collapses to a small size and is useful as a spare.

Repair Kit

However good your equipment and however careful a skier you are, breakage and damage do occur. I have never been on a tour of more than a few days when something hasn't failed or broken. At times I have had to deal with snapped poles, broken baskets, ripped-out pin-holes, delaminating ski tips, even broken skis. In remote places such breakages can be very serious, especially if the snow is deep and walking isn't easy or perhaps not even feasible. Being able to effect a repair that at least enables you to ski out by the easiest route requires a fairly comprehensive repair kit. Only one kit is needed in a group, though you need to be sure you have the means to repair or replace different sorts of gear. Over the years I have put together the following selection of items that I carry in a tough zippered nylon bag:

Posidrive screwdriver for tightening ski-binding screws—different bindings have different-size screws, so make sure you have the right size screwdriver or one with various replaceable bits, such as Black Diamond's T-Grip Posi-Driver.

Vise-Grip for use as pliers and to hold ski edges together after gluing.

Strong wire for jury-rigging bindings—thin wire can even be used for stitching split boot soles.

Quick-drying epoxy for gluing delaminated skis is essential. Swix manufactures packets called Ski Rep.

Duct tape—strong and waterproof, it is useful for all types of repairs, especially broken poles.

Emery cloth for smoothing rough edges.

Binding screws in case of loss.

Hose clamps, small and large, for holding together repaired poles and skis.

Empty drink can—ideal as a splint for broken poles when cut in two.

Section of wooden pole for jamming inside broken poles.

Steel wool packing for binding holes.

Spare binding—more than one for a large group.

Spare cable if relevant.

Spare basket—two or three for a large group.

Spare plastic slip-on ski tip.

P-tex candle for filling in gouges in ski bases.

There are many other items that could be useful, but remember they all have to be carried. I also carry a Rucksack model Swiss Army knife, a multipurpose tool with so many uses that I keep it easily accessible in a pants pocket or the pack lid pocket rather than in the repair kit. A Leatherman tool or similar would be an alternative. Repair items for clothing and camping gear are also needed. These are discussed in Chapter 9.

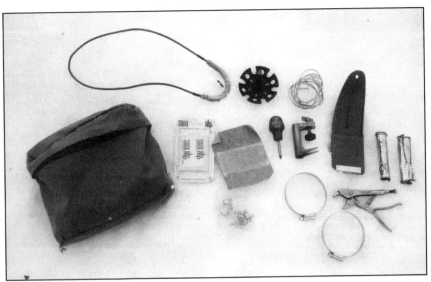

Repair kit showing some of the items needed on a tour.

Some breakages can't be easily or successfully repaired, of course, and you have to decide at the time whether it is worth trying. On our descent from the Columbia Icefield (see Chapter 10) a ski snapped completely in two under the binding. Because we were less than a day from the road and in an area where the snow was patchy so we had to walk in places anyway, we didn't bother trying to repair the ski. If we had been high on the ice field we would have had to do something, probably open up the rear half of the ski at the break, jam in the front half, and try to glue, tape, and clamp it together so it could at least be used for walking. On tours in really remote areas a case can be made for carrying a pair of snowshoes or even, if large pulks are being used, a set of skis in the event a ski breaks.

In other situations a quick repair is worthwhile. Our party was just starting the descent of the Hardangerjokul ice cap in Norway when one of us broke a fiberglass pole. As the descent is long and in places steep, we headed for a small shelter hut below the summit plateau to see if we could patch it. Typically for a fiberglass pole, it was still in one piece but had lost all rigidity where it had split. Luckily, the myriad longitudinal cracks had not spread far. First I taped the split with duct tape, then I wound half a metal can around it as a splint, clamped that tight with two small hose clamps, and

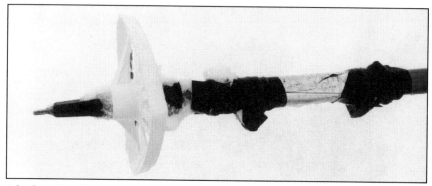

A broken ski pole repaired with a tin-can splint, hose clamps, and strong tape.

finally taped up each end of the splint. This crude repair rendered the pole usable for the descent. It would not have lasted long, but the skier was able to buy another pair at the mountain lodge where we were staying. The next time I had to make such a repair (fiberglass poles break with alarming regularity) I also jammed a section of wooden pole into the pole halves for extra strength. On this occasion

Repairing a ski base with a P-tex candle.

the pole lasted for three days before breaking again in a fall in which both the metal splint and the wood core snapped in two.

While you can't predict failures, keeping your gear in good working order helps prevent them. Before a long tour I check that my binding screws are tight, that my skis don't have gouges in the base or show any signs of delamination, and that my boot soles aren't coming off. I also check my pole grips and baskets for wear or damage. It is much easier to effect repairs at home than halfway down a mountainside in a blizzard.

Some Final Thoughts

While it is worth taking care over your selection of gear, skiing isn't about equipment, and you can get by with almost anything as long as you accept its limitations. The best gear of only a few decades ago would be rejected as inadequate now, but people skied happily on it then (some still do!). Over a century ago Sondre Norheim invented the telemark turn using heavy wooden skis and crude cable bindings. While good equipment will make life easier, it won't make you a good skier. Nor should you think that you have to have the best before you can go touring. I did my first tours in Scotland, the Alps, and the Rockies on the mediocre gear described at the start of the chapter. I didn't have skins either. But although I shudder now at some of the things I did, I enjoyed myself. And that's what it's all about.

Skiing Skills

*"Tighten up the toe strap, adjust the heel strap
and away you go," he said confidently.*
—*Guy Sheridan,* Tales of a Cross-Country Skier

The better skier you are the more you will enjoy your skiing, the farther and faster you will be able to go into the wilderness, and the more rugged the terrain you will feel confident skiing on. Once you have learned the basics, you improve mostly by practice. Occasional lessons are worthwhile too, especially if you have a problem or a barrier you can't work through by yourself. An instructor or experienced friend may well be able to point out what you need to do. Rather than dash off on a long, hard route on your first day out after a long hiatus, choose an easier, shorter route so you can familiarize yourself with being on skis again and practice some techniques without the pressure of having to travel far.

In this chapter I have outlined the basic techniques and indicated where I think they fit into touring. I have also emphasized those points that I have noticed can cause problems (from my own skiing as well as from instructing and watching others) when skiing with a pack in the mountains. Touring is different from track or piste skiing. Techniques that work well on prepared snow when you have only a light pack must often be modified for touring.

The Beginning

The first challenge, if you have never been on skis before, is to get used to having long, slippery boards strapped to your feet. Remember that skis are meant to slide—that's what they're for. As you learn to ski, you will learn to control the skis so they slide where and when you want them to. Practice the following exercises without your poles, so you learn to keep your balance over your feet.

Positioning Your Body

Before you move the skis think about your body position. Are you standing stiffly, with every muscle tense, because you know that if you relax for a second your skis will shoot away from you? Quite probably—but you can't ski like that. Instead, adopt a more relaxed yet athletic stance with your stomach pulled in, your shoulders down, and your knees and ankles flexed forward. If you keep your ankles straight, you will sit back onto an invisible chair, an uncomfortable position that puts your weight too far back. You should be able to bounce up and down on your skis, using your knees as shock absorbers.

Avoid developing the habit of watching your skis. You can't control them with your eyes, though many beginners try to. Apart from preventing you from seeing where you are going or admiring the scenery, watching your ski tips also tilts your body forward and puts you in a position where you are more likely to fall.

Warming Up

It is best to move in place at first. Slide the skis backward and forward, then pick up each one in turn. Speed up the movements as you begin to feel more confident. If this makes you feel unstable (at this stage just being on skis is bound to make you feel a little wobbly), flex your knees more. Stiff, straight legs make any ski technique—from slow shuffles on the flat to the fastest downhill turn—very difficult. To ski well you need to be relaxed.

Falling

Oddly enough, one way to relax is to fall deliberately. All skiers fall, and if you learn to fall safely you will be far less likely to hurt yourself. Flex your knees and slowly sit down sideways, keeping your hands out in front of you. Try it again with your poles, keeping them out of the way. When you are skiing and you know you are going to fall (more often than not during a descent), it is better to fall deliberately than to lose control and do a painful face-plant over the tips of your skis.

Falling is very easy. It is getting up again that is difficult. First get your skis parallel and at a right angle to the slope, if you are on one. Otherwise, on even the slightest slope, your skis will slide away from you as soon as you start to stand. If you fall on a slope with your body below your skis, swing yourself around on the snow and plant your skis below you. Once your skis are parallel and close together, simply push yourself up with your hands into a kneeling position and then stand up, using the slope to help you. If the snow is soft, cross your poles on the surface of the snow and push down on them for better support. Do not try to heave yourself up on your poles; it is very hard work, and you may easily bend or break a pole.

Star Turns

Once you have fallen over and gotten up a few times, try a star turn; leave your poles to the side so you are depending on balance. Lift up the tip of one ski (just the tip, not the whole ski) and move it out a little from the other ski. Then move the other ski parallel with it. Keep repeating this until you have turned a full circle. Look at the pattern you have made in the snow and you will see why this is called a star turn. If you find yourself crossing the tails of your skis, your steps are too big; if you are crossing the tips, you are moving the wrong ski first or moving it the wrong way. If you feel very insecure and keep falling over, try flexing more at the knees and placing the ski down more firmly after moving it. Don't lean back or sideways—keep your weight over your feet.

Kick Turns

Star turns are slow and require a wide, flat area. Imagine trying to do one on a narrow forest trail or, even worse, a slope. You can turn directly from front to back with a kick turn, using your poles as supports. Place the poles almost at arm's length on either side of your skis (Figure 3-1a) and then kick one ski forward and up so it is upright on the snow (Figure 3-1b). Next pivot it away from you and turn it until you can put it back down on the snow facing the other way (Figure 3-1c). This position is very awkward, so as quickly as possible (but carefully, carefully!) swing the other ski around next to the first one (Figures 3-1d and 3-1e). The kick turn may at first seem possible only if you are a contortionist, but it is an important maneuver, so it is worth persevering until you can do it readily in both directions.

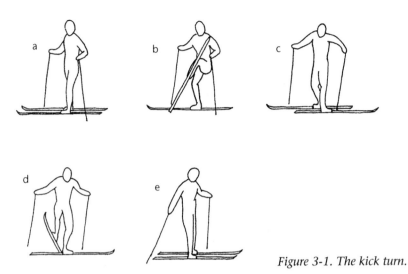

Figure 3-1. The kick turn.

Sidestepping

Sidestepping is normally used for ascending or descending slopes, but practicing it on the flat at this early stage helps you learn to transfer weight from one ski to the other. To sidestep, stand with the skis parallel, then pick up one ski and move it a short way directly to the side, following it with the other and keeping them parallel. You will find that you have to weight the stationary ski and then transfer your weight to the ski you have just moved. Do a few steps one way and then a few the other. If you keep your knees flexed, you will be less likely to fall and are more able to react quickly if one of the skis slips. Remember that stiff legs make it difficult to ski well.

First Steps

By now you are probably getting bored with standing on the same spot, so it is time to go for a walk, or rather a glide, on your skis, sliding each one forward in turn. You will find that the looser and more relaxed you are the more stable you will feel. Try skiing with all your muscles tense, then with all your muscles relaxed, and note the difference. If you find that your forward ski shoots off ahead, leaving you behind, flex your knee and push it forward as you glide so that your weight stays over the ski. This basic principle underlies all ski techniques: *your weight must be over the lead ski if you are to stay in balance.* It is better to exaggerate this stance than to edge the ski forward with your toes. Once you have made a track in the snow, ski up and down it a few times to get used to the feeling of moving. As you relax, you should feel a flow developing, a feeling of moving effortlessly with the skis and the snow rather than against them. Practice moving without poles first. Then add poles to the movement.

Holding Your Poles

To hold the poles correctly, put each hand through the pole strap from below, so that when you grasp the handle of the pole the strap lies between your thumb and forefinger (see Figure 3-2). Using the strap this way allows you to relax your fingers and hold the pole loosely. This in turn will allow you to relax your arms and shoulders and reduce the tension in your whole body.

A First Descent

The thought of a descent fills many nordic skiers, including some experienced ones, with trepidation, yet this experience can be the most enjoyable part of the day.

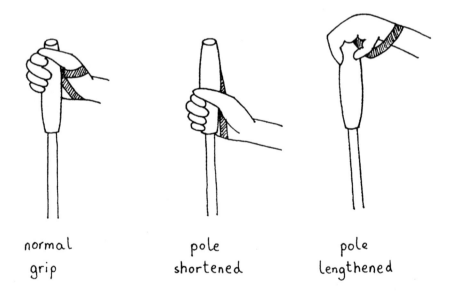

normal grip   pole shortened   pole lengthened

Figure 3-2. Holding the pole.

To get used to the sensation of sliding effortlessly down a slope, try some direct descents on short gentle slopes of soft snow with good long run-outs. Push off with your poles and allow gravity to bring you slowly to a halt. As your confidence grows, practice from higher up and on steeper slopes and try changing your body position to see how it feels: stand up straight, then flex your knees and sink down. Which feels most stable? To get used to balancing on one ski, lift one off the snow, then the other.

Once you can shuffle along comfortably, get up when you fall over, do kick turns, and slide down easy slopes, you are ready to go on your first short tour. You are no longer a complete beginner.

Travel on the Flat

The Diagonal Stride

The fast, athletic diagonal stride—the kick and glide of the track skier—is not something you will do often when touring. That stride doesn't go with unbroken snow or a heavy pack. The basic technique is the same, however, and the better you are at the diagonal stride

The basic stride.

the easier you will find touring on flat and gently undulating terrain. The diagonal stride is much more dynamic than the sliding walk you have probably been doing so far. The idea is to glide as far and as fast on each ski as is possible.

Push off with one foot (Figure 3-3a) and then put all your weight on the other ski as it starts to glide (Figure 3-3b). Push your knee and your hip forward over the leading ski, keeping your weight centered there, and glide as far as possible. The more tentative you are at getting your weight over the front ski, the slower you will glide and the less distance you will travel. Let the skis do the work. As you slow down, push off on the other foot (Figures 3-3c and 3-3d). If you hear your ski making a slapping sound on the snow just before you kick down, your ski may be coming down on the snow too soon and too far behind the other ski. Concentrate on pushing your hips over the gliding ski so that the rear ski hits the snow as your feet pass each other.

Figure 3-3. The diagonal stride.

Practice at first without your poles so you can concentrate on the leg and foot actions and not be confused by trying to do things with your poles at the same time. You will probably find that your arms swing back and forth naturally as you ski along. If not, swing them from your shoulders like pendulums, keeping them slightly bent at the elbows and letting them drift well back behind your body. Force isn't needed. Your arms should be relaxed.

Once you are happy with your basic glide, you can pick up your poles again. It is surprising how many skiers waste a lot of energy by using their poles as outriggers, holding them away from their body to the side. If you hold them out that way, the push you get from them will be sideways rather than forward. For maximum efficiency, your pole should be planted almost at arm's reach out in front of you, with the basket no more than 6 to 10 inches/15 to 25cm from the edge of the ski. The pole should be planted with the tip to the rear so that when you push down on it you are pushed forward (Figure 3-3b). (If you angle the pole away from you it will act as a brake.) To gain the most power from each pole plant, let your arm go back past your hip (Figure 3-3d). Remember how your arms swung when you skied without poles. They should be moving in just the same way now. If you stop your arm at your hip, it will act as a check and result in a shorter glide.

When you are carrying a heavy load you will need to modify your pole technique slightly. Keep your arms lower in order to avoid tiring your shoulders, and plant your poles not quite so far in front.

Double Poling

Double poling is very useful for gaining speed when you are on hard snow or in other skiers' tracks, especially on slight downhill slopes. The technique also gives your muscles a break from diagonal striding. To double pole, keep your skis parallel, plant both poles almost at arm's length—angled to the rear—and push the handles away from you forward and downward, bending forward from the waist and almost falling onto the poles as you do so (Figures 3-4a, 3-4b, and 3-4c). Again, let your hands go back past your hips for greatest efficiency (Figures 3-4b, 3-4c, and 3-4d). If you are double poling with a heavy pack, it is easier if you do not bend quite so far forward.

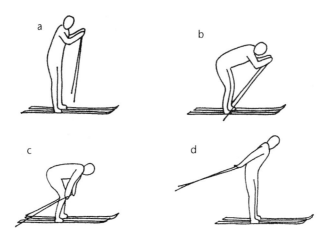

Figure 3-4. Double poling.

Mixed Techniques

Pure diagonal stride and double-poling techniques are fine when practicing. When touring, a mixture of techniques is often more efficient; you may want to switch from one to another according to the terrain and the snow. You can also rest both arms or double pole while diagonal striding.

I discovered a useful technique when one of my students broke a pole beyond repair and I loaned him one of mine. I quickly found that diagonal striding with only one pole was awkward and unstable. The easiest way to travel was to glide continuously on one ski, propelled with kicks from the other ski and pushes from the single pole. Since then I have found that this "scootering" technique works even better with two poles, and I use it often, especially on packed snow or icy tracks when double poling is tiring to maintain but the diagonal stride is a little slow. You may hear the technique described as "one-push-double-pole" or "kick-double-pole." Alternating the legs is often recommended, but I have found it easier and less tiring to kick off one ski several times in succession, only changing to the other when my kicking leg begins to tire.

V-1 Skating

Skating isn't an essential touring skill, but it is a useful and enjoyable one. Even more than double poling, skating requires a hard-packed surface. You may not use the technique often, but when you come upon a frozen lake or a meadow covered with wind-packed snow, no other technique will speed you across with so little effort, especially if your wax is wearing thin. Skating is estimated to be twice as fast as diagonal striding. The key to effortless skating is rhythm, which is important for all skiing but is absolutely essential for skating. If you know how to ice-skate, the easiest way to learn to skate on skis is to pretend you are on ice skates. I have seen a number of people pick up ski skating within minutes this way. If you are not an ice-skater, you have to start from scratch.

There are many different styles of skating and even more names for them. For touring, concentrate on the one variously known as V-1 skating, two skating, or asymmetrical skating. The technique involves double poling over just one ski, and it is an easy, relaxing, and fast way to skate with a pack. As with the diagonal

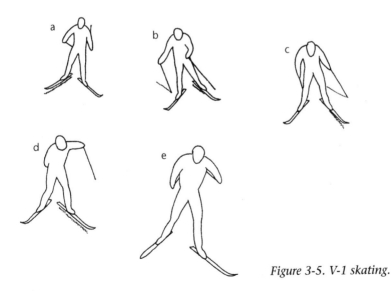

Figure 3-5. V-1 skating.

stride, when skating you glide on one ski, pushing off with the other ski. Because your skis are at an angle to each other, one has to be set on its edge, making a platform that you can push off against (Figure 3-5a). (Most people find when they try skating that the ski goes onto its edge automatically when they push on it without conscious effort.) Because skating is so efficient, the forward ski is quite likely to shoot out ahead of you. To counter this movement, flex your knee and really throw your hip over the ski (Figure 3-5b). Make sure all your weight is over the gliding ski.

Try V-1 skating by pointing your ski tips out in a V, then pushing off one ski with both poles, making sure that they are outside your skis, and throwing your weight over the other ski (Figure 3-5b). As this ski slows, shift your weight back to the first ski and, without using your poles, glide (Figures 3-5c, 3-5d, and 3-5e). Then with a double-pole push, shift back to the ski you started with. Because your skis are farther apart and at an angle to each other, moving from one ski to the other feels much more dynamic and positive than when diagonal striding. By poling over just one ski, you can develop a fast yet relaxed rhythm. Try double poling over both skis (V-2 skating) to see why V-1 skating is better for touring. If you are having problems coordinating pole and ski movements or find that you are not getting much glide, try skating without your poles. You will have to get your weight onto the leading ski to move at all.

Uphill

You can diagonal stride straight up short, gentle slopes by leaning forward, picking up your skis, and slapping them down harder on the snow. You will slow down and glide less, but for a time you can keep going. On most slopes this technique doesn't work for long, and whether waxed or waxless, your skis will soon start slipping. For long climbs the solution is to use climbing skins. For short ascents you do need to know some uphill techniques; you will also need them for slopes too steep to ascend directly even with skins.

Herringbone Climbing

The herringbone technique works well for very short steep climbs (Figure 3-6). You can change to the herringbone position without stopping, as soon as your skis start to slip. Simply angle your skis out-

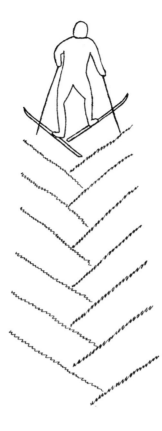

Figure 3-6. The herringbone.

ward, placing the skis on their edges to form platforms that you can push off from. This may sound similar to skating. It is, and a good skater can skate up quite steep hills. When the skate slows to a walk and the glide fades away it becomes a herringbone. Your poles are important when herringboning, and you need to keep moving. Most backsliding, a literal description, is due to a lack of aggression and commitment. Don't hesitate! On the flat if you fail to get your weight over the leading ski you simply go slower and have to work harder. If you fail to do so while herringbone climbing you will start to slip and will probably find yourself down in the snow. You can't tiptoe up a slope. Put the whole weight of your body on each ski as it hits the snow, throwing your hips over the ski to get your whole weight on it quickly. Leaning your torso forward puts your weight ahead of your skis, so try to keep upright, bending at the knees and ankles rather than the waist. Look ahead rather than down at your skis.

Because herringboning is hard work it is only suitable for short slopes, unless you are very strong and determined. I have seen Norwegian skiers herringbone for many hundreds of feet up steep slopes—not something I would like to try. Also, unless you take care—not easy as you sweat and grunt up a slope—you can chop your ski tails to bits as the metal edges slice into the top plates.

Sidestepping

Sidestepping is a less strenuous, slower, and more relaxed way to climb short steep slopes (Figure 3-7). This technique is also a good way to learn about both weight transfer and edge control. Unless I am in a hurry I prefer to sidestep rather than herringbone. Sidestepping is less tiring and allows you to look around. On all but the steepest slopes you can stop to catch your breath, take photographs, or watch the snowshoe rabbit that has just appeared.

To sidestep, stand with your skis parallel and at right angles to

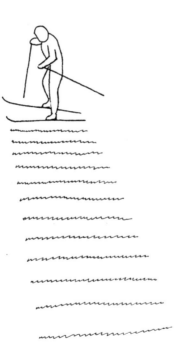

Figure 3-7. Sidestepping.

the slope, then step sideways up the slope one ski at a time. To prevent your skis from slipping, keep them tilted onto the edge nearest the slope (the inside edge) to make a platform on which to stand. As you roll your ankles and knees into the hill, the skis will move with them. You also need to ensure that your weight is over one ski when you place it on the snow. Keep the steps short to avoid overbalancing, especially on steep slopes. If you find the skis slipping forward or backward, it is because they aren't at 90 degrees to the fall line (the direction a snowball would take if rolled downhill).

Although you may have to balance just on your edges, you can ascend very steep and icy slopes that it would be impossible to climb with the herringbone technique. When the slope gets this steep it helps to slip your upper hand out of the pole strap and grasp the pole much lower on the shaft and place the palm of your lower hand over the top of the pole.

Traversing

You can climb long slopes by traversing them, sliding forward at an angle at which your skis won't slip. At the end of each traverse, do a partial kick turn—you don't want to end up facing the way you have come but at an angle to it. A partial, say two-thirds, kick turn is usually enough. At the end of an upward traverse kick the uphill ski around and place it on the snow in the direction of your next traverse, then follow with your other ski, placing it ahead of the first ski so you can keep moving. On gentle to moderate slopes you can climb continuously by this method. On steeper slopes you may need to stop and stamp out a platform before you can do a kick turn. Traversing may be necessary even when using skins on a long steep climb where going straight up is either too tiring or simply impossible.

On icy snow you may find you are skiing just on your edges. Then it is best to look for softer snow or a flatter area for your kick turn or else stamp out a platform. On steep traverses you can also slip your uphill hand out of your pole strap and hold the pole lower down to reduce strain on your arm. When traversing, it is best to use the whole width of the slope. Long traverses with a minimum number of kick turns are quicker and less tiring than short traverses and endless kick turns.

Combining traverses with sidestepping lets you ascend steep

slopes more quickly, particularly if the slope isn't wide enough for long traverses. To combine the techniques, move your ski forward as well as upward when you sidestep.

Downhill

In the mountains, being good at downhill skiing means being able to stay in control and choose the best turn for the snow and the terrain rather than swoop at full speed into the unknown. While the function of turns is to check your speed, making fast linked turns down open slopes or powder-filled bowls is always exciting and satisfying.

The first thing to do before starting a descent is to consider how you are going to handle it. Cautious traverses? High-speed telemarks? Stem turns? Jump turns? However you start, unless you climbed most or all of the entire length of the slope beforehand and observed the conditions, be prepared to change tactics very quickly if the snow changes. The firm hardpack at the top, ideal for stem or even parallel turns, may turn, halfway down, to breakable crust on which only kick turns are safe. I have descended gullies shaded on one side and sunlit on the other where I could turn easily one way but not the other. The resulting mixture of kick and stem turns didn't produce a smooth rhythm, but it did work. How you are feeling makes a great difference too. If you are tired and aware you have not been skiing well for the last few hours, it is wise to be cautious. I have started on descents and realized quickly that I was not in the right mood for tackling them head-on and instead made my way more slowly. At other times skill and confidence come together and I can soar down slopes wondering why I ever find descents difficult.

The Downhill Stance

Body position is even more important for downhill skiing than it is for skiing on the flat or uphill. A rigid, straight-legged stance will throw you all over the slope and make you feel very unstable. Your knees and ankles should be flexed forward, and your torso should be upright. Check this position by seeing if you can feel pressure from the tongue of your boot on the front of your ankles. If you can't, bend your ankles more. Alpine ski boots force you into this position, but nordic touring boots do not, so you have to concentrate on maintaining it.

Straight Running

When the slope isn't too long or steep and you can see a good, long run-out at the bottom, the simplest, fastest, and most exciting way to descend is to point your skis down the hill and go. If the snow is soft and even, a straight descent may be quite easy. Where the snow varies, however, and where there are bumps and dips on the slope, a little more technique is needed. In particular the knees should be well flexed so they can absorb bumps. On very bumpy terrain, pushing one ski a little ahead of the other and raising the rear heel in a hint of the telemark position (see the section on telemark turns) will aid stability.

If you feel yourself starting to fall or if your weight moves back over your skis, flex your knees even more and lower your center of gravity. Push your hands forward as well. If your hands start to drift behind you, you will straighten up and your weight will go back too.

Ultimately, for maximum stability at high speed, go into a tuck position, just like a downhill racer. Bend your body forward, push your derriere high in the air, rest your elbows on your knees, and tuck your poles under your arms, bracing them against your body. Point your poles backward, for safety if nothing else—you don't want to stab other skiers as you zoom past them.

Traverses and Kick Turns

The easiest and safest but often the slowest way to descend a slope is by traverses (Figure 3-8a) and kick turns. In breakable crust where the snow collapses as soon as you put weight on it, or on slopes where the snow is thin and there are many rocks visible, this may be the only sensible way to descend. It is certainly the best method to use on any slope where you don't feel confident. Ignore what others do. If you feel best being cautious, then be cautious. On a wide slope you can pick up quite a bit of speed in a traverse, and with kick turns you can sometimes get down quite quickly this way, certainly faster than if you keep falling over as you try to link turns on the move.

Staying in balance during a traverse, especially on hard-packed snow, can be difficult. The key is to keep most of your weight over the edge of the downhill ski. On steep slopes this means you will feel as though you are leaning away from the hill. That's OK. If you lean into the hill you will fall. Keep your torso upright, angling your

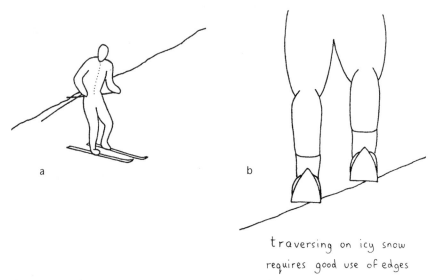

traversing on icy snow
requires good use of edges

Figure 3-8. The traverse.

knees into the hill. The idea is to put the skis onto their uphill edges (Figure 3-8b) so they don't skid downhill. Push the upper ski slightly ahead of the lower ski; this stance makes it easier to stay in balance and to keep the skis on their edges. In soft snow or on gentle slopes, edging isn't really necessary, and you won't need to push your knees into the hill so much either.

I prefer to kick turn facing downhill and across the slope or, as it is often called, the fall line. Many people prefer to kick turn facing upslope so they don't have to look down the hill, but this maneuver can be difficult on a really steep slope where your skis may catch on the snow. If your kick turns are a little wobbly or the slope is very steep and the snow hard packed, you might want to stamp out a platform first. In mixed snow, look ahead as you traverse for softer patches where it will be easier to turn.

On a fast traverse you have to stop before you can kick turn, and some people have a problem stopping. If you twist your knees up into the slope, the skis will pivot and the tips will turn in to the hill. You can also use step turns and telemarks (described below). Practice stopping traverses on easy slopes before you venture high into the mountains and onto terrain where it could be dangerous not to be able to stop at will.

Step Turns

A step turn is an extremely useful movement. You can use it to turn downhill across the fall line on gentle slopes, to stop a traverse, to round corners on trails and in narrow corridors in forests or rocky terrain, and to avoid rocks, trees, fallen skiers, and other unexpected objects that may leap in front of you. The step turn is basically a star turn done on the move.

To step turn, lift the tip of the inside ski—that is, the ski that will be on the inside of the turn (Figure 3-9a), point it in the direction you want to go (Figure 3-9b), put your weight on it, and then step the other ski next to it (Figure 3-9c). The steps should be kept short so you don't cross the tails of your skis. For sharp turns several steps are necessary. If you find you can't lift the ski you want to step it is probably because your weight is on it; shift your weight to the other ski immediately before you step. It is quicker, more efficient, and less tiring to lift just the tip rather than the whole ski: pull your toes upward toward your knees and press down on your heel; turn your shoulders in the direction of the turn so you can use your upper body to help steer the skis.

Sideslipping

Traverses work best on reasonably wide slopes. On steep, narrow slopes between trees or in gullies you can sidestep down. It works

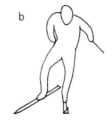

Figure 3-9. The step turn.

just as well going down as up. If you feel your downhill pole is a little short, put your palm over the top of the grip. Where the snow is hard packed, sidestepping can become sideslipping, a technique that requires good balance and edge control. To sideslip, flatten your skis onto the snow by rolling your knees down the slope, allowing your skis to skid downhill. To stop slipping, roll your knees up into the hill to set the skis back onto their edges. By rocking backward and forward on your skis you can weight either your toes or heels and thus sideslip backward or forward, a useful way of rounding obstacles.

Mixing Techniques

In difficult snow all the above techniques can be combined. A party of us once came off a 6,500-foot/2,000-meter peak in Norway's Jotunheimen Mountains on some of the worst snow it has ever been my misfortune to descend. Patches of ice were mixed with breakable crust, soft, windblown snow, and hard ridges. At times our skis shot across the slopes at high speed, bouncing over the ridges, while at other times they buried themselves deep under the crust and we stopped abruptly. Downhill turns were out of the question. It was not the place to risk an injury.

Traverses and kick turns were the obvious method of descent, but in those conditions even traverses were unpleasant as we worked to hold our edges on the bone-shaking rippled ice and then strove to avoid face-plants as we hit the soft snow. I soon discovered that sideslipping down the channels of icy snow was easier and faster than traversing. I probed ahead with my downhill pole as I progressed, so I could stop when a patch of soft snow appeared below me. Then I would traverse across to the next bit of hard snow, using step turns to stop when I reached it, then sideslipping again. Instead of straining muscles by holding one position all the way down, I was able to vary the position and lessen the strain.

Preparing for Downhill Turns

Often (very often, hopefully) you will encounter slopes of good snow on which it is possible to descend quickly and enjoyably by linking downhill turns. This is when those who can manage only kick turns and traverses watch jealously as those with more skill soar effortlessly along, relishing the freedom their skills grant them.

Some of the most important elements of descent are incorporated in the traversing and sideslipping skills described above. However, the most important factor of all is your commitment. You cannot ski downhill successfully while holding back. I have already said that getting your weight over the leading ski is important. For downhill turns it is crucial. Hesitate here and all is lost.

Upper-body position is important too. Bent double with your backside poking out is not the best way to ski, though many skiers adopt this pose. Instead, you should be upright with your stomach pulled in, your back fairly straight, and your shoulders dropped and relaxed. When your shoulders hunch up and stiffen, the rest of your body tends to do the same. If I find myself tensing up and starting to lean forward at the waist, I drop my shoulders. The movement works wonders. Remember, too, to keep your knees and ankles flexed. Turning skis with your legs rigid is just about impossible.

SLOPE PREPARATION

Firm snow and a smooth slope are best for learning and practicing downhill techniques. If you don't mind the paraphernalia and the other skiers, an alpine resort is an ideal place. Using the lifts saves energy and enables you to concentrate on downhilling. Elsewhere you may need to prepare your own slope by sidestepping up and down until it is well packed. The more people available to do this job the quicker and easier it is. Once you have a prepared slope, it is best to climb it at the sides rather than up the center, both to avoid damaging it and so downhill skiers won't need to look out for ascending skiers. Making such a slope and practicing downhill turns on it can be done on a tour on days when the weather is too bad for touring or you feel like a break from skiing with a pack. To make it more fun, you can set up a slalom course with your poles and have races, or try cutting figure eights or matching turns. Practicing without poles is a good idea; it helps with balance and prevents you from worrying about what to do with them.

THE WEDGE OR SNOWPLOW

Most nordic skiers want to learn to telemark, but you need to learn a few more basic techniques first. The easiest, most stable, and overall most useful downhill technique is the snowplow or wedge, so called because of the V-shape made by the skis. Before you can learn to

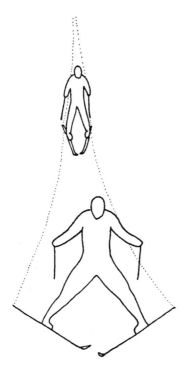

Figure 3-10. The snowplow.

turn, you need to be able to snowplow straight down the slope (a useful way of descending narrow gullies and tree-lined corridors), controlling your speed as you go.

Push yourself off down a gentle slope of firm snow with the skis parallel and about hip width apart and your weight equally on each ski. Once you are moving, push outward on your heels to force the tails of your skis apart (Figure 3-10). Your ski tips should be about a basket width apart while your knees should have enough space between them to hold a basketball. A knock-kneed wedge will set your skis too much on their edges, and they will run as though on rails and probably converge, picking up speed as they do so. Keep your body upright, flexing your knees and ankles rather than bending at the waist. Look ahead; if you look down at your ski tips your body will tip forward, becoming unbalanced. Looking up also helps you see what lies ahead. You also need to keep your weight over your heels. Think of trapping something, an important piece of paper, say, firmly between your heel and the ski, or of squashing a bug under your heel. Your hands should be out in front where you can see them, roughly where they would be if you were riding a bicycle, with your poles pointing backward along the line of the skis so they don't catch on trees or bushes or stab other skiers as you go past.

If you have problems getting into the wedge position, try practicing it on the flat, stepping the skis into place, so that you know how it should feel. You could also try jumping into the air and landing in a wedge position. Repeat the exercise until you can slide your skis into position rather than jump there. This maneuver is also a good way to start downhill in a wedge position. A gentler method is to support yourself by your arms in the wedge position by placing your poles in the snow down the slope in front of you, then slowly taking your weight off your poles so you can ski between them.

The wedge can be either a braking or a gliding technique. For braking, sink down and press harder on your heels to push the tails farther apart until you come to a stop. You will be surprised at how steep a slope you can stop on like this, though you won't be able to stop very quickly. (If a rock appears in front of you, a step turn works

If you can, practice the snow plow on an open slope; if you miss a turn, you won't hit anything.

much better.) By sinking down, you put more weight on your skis, which widens the wedge and slows them down. To glide, relax your heels and rise up slightly, allowing the wedge to narrow and the skis to speed up. Practice varying your speed by rising and sinking as you descend a slope.

Poles serve no purpose in the wedge position. Waving them around will make your upper body feel unstable; if you can't keep them still, practice without them. If you find you still wave your arms around, put your hands on your thighs and keep them there. (This position is not ideal, but it is better than windmilling down the hill.) An alternative is to ski holding your poles horizontally steady in front of you, as if holding a tray of food (the poles are held across the body, not pointing forward).

The wedge position can get you down long steep slopes. It is tiring though, and after a time your thigh muscles will start to scream. I found this out on a descent of the Vallee Blanche, in the French Alps. I was barely more than a novice at the time, and I had borrowed alpine gear on the advice of the expert skiers who were accompanying me. The ski down the glaciers that make up the bulk of the route went well, and I was carefully guided and supported by my companions. However, at the end we came to a long descent on a winding and, to my eyes, very steep and narrow track through a forest. To the others the serious part of the day was over and they zoomed off, cutting turns through the trees. All I could do was snowplow, so that is what I did, for what seemed hours, while an endless procession of skiers skimmed past me. By the time I reached the bottom my legs felt as though they would never straighten again.

Downhill Turns

WEDGE TURNS

To relieve the strain of a long descent in the wedge position, you need to be able to turn the skis, pointing them across the slope and transferring your weight from one ski to the other. To shift your weight when in the wedge position, press down on one heel only, sinking your torso down on that side, pushing that knee forward, and facing the way you want to go. You will then turn in the direction that the ski is pointed: weighting the right ski turns you left; weighting the left ski turns you right. To then turn back across the

*The snowplow is a good way
to descend hard-packed snow.*

slope, transfer the pressure to the other heel. If you apply the pressure quickly, you will stay close to the fall line and make abrupt turns called short-radius turns. If you apply the pressure gradually, you will make much wider, long-radius turns. If you keep the wedge narrow, which means the skis will be flatter on the snow and less on their inside edges, you will come around the turn quicker and the tails of your skis will slip or skid down the slope as you cross the fall line.

A good exercise for learning to turn when and where you want is to make a slalom course with poles and practice skiing between them, starting with a turn one way, then repeating the descent starting your first turn in the other direction.

STEM TURNS

Long-radius wedge turns involve a traverse between the actual turns during which your weight is on the ski that led into the last turn and

Figure 3-11. The stem turn.

which is now your downhill or outside ski (so called because it is on the outside of the turn). Traversing in a wedge position is awkward and puts a strain on the leg muscles. It also limits how fast you can go. It is easy to change the long-radius wedge into a stem turn, in my experience the most useful and stable turn on firm snow or ice.

The stem turn (sometimes called the stem christie or wedge christie) is a turn that starts with a wedge but finishes with the skis parallel. To move from the wedge turn to a stem turn, start off in a traverse, making sure that all your weight is on the lower ski (Figure 3-11a). Once you have picked up a bit of speed, slide, or stem, the uphill ski out into a wedge position (Figures 3-11b and 3-11c), then put all your weight on it and come around the turn (Figure 3-11d). As you return to a traverse you can bring the new uphill ski back parallel with the downhill one (Figure 3-11e). In soft snow you may need to lift both this ski and the stemming ski and step them into position, but whenever possible you should slide them.

If you find it difficult to turn across the fall line from a traverse, pick a gentle slope, ski down the fall line with your skis parallel, stem out one ski, put your weight on it, and turn into the slope, bringing your skis parallel. Once you feel confident with this movement, try it from a traverse.

As your ability improves, you can move farther up the slope and try linking a series of turns. The longer the traverse, the faster you will go. If you want to keep the speed down, stick to short-radius turns with very short traverses. If you have a wide slope to play on, try some long-radius turns to get a feel for faster skiing.

Once you are comfortable linking basic stem turns like this, you can speed up your turns by emphasizing the weight shift to the outside ski and by bringing the skis parallel earlier in the turn. Because a faster turn means less time spent crossing the fall line, it feels and is more stable. You can now start to think about unweighting the skis. Stand up just before you start a turn to take the pressure off the skis; this movement makes stemming the outside ski easier. Then, sink down to drive the ski around the turn. As your turns become more dynamic and faster, you will find you can bring the skis parallel sooner, even before you cross the fall line. You are well on the way to parallel turning.

You can see how your skis are turning by looking back at your tracks. In both wedge and stem turns, especially fast ones, the tails of the skis slip sideways—or skid—as they come through the fall line. When the skis are parallel, however, they can carve, or turn on their edges, without skidding. In the stem turn, the sooner you bring the skis parallel the more you carve the turn and the less you skid. Because of their construction, however, double-cambered nordic skis will always skid, and any carving will be minimal. Alpine-cambered telemark skis can carve.

I haven't mentioned poles at all. They are useful in the stem turn but can get in the way initially, so it is best to practice at first either without them or holding them as you would for wedge turning. Once you work out the basics of stem turns, however, you can use the downhill pole to start or trigger the turn. Plant your downhill pole a split second before you stem the uphill ski. Don't rely on the pole for support, because on all but the hardest snow you won't get any.

As always, your upper-body position is very important. You should be upright and aligned with your skis. If you twist your shoulders across the fall line and into the slope ahead of your skis, your ski tails will skid too far and you will find it hard to get into the next traverse. You may even come to a stop. Instead, keep your body facing down the fall line in preparation for the next turn. This position speeds up turns, helps you see what lies ahead, and proves useful as you tackle the more advanced parallel and telemark turns. In short-radius turns it is essential to face down the hill. If you turn away from the fall line, you won't be able to link turns quickly enough, so look down the slope at something in the distance, preferably something immobile like a rock rather than another skier.

PARALLEL TURNS

The basic skidded version of the stem turn is possibly the most useful turn you will learn. It is certainly the most stable when you are carrying a big pack. Parallel turns are fast and fun but not as stable or useful as stem turns. They are also more difficult to do. If you want to progress to them, the best way is by gradually reducing the stem of a stem turn until the skis are parallel throughout the turn. But how do you initiate such a turn if you don't stem the uphill ski? The answer is by rising up from a flexed knee position (Figure 3-12a) and extending your legs to unweight the skis (Figure 3-12b). At the same time

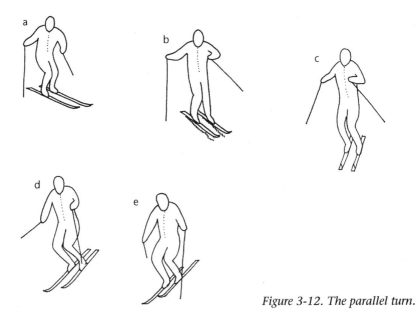

Figure 3-12. The parallel turn.

twist the skis with your boots and drive your knees into the turn (Figure 3-12c), sinking down as you come across the fall line (Figure 3-12d). This up-and-down movement ("stand tall and sink small") is crucial to successful parallel turns on nordic skis. Driving your knees and hips into the hill is critical too, but don't follow them with your shoulders and upper body. Keep your upper body upright, away from the slope. This position is called *angulation*, because there is an angle between your legs and upper body.

If you find it hard to avoid initiating the turn with a slight wedge, try steering the inside ski first. This should also help you avoid overrotating your hips into the hill.

As with stem turns, long-radius parallel turns are faster and get you down more quickly than short-radius ones. Although short-radius turns are slower, something you might like, they require more effort because they are tighter and follow on each other more quickly. Initially it is easier to learn long-radius parallels. Before you try short-radius parallels, practice short-radius wedge and stem turns to get the feel of quick, linked, rhythmic turns back and forth across the fall line. Keep facing straight down the hill so you feel your legs swinging from side to side under you. Reach forward and plant the pole close to your ski to initiate the turn (Figure 3-12e). Alpine-length poles are useful because they put your hands at the correct level. If your poles aren't adjustable, cock your wrist slightly rather than lift your arm, or grasp the pole below the grip. (While practicing, you may want to run a few lengths of tape around this area below the grip so your hand has something to grab on to.) Your hands should be kept low but always in view.

A steep slope is required to execute parallel turns because they work only at reasonably fast speeds. Parallel turns are difficult to perform with sloppy boots or stiff-cambered skis. Stiff boots and soft skis make them easier, but if you really want to learn to parallel well, it is probably best to learn on alpine skis at a ski area and then transfer your skills to nordic gear. I have seen many experienced alpine skiers learn to parallel very quickly on nordic gear by simply exaggerating what they are used to doing (how they manage with telemark turns is another matter). If, as I did, you learn to parallel on double-cambered skis, you will probably end up with a fairly crude wide-legged style that often verges on a stem.

9 7

TELEMARK TURNS

In recent years, being able to telemark has become the touchstone of competence for many nordic skiers. Nordic downhill is often called telemark skiing, as though no other turns were possible on free-heel equipment. While the telemark turn is a very useful technique for descending certain types of snow, and linking telemarks down a steep bowl of deep powder is one of the most wonderful of skiing experiences, you can be a perfectly competent tourer without being able to do it.

Indeed, I would rather be high on a mountain in poor storm visibility with a nontelemarking companion whose navigation and winter survival skills were good than with the best technical tele-marker in the world who couldn't tell the front of a compass from the back. If you have good snow travel skills and can do wedge and stem turns, you can undertake tours that are just as adventurous as those of someone who can telemark. While I heartily recommend learning the telemark turn, you shouldn't restrict your touring if you have not mastered it.

The advantage of the telemark turn is that it is very stable fore and aft because it is almost like being on one long ski. The turn can be used on all types of snow but works best in soft snow and powder, where it may be the only feasible turn, especially if you are carrying a heavy pack. The telemark position is also a stable running stance for riding over bumps and dips on gradual descents where the terrain is rough but you don't need to turn. The telemark can be done on any nordic gear, but is easiest on soft or alpine-cambered skis. With the latter you can make carved rather than skidded turns and stay in control on steep icy slopes.

To start, you need to be comfortable running downhill in the telemark position. Practice on a gentle slope with a good run-out. Face down the fall line, start gliding, and push one ski out in front of the other, sinking down on your skis so that each knee is bent at about 90 degrees. Your rear heel should be raised. (Telemark turns cannot be done on alpine skis because you cannot raise your heel.) Your rear ski tip should be about halfway between the binding and tip of your lead ski. Glide for a while in this position, then rise up and drop into a telemark with the other ski advanced. Your upper body should be upright and square over the skis, with your

The finish of a telemark turn. Note the position of the right pole; it is about to be planted as a trigger for the next turn.

hands out in front where you can see them, as if holding bicycle handlebars.

If you find the front ski running away from you, put more weight on it by really pushing your knee forward. When you look down you shouldn't be able to see the toe of your boot. Much advice is given about how your weight should be split between the front and rear skis. Should it be 50/50 or 70/30? When you are learning to telemark, the exact ratio is irrelevant. The biggest problem most novice telemarkers have, and the one I remember from when I was learning, is committing themselves to that front ski. I advise leaving the back ski to look after itself and concentrating on getting weight over the front ski. If you eventually find that the rear ski is wandering because there is no weight on it, put some pressure on the ball of your rear foot.

Although you may be impatient to move on to turns, continue to run straight with lead ski changes until you feel thoroughly comfortable. If you cannot sink into the position naturally, you will have great difficulty turning. To make the skis turn, you need to set them on their edges slightly and also to steer and pressure them (Figure 3-

13). Twist your knees, driving them in the direction of the turn. Remember that the ski out in front is the outside ski in the turn. So as you drop into a telemark position with your right ski advanced, twist your knees to the left (Figure 3-13a). The skis will then go onto their edges and begin to turn (Figure 3-13b). Let them take you through the fall line (Figure 3-13c), then rise up (Figure 3-13d), allowing them to run parallel, before sinking down and advancing the other ski for the next turn. The sequence should be fluid and rhythmical, not jerky, a dance down the snow.

As with other techniques, concentrate on the leg movements at first and don't worry about your poles. In fact, if the poles get in your way or you find yourself using them for support, practice without

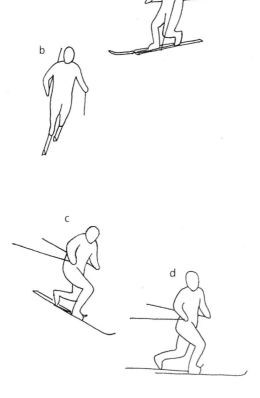

Figure 3-13. The telemark turn.

them. Keep your arms out in front and your hands where you can see them. If your arms, especially your inside arm, drift back, your weight will too, and chances are you will fall. Once you can link a few teles without too much difficulty, you can use your poles to trigger turns by reaching down the hill and touching the snow with the tip just before you sink into the telemark and start to turn. This movement is more important in short-radius than long-radius turns.

The upper body can follow the skis in long-radius turns, but you need to face down the slope more in short-radius ones. Creating tension between your upper body and your legs in this way (called counterrotation in skiing jargon) helps with quick turns because the legs want to unwind and follow the body. If you have difficulty with this maneuver, try touching the calf of your forward (outside) leg with your inside hand as you go into the turn. This position will force your body out from the slope and prevent you from leaning in; leaning in may work in long-radius turns in soft or powder snow but is a sure way to fall on hard snow and in short-radius turns.

To help with edging and pressurizing the skis, think of pressing down on the big toe of your leading foot and the little toe of the rear one. This effort will weight the edges of your feet and thus the edges of the skis. More edging is needed for short-radius turns on hard-packed snow than for long-radius turns in soft snow. In the latter case, you may only need to steer the skis with your feet and knees. In powder snow keep the skis as flat as possible and the telemark stance low for greater fore and aft stability. The high stance of the telemark racer is designed for maximum edging on the hard-packed prepared slopes.

Once you can link basic teles you are ready to explore all the various types and styles of telemarking. As with parallels, the best place to practice is probably on lift-served runs so you don't expend too much energy climbing up the slope. There is much argument among experts about what constitutes a good or even proper way to telemark. Don't worry about the latest deliberations. The telemark turn allows for a great deal of individual style. If your version lets you ski in control and make turns when and where you want, then there is nothing wrong with it, whatever others may tell you about your stance being too upright or too low, your rear knee too low or too high, or your skis too close together or too far apart.

Aggressive and fit skiers can tackle very steep slopes and diffi-

Telemarking in powder snow.

cult, cruddy snow with step or jump telemarks. To do a step telemark you step the lead ski across the fall line, creating a wedge shape, then bring the back ski in next to it. On really difficult terrain, coming to a complete stop after each turn is a good idea for the best chance of staying in control. In jump telemarking, as the name suggests, you actually unweight so forcefully that your skis come up off the snow so you can turn them in the air. Both styles are hard work, especially when carrying a pack, but can be the only way to descend some types of snow other than traversing and using kick turns. (Jump and step parallels are also possible but are not as stable fore and aft.) Long descents using these techniques require superhuman strength. With a heavy pack, even the superhuman may find them impossible.

Last Thoughts on Ski Techniques

The final thing to remember with all ski techniques, especially downhill ones, is that the more you practice the better you get, especially if, whenever possible, you have an instructor or good skier watch you and comment on how you are doing. If you don't have anyone to do this, reread the instructions and make sure that each part of your body is in the proper place and feels "right." Does your front ski wander? Put more weight on it. Does your back ski wander? Put more weight on it. Do you use your poles to maintain balance? Practice without the poles, keeping your hands down and in front of you. Check each movement. It is surprising how much difference moving your arms just a few inches can make. Also, use every opportunity. On a tour, if bad weather keeps you from moving on, look for a slope near the lodge or camp that you can ski on for a few hours.

And as a last word, don't forget that skiing is meant to be fun. It is all too easy to get wrapped up in trying to perfect a new technique and lose all the enjoyment in the process.

Into the Mountains

The most sophisticated equipment is only an aid to, not a
substitute for, our physical and mental resources.
—Galen Rowell, High and Wild

The planning is complete, the long journey to the mountains over, and you are finally standing on the edge of the snowy wilderness, your pack on your back, your skis on your feet, excited at the thought of what lies ahead. What will the snow be like? Will the weather hold? How cold will it be? The answers to these questions and more will determine how well your tour goes and how much you enjoy it. You cannot change the circumstances, but you can make them work to your best advantage. Other factors, like route finding, do lie in your control.

Pace

A ski tour is more like a long-distance walk than a mountain run. You may want to speed off down the trail, eagerly putting some distance under your skis, but it is best to resist this temptation. If you are going to ski all day you need a steady pace you can maintain easily hour after hour. How fast this is will depend on the snow as well as your fitness and the weight of your load, but short bursts of speed followed by long rests while you recover are neither efficient nor enjoyable. If you can talk to companions, or sing or whistle, then your pace is about right. If you have no breath to utter a sound, slow down.

Ski tours aren't marathons. Stop occasionally to admire the view.

Leading

In a group someone has to go out in front, creating a trail for the others to follow. Everyone should have a turn at this; it is good for morale. Skiing with no one in front of you is totally different from skiing behind others and for many people more rewarding. When it is your turn to lead, remember the people behind you. Don't assume they will tell you if there are problems. They may not have the breath to do so, or the wind may whip their words away. There is nothing more frustrating than seeing the leader vanish into the distance while you are rewaxing your skis, so check occasionally that the others are following without difficulty, especially during climbs, when your tracks may become so hard packed and slippery that those at the back start to slip.

It isn't necessary to keep a group close together except in storms and poor visibility, when the slowest skiers should be at or close to the front so they don't get left behind. Skiers have their own pace; trying to keep up with faster skiers is a sure road to exhaustion, while skiing slower than you would like is surprisingly difficult and

Take turns breaking trail in soft snow and ski in single file.

tiring, so skiing farther apart is usually more enjoyable. It allows you to appreciate your surroundings without being aware of the proximity of others. At times you may find no one else in view and for a short while experience the exhilaration of being alone with the mountains.

If the group consists of more than four or five people, it is a good idea to have a back marker to ensure that no one is left behind. Then the leader won't have to count everybody, just find the back marker. A system of simple signals using ski poles can be arranged so the leader and back marker can communicate. The ones I use are a single raised pole for "Everything OK, continue" and crossed poles for "Stop, there is a problem." Back markers are particularly important on long descents, as that is when differences in skill (and boldness) become more apparent and it is easy for people to be left far behind. It is very important that the back marker never pass anyone for any reason whatsoever. That way no one gets lost. It is also a good idea to agree in advance on a rest place where people can regroup if they become split up.

BREAKING TRAIL

When the snow is soft and deep, leading becomes arduous and tiring, and there is little danger of leaving people behind. In fact, the leader, struggling to push through the snow, may go so slowly that skiers at the back of the group, gliding along the nicely packed track, may be heard to complain at the lack of speed—until it is their turn up front.

The best way to deal with breaking trail in difficult snow is to change leaders frequently. Ten minutes out front can be more than enough in some conditions. Rotating leaders is simple. Once the leader feels tired or when a timekeeper, usually the second or third in line, indicates the stint is up, the leader can step to one side, let the next skier lead through, and then rejoin the group at the back.

If you are carrying heavy loads and the snow is really deep, it may be necessary for someone to break trail without a pack and then return for it, a very slow method of progress. At times it may even be better to give up if you have the option. The slowest skiing I have ever done was in the Canadian Rockies when we attempted to ski up the Alexandra River valley in order to plant a food cache at its head. After an exhausting hour during which we traveled only a few hundred yards through the knee- to thigh-deep, loose, sugary snow, we abandoned the attempt.

Rest Stops

Very few people can ski all day without a break, and that is hardly the way to enjoy your skiing anyway. Most people like to have at least a couple of stops a day when they take off their pack and skis and sit down for a drink and a bite to eat. In sunny weather, scenic spots like the head of a pass or the top of a mountain are the obvious places to halt. In storms, shelter will be needed or you will cool down very quickly. Large boulders are good, or you can dig into a bank with your snow shovels. In trees a tarp can be erected as a windbreak, and in flat, open terrain a wind shelter can be built quickly by standing your skis up in a line and then heaping snow or cut snow blocks against them. In really stormy weather, when you need to keep moving and shelter is hard to find, frequent short halts are better than a few long ones. You can stand while you have a drink or sit astride your pack with your skis still on. In all but the warmest weather it is important to put on extra clothing as soon as you stop, or you will soon feel chilly. Keeping warm is much easier than getting warm.

Apart from rest stops, you will need to stop occasionally to adjust clothing layers, tighten boot laces, rewax skis, put on and take off skins, check the map, and more. These halts can add up to a con-

At brief stops you can sit on your pack and keep your skis on.

Replacing fluids regularly is important.

Use your gear to the full!

siderable amount of time over a day, so it is best to keep them short. If you are thinking of stopping to do something and someone else stops, do your chore then too rather than wait. But don't neglect to stop if you really need to. In the long run waiting could cost even more time, and it won't do much for your enjoyment.

Reading the Snow

You will quickly realize when you leave groomed tracks and prepared runs that the nature of the snow greatly affects your skiing. Learning to read the snow, to interpret what lies ahead, is an important skill, especially on descents, where you may have to adapt your techniques very quickly when the snow changes.

POWDER. Snow is affected by the wind and the temperature both when it falls and afterward. Snow falls as dry loose powder in cold temperatures with little wind, and breaking trail in it is slow and difficult, with ascents usually having to be done by very shallow tra-

In spring you may have to link patches of snow.

Skiing in new snow.

verses. But it is great to ski down; its braking effect allows safe descent of steep slopes. Floating, almost in slow motion, through deep powder is exhilarating. For me the ideal turn in powder is the telemark, though some people argue that parallels are better. The telemark works best if you edge your skis less than on hard snow and, for once, keep your weight centered over both skis rather than throw most of it over the front one; this allows the tips to float to the surface of the snow. Pressure the heel rather than the toe of your lead foot to keep your weight centered.

PACKED POWDER. Wind causes powder to drift and pack. The resulting compacted snow is dull and off-white looking and doesn't sparkle. On the flat it is easier to ski through than powder, but on descents it can be a real problem because it is usually mixed with patches of hard-packed snow or even ice. When you hit compacted powder after speeding across hardpack your skis will slow abruptly, and unless you are prepared you will probably do a face-plant. In such conditions it is best to turn on the hard snow to keep your speed down and let your skis run across the compacted powder. The two types of snow look very different, so as long as you stay alert and look ahead you should be able to stay in control and on your feet. Skiing in the telemark position gives you greater fore and aft stability and makes it less likely that you will be thrown off balance when your skis hit the compacted powder. Even if you don't use the telemark position, a low stance improves stability. You need to be prepared to rock back on your skis to counter the forward propulsion of your body that will occur when your skis slow down. When descending continuous compacted powder, telemark turns work well.

HEAVY SNOW. Snow that falls in temperatures around and above freezing is heavy and wet. In spring, high temperatures commonly turn snow heavy, especially late in the day. Skiing in heavy snow on the flat is hard work, especially if it is deep. On descents it is potentially dangerous. Your skis can become locked in the snow and refuse to turn, leading to twisted ankles and knees. Kick turns or jump turns are best for this stuff if it is more than a few inches deep. Snowplow turns are slow and very hard work, if possible at all. An alternative to jump turns, which are exhausting with a heavy pack, is a step telemark, in which you step the lead ski down and across the fall line at an angle to your rear ski. This is a good turn for keeping your speed down, especially if you weight the back ski as it comes around the turn.

BREAKABLE CRUST. The worst snow to ski is the breakable crust that sometimes forms when the surface of wet snow freezes. You will bury your ski tips constantly. On the flat you can progress by lifting the tips of your skis at each stride and placing them on top of the crust. They will still go through when you weight the ski, but you won't bury the tips so often. Only kick turns and traverses are safe on descents.

CORN SNOW. When snow repeatedly thaws and freezes it packs down to form a hard surface called corn snow that is excellent both for striding and skating on the flat and for descending at speed. Any turns can be used, but stems and wedges are easier than telemarks unless you are very good at them. Beware of running into breakable crust as you descend into warmer temperatures. Sideslipping can be used for narrow sections in gullies or between rocks.

On the flat a gentle glide can be maintained for hours.

ICE. It is fortunate that ice is easy to identify, because hitting a patch unexpectedly can give you quite a shock. Any snow that gleams at a distance is probably ice, or at least snow with an icy glaze on the surface. On flat terrain such as frozen lakes that winds have blown clear of snow, skating is the most efficient technique. Ice will strip wax, except blue klister, off your skis quickly, leaving you slipping backward if you try to kick and glide.

You can ski long distances quickly on lake and river ice. Local knowledge is the surest indicator that the ice is safe. If snowmobiles or even trucks are on the ice, you should be safe on skis. To form a sufficient thickness of ice (at least an inch on lakes, more on rivers), prolonged cold temperatures (below 20°F) are needed. Knowledge of recent and overall temperatures is useful. Check local agencies for this information.

Often you won't be able to tell how much ice is under the snow, and in places the surface snow may have melted or the river may have overrun the ice in a thaw and left pools of water on top. These pools do not mean the ice is unsafe. I have skied (soggily) many miles along frozen lakes in several inches of water.

There are, however, warning signs that you should heed when skiing frozen lakes and rivers. Streams running into a lake or river you're on may keep the ice open or very thin, especially if the current is strong. Check your map for these areas and give them a wide berth, staying well out or even skirting the far shore of a lake and perhaps leaving the ice altogether when on a river. Rapids and other areas where the water flows quickly may also be open or inadequately frozen. Take great care in such places.

For safety, always keep a close eye on the ice or snow ahead. If you see tracks—whether those of animals or other skiers—skirting around an area, assume the ice is unsafe and do the same. Open water, which you may see on large lakes, shouldn't be approached. Ice that has been thrown up into cracked slabs or has slumped into hollows should also be avoided.

In spring, after anything other than a very temporary thaw, be extremely careful. Once ice starts to melt and break up, it can do so quickly, even though on the surface it still appears solid.

Overall, I'd stay off any frozen lake or river you're unsure about. My experience has mostly been on large lakes in areas with dependably cold winter temperatures. Yet in the same areas, rivers can still be open when the lakes will support trucks, never mind skiers. When water is frozen but you don't have information as to its safety, you could use an ice ax or snow shovel to chop through the ice to see how thick it is (do this at the edge!). And when traveling, use your poles to tap the ice ahead if you're unsure as to its solidity. If in doubt, retreat to the bank. When you decide the ice is probably safe but you're not absolutely certain, ski very carefully, keeping well apart and leaving hip belts unbuckled in case the ice begins to break up.

Sometimes ice creaks and groans as you cross it. This "settling" doesn't mean the ice is unsafe, although the sounds can be alarming.

Traversing patches of ice on a hillside requires using your metal edges. General touring skis without metal edges can be dangerous on ice. Once when climbing Glas Maol in the southern Cairngorm Mountains in the Scottish Highlands a group of us came on a long ribbon of steep ice about 15 feet wide that we had to cross. Those with steel-edged skis could just make enough of an impression in the ice to cross safely, but as soon as the one person in the party without metal-edged skis tried to cross, her skis slipped and she slid 150 feet down the ice. Luckily, there was a safe run-out and no harm was done.

When descending ice, wedge turns, or if you are happy with the speed, stem turns, work best. You will need to really edge your skis, which tires the ankles on a long descent. In narrow places or where there is a dangerous run-out, sideslipping is a safer alternative. Kick turns and traverses are not a good option on ice. Just think about trying to do a kick turn on steep ice with a heavy pack and you will see why. In bad weather or where there are many rocks poking through the ice, skins can help to keep your speed down. They also make it less likely that you will slip.

SASTRUGI. Windblown snow can become rippled with ridges (like sand dunes) known as sastrugi. If these ridges are soft and low, breaking through them is easy. Once they become higher and harder, though, take care; you may find your skis bouncing off them rather than cutting through. Aiming for them at right angles is essential, and a degree of speed is needed for the skis to ride over or cut through them—too fast, though, and your fall will be a heavy one. A half-telemark position provides better fore and aft stability.

Really hard, high sastrugi may have to be stepped over, a slow, laborious activity.

Flat Light

In cloudy or misty weather and early or late in the day, visibility may be such that, although you can still see distant features such as peaks or lakes, the snow immediately in front of you loses all distinctness, and it becomes impossible to tell what the angle of a slope is and whether there are drop-offs or even ridges of snow ahead. In such flat-light conditions, very slow, careful skiing is essential, especially when descending. Even on the flat, problems can arise. I have skied over short drops that were completely invisible. How to navigate in flat light is discussed later, but good route finding won't help you ski. With experience, you can learn to feel changes in the snow through your feet, which will help you react quickly even when the snow all looks the same.

Balling Up

In temperatures around and above freezing you may find snow sticking to the bottom of your skis. This "balling up" is extremely frustrating; it prevents all glide on the flat and keeps your skis from running downhill, making you feel very unstable, as if you had ministilts under each ski. (In ascents a little balling up can help with traction.) It happens because your ski bases are warm enough for the top layer of snow, which is also quite warm, to stick to them.

Ignoring slight balling up is unwise, though tempting, because it can worsen quickly, soon resulting in huge slabs of snow adhering to the underside of your skis. Then all you can do is stop, remove your skis, and scrape off the snow. If there are signs of balling up you can minimize its burgeoning by being careful not to lift the skis off the snow into the warm air. If you do, when you put them down the snow will stick even more. Instead, keep the skis in the snow and slide them forward, using a shuffle rather than a walk, and keep the skis moving constantly. When you are standing still, slide the skis back and forth; the friction will help prevent balling up. If snow does begin to stick, banging the edge of the ski with a pole can knock it off. Then kick the ski vigorously on the snow and slide it rapidly back and forth to remove the last traces. You can also scrape the base of one ski across the edge of the other to remove snow, but that is a good way to scratch the top plate unless you are careful. Avoid skiing through patches of slush or puddles of water even if it means a long detour. Wet skis are far warmer than the snow and ball up badly.

At times nothing works, and than you just have to remove some wax and cork in hard what is left or else apply a harder wax. This may cause slipping, leaving you with an awful choice between balling up or lack of grip. Paraffin or even candle wax can be rubbed on waxless skis that ball up, but that, too, can spoil the grip.

Bushwhacking

The hardest skiing I have ever done was in the Castleguard River valley in the Canadian Rockies after a descent from the Columbia Icefield (see Chapter 10). This valley is narrow, steep-sided, and densely forested, with the river dropping down through a series of gorges. In early April it was full of deep, soft, sugary snow, and there was no sign of the summer trail. Maintaining a straight line was impossible, and progress was very slow and exhausting as we skidded and slithered and scrabbled our way through the dense undergrowth,

Soft snow, steep slopes, and trees make for difficult skiing and slow progress.

constantly catching skis, poles, clothing, and packs on branches and twigs. Great fallen trees banked with snow on the uphill side often blocked our way; we would ski unknowingly onto them, only to find ourselves perched six or more feet above the ground on the other side. The rotten snow frequently collapsed under us, swallowing up our skis or, worse, just one ski, leaving the skier tipped sideways with one ski waving in the air. Extricating oneself from such traps was very difficult and usually involved removing the pack and sometimes the skis. When the frustrations grew too much we took our skis off and tried to walk, but that proved even harder; the skis strapped on our packs constantly became entangled in the foliage above us.

If at all possible, avoid bushwhacking. If there is an alternative, however long, take it. When you do have to ski through dense forest or bushes, be patient and move slowly so the inevitable falls don't do too much damage to you or your gear. The day after the episode described above a member's ski snapped under the binding, and a few days later a cable binding ripped out of another ski. Both failures were probably due to the stresses of bushwhacking. For safety, take your hands out of your pole straps so that when, as they will, the baskets catch on twigs and hidden snags you don't risk a dislocated shoulder. If you know you will be bushwhacking through dense forest you could use snowshoes, which are far more maneuverable and much less frustrating in dense bush or rotten snow. They will add weight to your load, of course, but if you will be mostly bushwhacking you could even leave your skis behind.

Stream Crossings

In midwinter and early spring, streams in most areas are frozen and covered with deep compacted snow, making them easy to cross. In spring and after any unseasonal temporary thaw the cover may thin and in places disappear altogether. The snow bridges left may or may not be safe. If you are at all in doubt, check from above or below to see if the center of the bridge looks thick and solid. Cross quickly one at a time, the first person probing ahead with a pole. Have someone unencumbered and ready to help if the bridge collapses. If the day is hot, bridges that were solid in the morning may be soft and unsafe by later afternoon. If the nights are cold and you are camping, you could pitch the tent and wait for dawn before

Rocks can be used as stepping stones for short stream crossings. Keep a good grip on your skis.

crossing; by then the bridge should be much stronger, having refrozen overnight.

Where a shallow stream has no bridge and there is plenty of snow on the banks, you can build your own bridge by shoveling snow into the water and stamping it down. As long as it is cold enough this is surprisingly efficient, but such bridges may not last long. I once crossed one with a group the day after it had been made, and it cracked and split just as the next-to-last person was crossing, holding together just long enough for the last person to cross.

Small open streams can be crossed, skis in hand, using rocks as stepping stones and a pole for support, but don't try it if the rocks are far apart or icy or the water is deep or fast-flowing. In wooded terrain it is worth prospecting up and down the banks for fallen trees that may provide a way across. A big, dry log can often be walked across, but sitting down and shuffling along is safer, and if the log is narrow or the wood wet or icy it is essential. Before you cross, always consider what the consequence of falling in would be.

Wading is the last alternative. It should be done only if the water is no more than knee deep and the current not too strong. If there is any danger of being washed away, don't cross. Heading upstream into colder air may lead to a snow bridge; otherwise you may have to turn back or camp on the banks and wait until early morning when the low overnight temperatures will have stopped snow and glacier melt and the water will be at its lowest.

If you decide it is safe to wade, keep your boots dry by wearing running shoes or other spare footwear or dirty socks, or even go barefoot if it is not too cold. Take care to secure your boots. I was once with someone who dropped a boot into a fast, swollen stream. It was whisked away out of sight. We were lucky enough to find it jammed against a branch not far downstream. We were high in the Sierras and several days from the nearest road—the loss of a boot would have been very serious. How do you attach a running shoe to a three-pin binding?

Before you begin your wade, unfasten your hip belt and chest strap so you can shed your pack if you slip—so it won't pin you under water. Fastening clothing reduces drag. Face upstream so the pressure of the water doesn't cause your knees to buckle, and move

At times you just have to wade.

carefully, one foot at a time, feeling for secure placements. Use your poles for extra support.

Groups can ford in a line, facing upstream, across the flow of the stream, with their arms linked, or in threesomes facing each other in a circle with arms around each other's shoulders, grasping onto pack straps. I have used this method and found it very stable, even though one person has to walk backward. You could also cross in a "chorus" line, with arms linked, using a ski as a brace, with everyone holding onto it with both hands.

If the crossing turns out to be more difficult than expected and you decide to retreat, turning around will be awkward and hazardous, and you may be better off proceeding backward. If you do slip and fall, all you can do is try to push yourself toward the bank, holding on to your pack, which, if (as they should be) the items inside are in waterproof bags, should be quite buoyant. Try to keep your feet downstream so your head and torso are protected from rocks. When a person is crossing individually, those on the bank should have their packs off and be ready to assist in an emergency, perhaps holding out a ski or ski pole for the person in the water to grab.

Using a rope to safeguard a crossing requires knowledge and experience. There is a growing view that the safety provided is to a great extent illusory because someone who falls in while being belayed across a river could be trapped under the water by the rope. I have found helpful a rope tied to trees or rocks on either side and used as a hand line. The first person to cross and the last may wish to do so without a pack, since they will not have the benefit of the hand line. This does mean they will have to cross two extra times to retrieve their packs while the hand line is in place. Clipping into the hand line with a carabiner attached to a waist belt (made from cord if necessary) can add to security.

Sometimes crossing a stream is the easy part, and climbing down to it and then up the other side is hard. If the banks are steep and icy, good sidestepping skills are required. Heavy packs can be handed down and up to make it easier. Don't be tempted to take your skis off: the ice or snow that supports skis may not support boots. On one occasion a party I was with in the Bergsdalen region of Norway had to cross a partially frozen stream in order to get back to the hut we were using as a base. Getting down to it was easy.

Even if the stream crossing is easy, climbing the bank may require some difficult sidestepping.

However, the far bank was nearly six feet high, almost vertical, and covered with hard, icy snow. A couple of people decided it would be easier on foot, took off their skis, and promptly went through the snow into the ankle-deep cold water. Only a narrow section of the far bank could be climbed, since the bank overhung everywhere else. When the first few people sidestepped up, they kicked off some of the snow with their skis, making the climb even harder. The group leader followed on skis but found as she balanced halfway up on one ski edge that there was nowhere to place the other ski. Exhibiting an acute sense of balance, she managed to execute a reverse kick turn in which she deliberately crossed her skis to end up facing the other way and higher up on the slopes. No one else attempted this maneuver.

Stream fords are potentially very dangerous and should never be undertaken lightly. In winter and spring the water will be bitterly cold, far too cold for swimming, and if you do fall in and manage to scramble to the bank you will then have potential hypothermia to deal with (see Chapter 5). Cross only if you are as sure as you can be that it is safe. On big rivers check upstream and down for easier fords, snow bridges, or fallen trees. A wide, braided area where the water is shallower and runs in many channels is easier and safer to ford than a narrow, deep section. Crossing above a waterfall is not a good idea unless the water is very shallow.

If by some mischance a skier does end up with a dunking, the most important thing to do is to get the person dry as fast as possible. Hypothermia could follow very quickly if nothing is done. Stripping off wet gear and putting on dry clothing is the first necessity. If the victim is starting to shiver, set up a tent or put the person in a sleeping bag or bivy bag, preferably with someone else. If necessary, build a snow shelter. Prepare a hot drink. In wooded country you could also light a fire, but that takes time, so leave it until after the other warming procedures have been carried out.

Carrying Skis

The easiest way to carry skis when you have to walk is to strap them to your pack, pointing upward. This is where side-compression straps

If you strap your skis to your pack, your hands will be free to use your poles for balance on approaches to the snow.

and wand pockets are useful. If you also clip the tips together with a short strap the skis will be less likely to wave about and upset your balance. However, skis protruding high above your head can be a big disadvantage in strong winds and when walking through forests. Then it might be preferable to carry the skis in your hands, strapping them together if the walk is any distance, perhaps using a pole as a handle.

Navigation and Route Finding

Navigation is an essential skill. It opens up the wilderness and enables you to ski safely away from marked routes and set tracks. Ideally, everybody in a party should be a competent navigator. Knowing the theory isn't enough: map and compass work have to be practiced. It is best to learn in the summer, when mistakes will probably not be too disastrous, rather than on a ski tour. Navigating in snow-covered terrain has its own special problems, and it is a good idea to go over the planned route beforehand. Check the map and compass regularly when on a tour, even if you are not responsible for the navigation, so you know where you are going and why you are taking that route. Apart from this being good practice, you might be called on to take over at some point. Here I have described the aspects of navigation of direct relevance to ski touring. For more information on general techniques, study one of the many books on the subject.

Guidebooks

While not as essential as maps, guidebooks, especially ski-touring ones if available, can provide much useful general information on an area, plus details of distance, time, elevation gain, slope angle and technical difficulty, potential avalanche danger, skiing abilities required, maps needed, whereabouts of roadheads, and even recommended equipment for specific routes.

Using Maps

Topographic maps are needed for ski touring. They show the shape or topography of an area by contour lines linking points of the same elevation. Planimetric maps (which give a plan of the area but don't have contour lines) such as Forest Service maps may have useful information on them, but their lack of contour lines make them suitable only for general planning or as backups to topo maps.

Topos are generally accurate and detailed. The contiguous United States is covered by Geological Survey maps at a scale of 1:24,000 (about 2½ inches to the mile). USGS maps of Alaska are on a scale of 1:63,360 (1 inch to the mile), while Canada's topo maps are 1:25,000 (as near to 1:24,000 as makes no difference). The largest scale available is generally best for wilderness travel; the more detail you have the better.

USGS maps are adequate but don't contain details useful to skiers, such as the whereabouts of cut ski trails or backcountry cabins. Better for that purpose are the Trails Illustrated series of topo maps that cover all the mountainous areas of Colorado and Utah and an ever-increasing number of national parks. These maps are also printed on tearproof and waterproof polyart plastic.

Before touring in an area new to you it is advisable to study the maps closely, not just to select a route but also to familiarize yourself with the special features of the map and to gain an idea of the type of terrain to expect. Contour lines are particularly important. First check the elevation distance, called the contour interval, between lines. It can be anything between 16 and 500 feet (5 and 150 meters), though it is usually 40 feet (12 meters) on 1:24,000 maps, 80 feet (24 meters) on 1:63,360 maps, and 100 feet (30 meters) on Canada's 1:25,000 maps.

Keeping the interval in mind, you can then determine what the terrain is like and where the steepest and gentlest slopes are. Where contour lines merge, the terrain will be very steep, far too steep for skiing. Note that cliffs of less height than the contour interval won't show up on the map. I know one attractive lake-filled cirque that can only be accessed from the valley below up the narrow ravine of the outlet stream because steep cliffs line the lake on either side. You couldn't tell this easily from the map, and the people who showed me this secret place admitted that the first time they visited the area they ended up on top of one of the cliffs looking down at the lake. However, a careful study of the map shows a contour line touching the water's edge, which suggests a sheer drop into the water and therefore perhaps a cliff above. This is where a detailed perusal of the map by an experienced eye can be rewarding.

Once you have an idea of the general terrain you will be in,

Check your map regularly.

study your proposed route carefully. Look for obvious features that will aid with route finding on the ground, and look for places where navigation could be difficult, such as flat open areas. I like to work out possible escape routes in case bad weather forces a retreat, and I always like to know the quickest way out of an area in case of emergency or accident. It is much easier if you know which way to go when a blizzard blows in out of nowhere than to have to start figuring it out at the time.

Refer to the map frequently during a tour even in clear conditions and when you are on a known or marked route. The weather can change rapidly, or you may return in poor visibility when knowing exactly where landmarks lie will be a great help. Look behind you occasionally to gain an overall picture of your surroundings. I do so whenever the route changes; for instance, on reaching a distinct feature such as a lake or stream. You should then be able to recognize key features on the way back and know at what point you need to leave the lakeshore or streamside.

When checking the map, allowances should be made for the effects of snow on the terrain. Stream gullies, hollows, and dips can fill up and flatten out or even become higher than the surrounding terrain. Small lakes may be very difficult to locate in large flat valleys. Their surfaces may not even be flat because of wind-built snowbanks. It is quite possible to ski uphill on a lake!

If you do get confused, check the surrounding features to confirm your position. Once, on a reasonably clear day, a group of us headed for a minor summit through complex terrain ideal for navigation practice. The summit was out of sight at first, so initially we aimed for the head of a small lake in a high bowl. We reached the lake without difficulty, but one of the group found it hard to believe we were there. "Where is the outlet stream?" he asked. "We're standing on it," came the reply. He stared down at the white expanse of the lake, some 15 feet below us. "We can't be." We were, though, deep snow having not only filled the stream bed but also built it up higher than the lake.

Route Finding

To be a good navigator you need to know not only where you are on the map and which direction to go to reach your destination but also how to work out the best route to get there. From the map you may know that you are at one end of a long valley and that the pass you wish to cross is at the other, but the map won't necessarily help you identify the best route between the two. You need to work that out on the ground by keeping a close eye on the terrain ahead and selecting the best route as you ski. Remember that the best or most obvious walking route is often not a good one on skis. Summer trails frequently traverse the steep sides of valleys, but avalanche danger is high there in winter and skiing is difficult. The valley bottom or the ridge above usually makes a better ski route.

Being able to estimate how far you have skied is very useful, especially in poor visibility, but it is harder to make an accurate estimate when skiing than when walking because your speed will vary greatly according to the nature of the snow and whether you are going up or down. Even so, it is worth figuring how long it should take to reach a certain easily identifiable feature and then keeping a check on the time. Allowances can then be made for time lost because of unforeseen obstacles or difficult snow.

A good way of estimating time and distance when walking is by a formula known as Naismith's Rule after the nineteenth-century Scottish mountaineer who invented it: allow an hour for every 3 miles/5km traveled and half an hour for every 1,000 feet/300 meters of ascent. This formula can be broken down into the more useful figures of 20 minutes per mile/1½km and 1 minute per 30 feet/10 meters of ascent. I have found Naismith's Rule to be accurate when skiing through softish unbroken snow over undulating terrain, but on hard-packed snow or skied-in tracks I travel faster; and in deep, soft snow or thick brush I progress much slower. Descents are nearly always much faster, too, because the rule is for hikers, not skiers, and ascents are about the same unless a lot of zigzagging has to be done. Overall, I suggest using Naismith's Rule as a basis for your calculations until you are familiar enough with your skiing speed in different conditions to do your own estimates.

The Compass

A compass is essential in flat light when landmarks are obscured, and even more so in whiteouts when the ground and the sky merge and it can be difficult to tell whether you are skiing uphill or down. I learned just how essential a compass can be a year or so ago when, to my embarrassment, I inadvertently left my compass at home when I changed packs at the last minute. I was on a solo camping tour in the Cairngorm Mountains in the Scottish Highlands, so no one else's compass was at hand. I didn't miss it the first day because I was on a familiar route and the weather was clear. I camped near some small mountain lakes known as the Dubh Lochan. The following morning I awoke to thick mist on the mountaintops and a cold wind. Rather than move on, I decided to ski over two rather featureless hills that lay to the south, Beinn a'Chaorainn and Beinn Bhreac, then return to camp over a pass called the Lairig an Laoigh.

The ascent of Beinn a'Chaorainn was steep and direct, so although I was soon enshrouded in mist with visibility no more than 30 feet, I didn't bother to check the map. But on the summit I needed to take a bearing on Beinn Bhreac. That was when I discovered I hadn't brought a compass. I should have followed my tracks back, but instead I decided to see how well I managed without a compass. I skied down in the opposite direction onto a flat featureless expanse between the two hills called the Moine Bhealaidh. I continued purposefully across, only to quickly come across fresh ski tracks. I went on and began to climb, sooner than I had expected. More fresh ski tracks appeared, heading downward. The realization dawned. They were my tracks! Knowing this didn't help, and over the next hour I crossed them several times and once reascended Beinn a'Chaorainn, convinced I was going in the opposite direction. I even resorted to leaving marks in the snow to show which way I had gone the last time I had crossed my tracks at a particular point, but try as I might I could not escape from my own spider's web and hold a southerly direction. Eventually I gave up and, using Beinn a'Chaorainn as a marker, descended to the west and out of the mist. It was a salutary lesson. Without a compass I had been completely unable to cross 2½ miles of easy ground in a straight line. Instead I had gone around and around in circles. I won't forget my compass again.

The Silva-type orienteering compass is ideal for ski touring. The standard design is adequate, though some experienced skiers prefer one of the optical-sighting versions because they are more accurate and easier to use for taking bearings from the ground. However, they are harder to use when taking bearings from a map, so I recommend the simpler, standard design to beginners.

MAGNETIC DECLINATION. Before you set off on a tour, remember to check the map for the magnetic declination. This is the difference between true north, to which the top of your map is aligned, and magnetic north, which is where your compass needle points. The declination is marked on most good maps. In many places it is significant and must be taken into account. To make matters more difficult, magnetic north moves, and the declination is not the same from one year to the next. Check your map key for details on this point. Because magnetic north lies in the far northeast of Canada, it is always west of grid north in eastern North America and east of grid north in western North America. In Europe, too, magnetic variation changes from area to area. In countries such as Britain magnetic north is significantly west of grid north. In the Alps it is so little it can be ignored; further east still it is east of grid north. Again, the best advice is to always check your map.

BEARINGS. To use a compass for anything beyond indicating where north, south, east, and west are, you must be able to take bearings. A bearing, measured in the degrees of a circle, is the angle between north and a line pointing the way you want to go. This is where

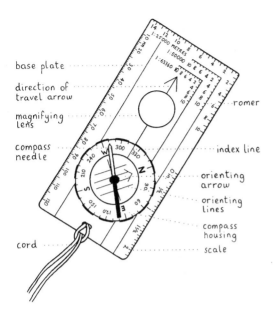

Figure 4-1. The parts of a standard compass.

magnetic declination comes in: the compass measures the angle between magnetic north and your direction line, while the correct bearing on the map is between grid north and your direction line. When you take a bearing on the map by measuring the angle between north and your direction, you then need to *add* the magnetic declination to get the right bearing if you are east of magnetic north but *subtract* it if you are to the west. To avoid making mistakes (easily done), you can get compasses with adjustable declination arrows or mark your compass with a strip of sticky tape. When you ski on a bearing you can then line up the compass needle with this declination arrow instead of the orienting arrow on the compass base.

To take a bearing on a point you can see, point the direction-of-travel arrow on the front of the compass base plate toward your destination, then twist the compass housing until the orienting arrow (or declination arrow if you have one) aligns with the magnetic needle. You can now ski to your destination, whether it remains visible or not, as long as you can follow the direction your compass points you in.

If you can't see your destination, you need to take a bearing from the map. To do this, place your compass on the map and lay

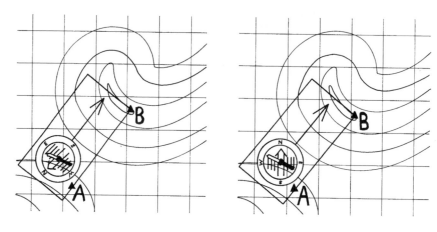

align the compass with your objective on the map,

then rotate the housing to line up the orienting arrow with the N-S grid lines

Figure 4-2. Taking a compass bearing from a map.

the edge of it along a line running from where you are to your destination. Then twist the compass dial so the orienting arrow is aligned with the sides of the map or with the north-south lines marked on it, if any. The bearing is the number of the tiny dash on the compass dial aligned with the direction-of-travel arrow. Up to this point both the magnetic needle and declination are ignored, but if you want to use this bearing in the field they must be taken into account; so when you remove the compass from the map, turn the entire compass until the magnetic needle is aligned with the declination arrow, if you have one. If you don't, align it with the orienting arrow and then adjust for declination. The direction-of-travel arrow now points the way you want to go. Once you know in which direction your destination lies it is best to break up your route into small stages and take compass bearings on features to which the way is relatively clear. If any of these lie some way off the straight line to your destination you will need to take another bearing to it when you reach them.

WHITEOUT NAVIGATION. Compass work is easy as long as features are visible on the ground. In mist or a whiteout, when there is nothing to take a bearing on, it becomes much harder. Unless you are alone, the easiest and surest though slowest way to navigate is by dead reckoning, with a skier substituted for the invisible features. To

Good navigation skills are required in conditions like this.

do this, someone goes ahead in the rough direction of the bearing until almost out of sight. Then the navigator can motion to the left or right until the skier is exactly on the bearing before joining the first skier and repeating the process. This is the only way to progress safely during descents.

On a crossing of the Columbia Icefield in a whiteout we used hand signals for communicating when skiing on a bearing because we couldn't hear our shouts in the wind. We were roped together because of crevasse danger, and a tug on the rope signaled to the leader that he was veering off course. I was out in front most of the time and often knew I was ascending or descending only when I looked back and saw the rest of the party slightly above or below me. I also found that it was impossible to ski in a straight line for even a rope length (about 100 feet/30 meters). At other times I have resorted to throwing a snowball to see what lies ahead. If there is a slope it will appear to hang suspended in the air. If the snowball disappears from view, retreat! You could be on the edge of a long, steep drop or, worse, on a cornice.

MEASURING DISTANCE. By keeping a close check on the time and estimating how far you have come, you should know when it is time to change your bearing. Pace counting is useless when on skis, but one way to measure distance on flatish or gently undulating terrain is by pole plants. If you know the usual distance between plants on one side, then all you need to do is count the number of plants you make to work out how far you have gone. It may be easier to count all your pole plants, then halve the number. Estimating distance on downhills is much harder; however, it is on flat, featureless terrain that you are most likely to need to know exactly how far you have skied.

If you can estimate the distance skied accurately, you can use the dogleg technique for navigating when skiing in a straight line isn't possible because of steep avalanche slopes, cornices, or other hazards. To use this technique, ski on a bearing to a point that you know from the map is beyond the barrier lying between you and your destination. There will probably be no clear feature at this point, since you selected it on the map. You know when you are there by the distance you have traveled, so this is a situation in which accurate measuring is important. To minimize any inaccuracy, it is best to keep navigation stages as short as possible when using this method.

AIMING OFF AND ATTACK POINTS. When you are heading for a specific spot but poor visibility makes hitting it exactly unlikely, there are a number of techniques you can use to aid you. If the point you want to reach lies on an identifiable linear feature such as a river, you could deliberately aim to reach the river above or below your target. When you reach it you will know which way to ski. This technique is called *aiming off*. An alternative method is to choose as an attack point an easily identifiable feature close to the point you want to reach. First navigate to the feature, then take a bearing from it to your target. Remember that features may be hidden by snow, so use only those that are distinct.

A Solo Journey

Navigating solo in poor visibility is much harder. It can also be a very strange experience. I once made a solo circumnavigation of the Hardangerjokul ice cap in Norway. The first day was easy: the weather was clear and I was on a well-used track marked with birch wands. I spent the second day in a hut during a snowfall. The third day dawned calm with good visibility, the cloud cover being high

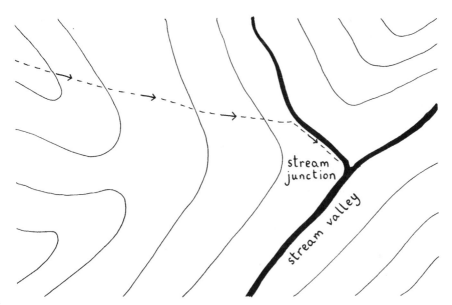

Figure 4-3. Aiming off.

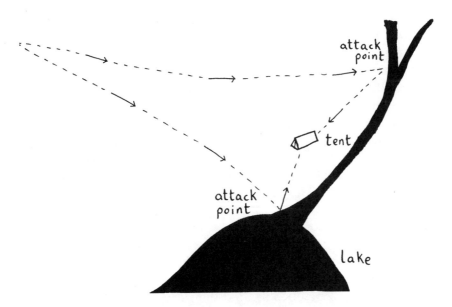

Figure 4-4. Attack points.

above the mountaintops. I set out northwest toward Rembesdalseter, another hut, to which in winter there are no marked routes. If anyone had been that way recently, the previous day's snow had covered the tracks. The terrain was complex, with many small lakes, stream valleys, and minor summits. The visibility remained good until I reached Hellevatnet, one of the lakes. Here the cloud base dropped and snow began to fall. From then on the visibility remained poor. My journal entry, written that evening, is perhaps worth quoting to give a flavor of solo navigation in rugged terrain:

> It was like traveling in a dream world. . . . I navigated on compass bearings and what I could see of topography. The route lay basically on a wide sloping shelf between the steep edges of the ice cap and the slopes down to the Hardangervidda proper. After crossing Helleelvi [a stream] I picked up occasional cairns of the summer route. Steep crags and corries loomed up on my right every so often. I skied from visible rock to visible rock with no idea of terrain between, running suddenly into a steep bank or plummeting into an unseen dip. Eventually worked my way around Skykkjdalsfjellet [a peak] to start descent to Rembesdalsvatnet [a lake]. Top of descent easy—slow telemarks in ankle-deep, heavy snow on open slopes. Bottom harder, with many boulders and sudden drop-offs—one I went into thigh deep. Ahead the broken blue ice of the snout of the Rembesdalskaki glacier—very impressive. Getting down to lake complicated, and I began to worry about avalanches—steep slopes here, and I set off sunwheels and could feel ice under the top foot or so of snow, which occasionally slipped away under a ski. Lakeshore traverse very difficult and dangerous: huge cracked ice slabs half-covered with recent snowfall lay on boulders at crazy angles. [Rembesdalsvatnet is a reservoir, and water is extracted after the surface has frozen, leaving a large gap between the ice and the lake. The ice then cracks and splits, making skiing across the lake too dangerous to attempt.] I teetered along slowly, skidding off slabs and poking poles and once a ski into cracks. Tried a higher line, but snow sliding off steep, ice-covered rock slabs forced me down again. Eventually reached final slopes to hut. Used skins during this section and took an hour to do a mile.

I had the hut and the magnificent scenery that surrounds it to myself. No one had been there for twelve days. The next day the visibility remained poor, but faint tracks led over the difficult ground to the west. I followed a network of lake-dotted valleys north and then east, knowing I would eventually reach the marked track that ran east-west to the north of the ice cap. If by some mischance I missed it, the Bergen-Oslo railway line lay beyond, so I wasn't too worried about getting lost. Again I had problems determining whether the ground ahead dropped or rose, and I skied on compass bearings all day. With nothing solid to focus on and no sound except the *swish, swish* of my skis, it seemed quite eerie. Only by constantly checking the time did I know that I had made any progress. Judging by the uniform surroundings, I could have been skiing the same few feet over and over again.

Altimeter

An altimeter can be useful, especially on tours in high mountains, though I have rarely carried one. Knowing your altitude is helpful for determining exactly where you are in poor visibility. An altimeter could also be used for pinpointing the spot where a traverse needs to be made off a snowfield or around a spur in order to avoid difficulties lower down. Thommen, Peet, and Gischard are quality names in traditional mechanical altimeters with jeweled bearings. Cheaper and seemingly just as accurate are digital watches with altimeter functions from manufacturers such as Casio. If you use an altimeter, remember that they measure air pressure and are vulnerable to weather changes. Don't be surprised if you discover your tent has levitated during the night! Check the altimeter against known heights whenever possible and reset it if necessary.

The most useful altimeter-type instrument I have seen is the Avocet Vertech Ski. As well as altitude and temperature, it measures vertical feet/meters skied and current and average vertical rate of descent, which would be very useful information for navigation purposes. When climbing you can switch to the alpine function and record feet/meters ascended and rate of ascent.

The Vertech can be worn on the wrist over clothing and is designed to be used while wearing thick gloves. It weighs just 1½ ounces/70 grams, and it tells the time too! I'm impressed enough to plan on buying one in the near future.

Getting Lost

Being lost means being unable to find your way to where you want to go or unable to find your way back to your starting point. Unless you have been parachuted from a plane into an unknown area, however, you will know which mountain range or forest you are in; and unless you ski amazingly fast, you won't be very far from the last place you recognized before you lost precise track of your location. By checking the map and compass you should be able to determine the approximate direction you need to ski in to reach an identifiable feature such as a river or lake. Unless the weather is so bad they have been obliterated, one great advantage of being on skis is that you can simply turn around and ski back along your tracks to a place you recognize (but remember my story of attempting to ski without a compass in a whiteout as evidence of how confusing even your own tracks can be).

The main thing to do when lost is not to let it disturb you too much. Panicking is the surest way to disaster. Whatever you do, don't push on mindlessly in the hope that somehow you will reach your destination. You might, but chances are you will expend a lot of energy and time skiing farther away from where you want to be. Instead, stop and have a hot drink or a snack while you consider the situation and study the map. How long is it since you last knew where you were? If not too long you might be able to reverse your direction of travel and retrace your route to that point. If it is late and you have camping gear, set up camp. In the morning you will have the whole day to find out where you are. I have spent many nights unsure of exactly where I was. It is always exciting to find out. You may have to bivouac even on a day tour if you have been skiing for hours in the wrong direction (but this shouldn't happen if you check the map and compass regularly), a good reason for always having the means with you to survive a night out in relative comfort.

Weather Forecasts

The weather is far more important on a ski tour than on a summer backpacking trip. Blizzards can keep you trapped in one place for days at a time, while heavy snowfalls can make travel extremely slow and lead to high avalanche danger.

Before visiting a new area I like to find out about the usual weather for the time of year I'm going so I have some idea what to expect. Guidebooks and national forest and park information leaflets can provide this information. Local forecasts from radio, newspapers, or ski resorts are useful once you get to your destination, but I don't rely on them. When we set off to cross the Columbia Icefield, the forecast, obtained from the local national park ranger station, seemed quite reasonable, but a five-day storm with heavy snow, high winds, and minimal visibility ensued. Staffed mountain huts generally post a daily forecast, and I have found them to be quite accurate. If you meet other skiers it is always worth asking if they have heard a recent forecast.

An altimeter can be used as a barometer for crude weather forecasting. In the morning or after a side trip from camp, if your altimeter indicates that your camp is on a higher level than it was at your last measurement, then pressure is falling and a worsening of the weather can be expected. Conversely, if your camp appears to have fallen, pressure is rising and better weather should develop. The rate

On glaciers, take care when crossing snow bridges over crevasses, however wide they are (see "Glacier Travel" on page 138).

of change may indicate how soon the weather will change and how severe it will be. In particular be wary of rapid and steep drops in pressure. These probably indicate a major storm.

Glacier Travel

Skiing glaciers is not in itself difficult or dangerous. Only when there are crevasses present do precautions need to be taken. In Norway some, though not all, glaciers are mostly free from crevasses and can be skied without ropes and harnesses. In the Rockies and the Alps the opposite is true. Skiing on crevassed glaciers is ski mountaineering rather than ski touring and requires mountaineering skills. There isn't the space here, nor have I the experience or knowledge, to go into the techniques needed. If you intend venturing onto crevassed glaciers, take a course at an outdoor center or learn from an experienced friend. *Glacier Travel and Crevasse Rescue* by Andy Selters is a good book on the subject that is worth consulting.

Hazards

It is easy to avoid avalanches: don't go to the mountains.
—*Ben Gadd,* The Handbook of the Canadian Rockies

Snow country is beautiful and wild. It can also be deadly. Ski touring is a safe pursuit most of the time, but there are times and places when great care must be taken to avoid disasters.

Hypothermia

Being wet and cold can lead to hypothermia, the serious lowering of the body's core temperature. And hypothermia can kill. Even competent, well-equipped ski tourers are vulnerable. There are two types: sudden onset hypothermia, caused by sudden immersion into cold water such as by falling through ice into a lake, and the more common long-term onset hypothermia. The latter is usually caused by a combination of inadequate clothing, lack of energy because of insufficient food and liquid consumption, and exhaustion. Being wet, whether from sweat, rain, or melted snow, can hasten the onset of hypothermia, especially if the weather is windy. Low morale can play a part too.

The first defense is to have proper clothing and to use it. People have died with protective clothing in their packs. Don't let a desire to push on prevent you from donning needed clothes. The probable result of neglecting this important practice was demonstrated graphically on a day tour in Norway. The day was fine, and the steep climb out of the trees onto the open mountainside above was warm work. Above timberline, though, a cold wind was blowing, so we pushed on rapidly to a small locked hut that we used as a windbreak while we had a short break. Here we discovered that one of the strongest

Rest stops are important. In bad weather put on extra clothing and get out of the wind.

and most experienced skiers in the party, who had been up near the front throughout the morning, was feeling very cold and shivery because his thick pile jacket and stretch nylon tracksuit were not windproof.

We had to help him struggle into his rain jacket and rain pants because his hands were too numb to connect the ends of the zippers. If he had been alone he would have been in trouble. (This is possibly a reason for carrying pull-on rain pants and other garments that can be put on easily with numb hands, especially on solo tours.) Once into the extra garments and after having a hot drink and some food he warmed up quickly and was able to continue. The episode shows how easy it is to become cold if you are not careful. He explained afterward that he thought he would be able to ski fast enough to keep warm without taking the time to put on windproof clothing. He found out the hard way that you can't do this. A cold wind whips away heat at an amazing rate. If you start to feel cold, don't push on. Stop and put on more clothing. Always.

The initial symptoms of mild hypothermia are shivering, stiffness, lethargy, and irritability. The skin will turn pale and gray and feel cold because of slow circulation. The victim may act out of character, something that will be obvious only to someone who knows the person well. If nothing is done, severe hypothermia will develop with increasing lack of coordination and eventual collapse, coma, and ultimately, death.

If someone does show signs of hypothermia, always stop and do something about it without delay. Sufferers can be protected from further heat loss by being placed in a sleeping bag or bivy bag with an insulating mat underneath, preferably in a tent, certainly out of the wind if at all possible. Ideally someone else should get into the sleeping bag alongside the victim. Both persons should be naked (or nearly so) so that body warmth can be most quickly transferred. If this can't be done and the victim's clothing is wet, get the person into dry, warm gear as fast as you can. In wooded country a fire could be lit (see Chapter 9). Hot liquids and food come next, as long as the sufferer is conscious enough to eat and drink without assistance. If the person recovers quickly, continue skiing; exercise creates heat as long as the skier has eaten and has enough warm, dry clothing. If recovery is prolonged, it would be better to camp or bivouac where you are unless there is a hut nearby.

While you are looking after the victim, don't forget about yourself or the rest of the group. Hot drinks all around and huddling together in a shelter are a good idea.

What you shouldn't do is rub someone to warm the skin. While this will stimulate blood flow to the skin, it will direct it away from the core, where warmth is needed. Nor should alcohol ever be given; it expands the capillaries at the extremities, speeding up blood flow and heat loss. It gives a warm glow, but in the long run the person will be colder.

Hypothermia sufferers may act irrationally and will certainly have poor judgment of the situation, so never let them return to hut or camp alone because they will "be all right, really"; nor should you leave them alone. They might wander off while you are away.

A Cautionary Tale

I have only suffered mild hypothermia once, but that brush was enough to have made me very cautious since. Although it was many, many years ago, I remember it all too clearly. It was on a backpacking rather than a skiing trip, but it is relevant and worth retelling to show how a chain of seemingly minor errors over a few days led to the development of a potentially serious situation. The first error was starting out late in the day with a forecast for bad weather. It was calm and sunny when the five of us set out to traverse a mountain ridge, but 4 miles and 2,500 feet of ascent later a cold wind was blowing. Soon we were in dense, wet mist and squalls of sleet. As the ferocity of the storm increased we abandoned the ridge and descended into a cirque to find shelter for a camp.

The wind grew stronger and screamed down the cirque in great gusts, driving heavy rain before it and sorely testing the strength of our tents. Nobody slept, and it was a long, long night.

At dawn we packed up and retreated down to the nearest road. I didn't bother wearing rain gear for the three-hour march in the rain, relying instead on the heat generated by fast walking—very unwise and another error. I arrived at our sheltered valley campground soaked and shivering. The storm continued with more rain and hail, but we all had a reasonable night's sleep.

We all intended another ridge walk, but we had already encountered snow on the ridge and only two of us had ice axes and none of us had crampons (a mistake in itself, leaving us inadequately equipped for the winter conditions we were likely to encounter). Sensibly, those without ice axes decided to take a low-level route to our next campsite. The two of us with axes stuck to our original plan. Because of our long sleep we again left late. On the ridge it was cold and windy but clear, and the day was going well when we ran into some soft snow on a rocky section, where I put my leg into a hole and cracked my shin on a rock. Initially it felt sore but didn't hamper movement.

With ominous black clouds gathering in the west prompting us to hurry, the day became a gradually worsening nightmare. My leg began to throb, and I was limping as we pressed on into thick mist and more rain. The slopes at the start of the descent were covered in thin ice, which would have been easily negotiable in crampons; without them they were very treacherous, and we had to cut steps down the steepest section. My injured leg had gone numb and I no longer felt secure standing on it, so my companion went down, left his pack, and came back to guide me. It was now raining hard, and he had donned his rain jacket. Wanting to hurry—daylight was running out—I didn't bother putting on mine and continued in the acrylic and wool shirt and windproof jacket I had worn all day.

Once onto easy ground we stumbled around a lakeshore in the dark and slogged down the valley to the campsite. I arrived soaked to the skin, feeling very cold and drained of energy. The others were already firmly ensconced in their tents and not keen to come out into the rain. I began pitching my tent. The earth on the well-used site was rock hard, and the stakes wouldn't go in easily. Suddenly I became very frustrated, threw the stakes on the ground, and sat down. Realizing I was on the verge of collapse, my companions bundled me into one of the other tents, stripped off my wet clothes, replaced them with a pile jacket warm with someone else's body heat, and gave me a hot drink. Then they pitched my tent. Soon I was able to move into it, and after a hot meal and a few hours in my sleeping bag I felt fine again. But it had been a near thing. A very near thing if understanding help hadn't been at hand.

I had a nasty shock but was lucky enough to escape without serious harm. I made too many mistakes that combined to put me in a threatening situation. On that last day I should never have attempted a high mountain hike while still tired from the previous two days. We should have had our ice axes out and ready when we ventured onto the snow. I might not have hurt my leg if we had. I was unaware, too, of the shock and worry the injury caused me. Being tired, upset, frightened, or fed up makes you more vulnerable to hypothermia, and I was all of those. And I compounded the situation by continuing in inadequate clothing, getting colder and wetter. I shudder at the thought of what would have happened if I had been alone.

The lone skier should take extra care to respond immediately to even the slightest sign of hypothermia. If it snows or a cold breeze springs up, don't wait, put on a shell garment. If you even think you might be going to feel cold, put on extra clothes. If you still feel cold, make camp early. That is what we should have done, instead of pushing on to make a rendezvous.

Hypothermia shouldn't occur if you are careful. It is the unprepared and unthinking who are at risk.

Frostbite

Frostbite occurs when flesh becomes so cold that it freezes. Exposed parts of your body, such as ears, nose, and cheeks, are most at risk, plus your fingers and toes if they become wet or are not adequately insulated. Signs of frostbite are a colorless appearance and tingling pain. If your feet or hands feel very cold or painful for a while and then go numb, it is a very serious situation. The tissues may die, leading to infection and possibly amputation. The solution is prevention. Minor frostbite or frostnip of the extremities (tips of fingers and toes, nose, face) isn't serious if dealt with promptly. Deep frostbite can be. All frostbite should be taken seriously. In the authoritative book *Medicine for Mountaineering,* editor Dr. James A. Wilkerson says that "the extent and severity of frostbite are notoriously difficult to judge accurately during the early stages, particularly when the tissues are still frozen."

As with hypothermia, frostbite shouldn't occur if you are adequately equipped and take action as soon as any part of your body starts to feel cold. Many of the old remedies for frostbite are worse than useless. Don't rub the injured area with or without snow. You may damage the underlying tissue. If part of the body starts to feel very cold, don't ignore it; stop and warm it. Move the affected part vigorously to create heat. A good remedy for cold hands is to whirl your arms around and around. After a short while you will feel the blood flowing back into your hands. They may ache painfully with the returning heat, but that is better than frostbite. You can stamp your feet and flex your ankles and jump up and down. Donning extra clothing is a good idea, along with consuming food and a hot drink. Just hugging a mug of steaming hot liquid can warm up cold hands. Cold feet can be warmed on someone's stomach, hands warmed in armpits or crotch. You could even pee on cold fingers. Warm breath can be blown on facial frostbite or a hand cupped over it. If a serviced lodge can be reached easily, a warm (not more than 108°F) bath works wonders.

While warming cold extremities directly is obviously necessary, adding more clothing on the body can help. Frostbite occurs because the body shuts down some of the blood supply to the extremities in order to conserve heat in the core. Keep the trunk warm and you are less likely to have a cold nose.

Tight boots can be a cause of frostbitten feet. Nordic skiers have a great advantage over alpine skiers in this regard because the constant flexing of the foot in a nordic boot helps keep the blood flowing. In a rigid plastic alpine boot the foot is immobile, and plastic boots can't expand with your feet as leather can. In extreme cold don't wear too many socks—they can constrict the feet, reducing circulation. For more warmth it is better to use an insulated supergaiter or even pull socks on over your boots.

If someone's feet do become frostbitten and there is no other option such as rescue or retreating to a road or lodge, ski out before you try to warm them (in fact, get medical help before thawing them if you can), as they will suffer more damage (and cause great pain) if they are thawed out and then refreeze.

Snow Blindness

The reflection of the sun off snow can cause snow blindness, which is why wearing sunglasses is essential (see Chapter 9) at high altitudes and in all but the dullest weather at low ones. Snow blindness is caused by ultraviolet radiation burning the cornea and is reputedly extremely painful. A halfway stage can lead to sore eyes that feel as though they have grit in them. Don't rub them, this may cause further damage. Analgesics can help relieve the pain, as can cold compresses (tea bags are sometimes suggested). Otherwise, rest and wait. Healing can take several days. Prevention is much better; I always carry spare sunglasses. In an emergency, you can cut slits in an eyemask of cardboard or other stiff material and strap it to your head with a piece of cord.

Avalanches

Avalanches are probably the greatest and most-feared hazard in snow-covered mountains. Immensely powerful, they can destroy anything in their path. I remember well the shock of my first encounter with the awesome force an avalanche can unleash. I was on foot in the backcountry of Yosemite National Park in the late spring during the height of the snow melt. The rivers were running fast and high, and fording them was very difficult. However, in many places avalanches had ripped huge chunks out of the forest and left massive trees lying across the rivers that we were able to use as bridges. In one place an avalanche had crossed the valley bottom and continued for a hundred yards or more up the other side, reducing the large trees in its path to little more than matchwood. Staring

A skier surveys a wall of avalanche debris.

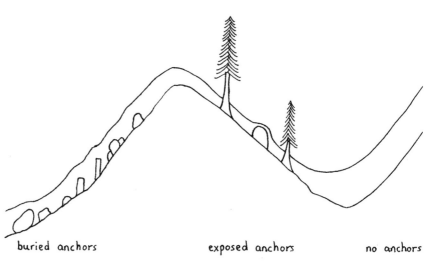

buried anchors   exposed anchors   no anchors

Figure 5-1. Terrain roughness.

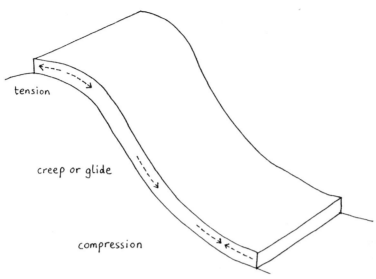

Figure 5-2. Forces within the snowpack.

at this swath of destruction, I thought how slight would be the chances of surviving the forces that could do this.

In many areas avalanches are not a problem. Where the snowpack has consolidated steadily throughout the winter without any sudden changes in temperature, it is likely to be very stable. A freeze-thaw cycle can also lead to very stable snow, but very warm temperatures can cause the snow to become wet and rotten. The nature of the terrain under the snow is important too. Regular smooth surfaces like steep grass and rock slabs hold snow less securely than rough broken ones with plenty of boulders and shrubby plants. Cirques with steep back walls can be dangerous, and convex slopes with snow pulled tight over the curved terrain are more prone to avalanche formation than are concave slopes.

While avalanches are not fully understood, and predicting them is an inexact science, there are many precautions that can be taken. To start with, understanding something of how and why avalanches occur is important. Here I can only touch on some of the major points. Every ski tourer should read one of the many books on the subject. Tony Daffern's *Avalanche Safety for Skiers and Climbers* is particularly good.

Avalanche Warnings

Most popular ski areas where avalanches are a danger put out regular avalanche warnings. They are usually posted at ski resorts, ranger stations, and in local mountain-equipment stores. They may also appear in newspapers and be available as recorded phone messages. Your first line of defense is to heed such warnings. They are based on fieldwork by experienced skiers and climbers who know the history of the season's snowfall. The scale of risk usually runs from low through moderate to high and very high. If it is either of the last two, potentially dangerous slopes should be avoided. Even if the risk is low it is not nonexistent, and you should make your own observations while you are out. Local information can also tell you where notorious avalanche areas are.

Danger Zones

Avalanches occur on steep slopes, usually between 25 and 45 degrees—far steeper than most nordic skiers feel happy descending, but they often traverse them. The angle of a slope can be measured with your ski poles (see Figure 5-3). Put one stick upright in the snow. Then hold the other pole at a right angle and slide the tip down the snow

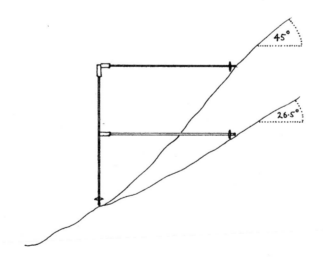

Figure 5-3. Using poles to measure slope angle.

until the handle touches the vertical pole. If the second pole touches the first at the handle, the slope is 45 degrees; if halfway down, 26.5 degrees. Stay off steep slopes unless the avalanche risk is low, skiing the valley bottom below, if it is wide, or the ridges above instead. Narrow canyons are dangerous. Ridges and buttresses are much safer than the back or sides of bowls. Avalanches often follow the same track. They can be identified by debris at their base or by the absence of trees on the lower hillside or in the valley below. Gullies are particularly prone to avalanche. Lunching or camping at the bottom of one is not a good idea.

Danger Times

Most avalanches occur during or soon after heavy snowfall, so dangerous terrain should be avoided for the 24 hours following a blizzard. Storms that start cold with dry snow but finish with warmer temperatures are more likely to lead to avalanche conditions than the opposite because dry snow doesn't adhere to or support the wetter, heavier snow on top of it very well. In spring, heavy rain can be a problem, saturating and destabilizing the snowpack. Warm temperatures can have the same effect. Strong winds blow snow about, dumping it on lee slopes to form potentially dangerous windslab and building cornices on the sides of steep ridges and cliffs. Even when skies are clear, snow plumes blowing off summits and cliffs are signs that the wind is moving snow about.

Windslab

Windslab is very dangerous. It may occur whenever strong winds have been blowing. Because it forms on lee slopes, knowledge of the wind direction for the period preceding your tour is useful. Windward slopes usually hold less snow and tend to be safer. If the snow settles or sounds hollow under your skis, or cracks appear, windslab is probably present.

Types of Avalanche

There are two types of avalanche: a loose-snow avalanche starts from a single point and grows as it descends, while in a slab avalanche a huge block of snow breaks away and slips all at once. Slab avalanches leave behind them a fracture line known as the crown wall. Both types of avalanche can consist of wet or dry snow,

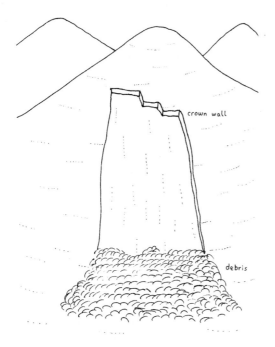

Figure 5-4. A slab avalanche.

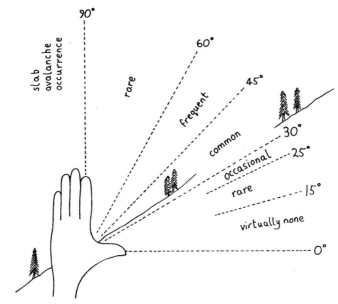

Figure 5-5. Slab avalanche occurrence related to slope angle.

and both can be tiny or huge. And whatever the size or the type of snow, both can kill.

Avalanche Tests

Where the snowpack is deep and consists of several layers, the adherence of the layers is important. A weak link in the layers is a likely cause of avalanches.

THE SHEAR TEST

The shear test is one of a number of ways to see if there are layers in the snowpack that will slide over each other. Dig a pit in snow that is at about the same angle as the slope you intend skiing and facing in the same direction, making sure your site is safe from avalanche danger. The pit should be several feet across and as deep as possible, at least several feet down. Next level off the back wall of the pit so it is vertical. Then mark out a rectangle above the pit about as wide and deep as your shovel blade. Cut down the sides of the rectangle to the ground (ideally) or to a very hard layer of snow, then cut out the back to the depth of the shovel blade. To carry out the shear test, put the shovel down the back of the area you have cut out and pull— don't lever—gently forward. Keep increasing the pressure. If there is a sliding layer present it will shear off. The amount of pressure needed

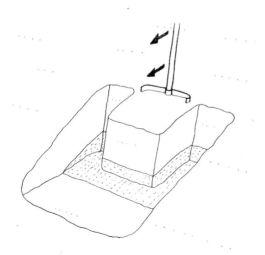

Figure 5-6. The shear test.

to cause it to slide indicates the degree of avalanche risk. Keep doing the test until you reach the bottom of the rectangle, as there may be other layers that slide. If there are no sliding layers, it doesn't mean the snowpack is safe: this is only a crude test, and the snow may well be different not far away. Several pits will give more indication of the nature of the snow than just one.

I once did this test on a day of minimal visibility high in the Norwegian mountains. Bored with sitting in the hut, we had set off to climb to a nearby pass. As the slopes steepened I felt the snow surface settle under my skis, indicating that windblown snow had formed into a slab resting lightly on the layer below, a sign of potential avalanche danger. Concerned, I suggested to the group that we retreat. This was initially an unpopular suggestion, until I mentioned avalanches. During the descent I noted some recent avalanche debris just to the side of our route. Back on safer terrain we did a shear test. I hardly had to pull the shovel at all for the top 4 or 5 inches of snow to slid off. Higher up I suspect that this layer could have been much thicker.

THE RUTSCHBLOCK SLAB-AVALANCHE TEST

Another test, specifically designed for skiers and for testing for slab-avalanche danger, is the Rutschblock test (also known as the Swiss or Jump test). Again find a safe slope with snow similar to that on the slope you suspect. The angle needs to be at least 30 degrees. Cut out a column almost as long and as wide as your skis and down either to the ground or to a hard stable layer of snow. Wearing skis, you then apply increasing pressure to the column until it slides. The different stability levels are:

1. Fails while being dug
2. Fails when approached gently from above
3. Fails when the column is stood on
4. Fails with a soft jump
5. Fails with a hard jump
6. Fails with several hard jumps
7. Does not fail

If the column fails on numbers 1 through 3 it suggests a high degree of instability in the snowpack and therefore avalanche danger. Failure on 4 or 5 suggests some areas of instability and the need for caution; 6 and 7 suggest low slab-avalanche risk on similar slopes.

The Rutschblock test sounds very useful, but I have not tried it. The above description is based on an article by one of Britain's foremost avalanche experts, Paul Thompson, that appeared in the January 1993 issue of *Climber and Hillwalker* magazine.

SNOW PITS

As well as the tests described above, a snow pit can be used for seeing how many layers and what types of snow make up the snowpack. By poking your finger into each layer you can see how hard it is. Little or no resistance suggests a weak layer in the snowpack, while a very hard layer may be ice and not bonded very well to other layers. If the difference between the layers is only slight and the changes are even, it implies a well-consolidated and stable snowpack. All snow pits should be filled in when you have finished with your tests, lest a skier coming by later finds them by catching a tip.

Avalanche Signs

Often small avalanches can be seen on steep slopes. Sunwheels, balls of snow that have cartwheeled down the slope, may be visible too. Both indicate unstable snow.

An avalanche fan on an ice field.

Crossing Dangerous Slopes

At times you may have no choice but to cross a dangerous slope. Before you do, think hard. Are there really no alternatives? What lies below? If there are cliffs or big boulders, turn back. If you do cross, stay well apart and aim for rock "islands" or slight ridges or flat areas. Watch each other cross, and watch and listen for signs of an avalanche starting. Fasten clothing but unfasten pack hip belts, unfasten ski safety straps, and take your hands out of the wrist loops of your poles. If you unclip your bindings, or at least loosen cables and put three-pin bails on the top notch, your skis can be kicked off if necessary. It is safer to go straight up or down a dangerous slope than to traverse it. Your skis slicing neatly through the snow could be the trigger for an avalanche. Remember that most avalanches are caused by the victims themselves. If you do have to traverse a suspect slope, do so as high as possible, above most of the snow.

Rescue Beacons

On tours in avalanche terrain, avalanche rescue beacons should be worn. These battery-operated devices send out and receive signals and make it much easier to locate buried avalanche victims. Their use requires practice, however, as explained later. Pieps and Ortovox are two of a number of makes. They operate at frequencies of 2,275 kilohertz or 457 kilohertz. Either will do, but all members of a party must have compatible beacons, and to be of any use, everyone in a party should have one. For this reason, dual-frequency beacons are a good idea. They should be worn around the neck inside clothing so they are not ripped off during an avalanche. Keep them switched to transmit while you ski, only switching to receive when you are searching for an avalanche victim. An older, less effective alternative is a brightly colored avalanche cord that you trail behind you.

If Disaster Strikes

What do you do if caught in an avalanche? I am glad to say I have no direct experience, though I have been close on occasion. In one frightening incident, two of us were on a late spring ski tour in Glacier National Park in the Rocky Mountains in Montana. A sudden rise in temperatures and a rapid thaw led to our doing more walking than skiing. We were traversing steep slopes of heavy wet snow well

An avalanche beacon.

above timberline on a day of rain when we stopped for lunch on a snow-free spur. As we were about to continue, the slope ahead of us suddenly avalanched with a huge roar and crashed down into the forest below. Almost immediately a second avalanche followed. Without hesitation we headed down our spur into the wet forest, shaken by this near miss.

In general, one is advised to ski to the edge of an avalanche as it begins, if possible. If you can't, thrust your ski poles into the snow and hang on, or grab a rock or tree if one is nearby. If you are swept away, try to jettison your skis, poles, pack, and any other item that could cause injury, and then try to stay on the surface, making swimming motions and perhaps rolling to the side as well. When under the snow, keep your mouth closed. As your fall slows, try to push to the top and also try to clear a breathing space in front of your face. Once the slide has stopped, see if you can push a hand or arm up through the snow (if you are so disoriented that you don't know which way is up, spit first to find out). If you can't quickly force a way out and it seems you are well and truly buried, it's important to

An impressive avalanche in the Alps.

conserve energy and air; there is no point in shouting or trying to move. All you can do is wait.

SEARCHING FOR VICTIMS

The fate of anyone buried is dependent on those left on the surface. If you see someone avalanched, try to keep the person in sight during the fall; locating someone in the avalanche debris afterward can be very difficult. Note the point at which you last see the person and begin the search below it. An immediate search is essential. If the victim isn't found very quickly, the chance of survival is slight, so there is no time to go for help. By the time a rescue party arrives it could be too late. Try to conduct the search in an organized manner, beginning by looking for signs on the surface such as bits of gear. Make sure that someone is watching for further avalanches. If you don't have avalanche beacons, ski poles can be used to probe for the buried person. Line everybody up and cover the area systematically. Once you find a victim, shovels are essential for digging the person out. Only if you fail completely to locate anybody after a very thorough search should someone go for help.

A beacon search can also be conducted in a straight line, after making sure everyone's beacon is switched to receive and the volume control is turned up full. Stop every few steps and swing the beacons slowly from side to side so you don't miss a signal. Once you pick up a signal, one beacon can be used to track it down to a specific spot. First orient the beacon in the direction where the signal is strongest, checking all possibilities. Then turn the volume down until the signal is just audible. This will enable you to pick up quickly the strengthening of the signal as you approach the source. Walk in a straight line until the signal stops rising and starts to fade, then reorient the beacon and repeat the process, walking in the opposite direction. The line you have walked marks where the signal is strongest in one direction. From the center of this line repeat the procedure at right angles to make another line. Start again at the center of this new line. Keep repeating until the ends of the line where the signal begins to fade are less than 6 feet apart. Now start crawling, moving the beacon backward and forward over the snow. Dig at the point the signal is loudest. This search system, known as bracketing, is the quickest way to find a victim, but it is not that simple and not something to learn after a real avalanche. Practice it well beforehand by

Starting a descent—take care when you can't see what lies below.

burying a beacon and then searching for it. Then practice it again.

Avalanches are a hazard that you must know about. However, the danger should be put into perspective. Much of the time nordic ski tourers don't travel in avalanche terrain. Alpine ski mountaineers and snow and ice climbers are far more at risk.

Cornices

Cornices, those great curls of snow that can form on the edges of ridges and cliffs, are spectacular and impressive. They can also be very dangerous. If they collapse they can cause avalanches, so camping or lunching below them isn't sensible, especially in spring or warm weather or when the sun has been shining on them for hours.

The greater danger is of skiing onto or even over a cornice.

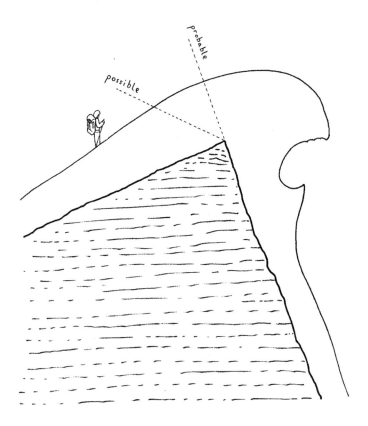

Figure 5-7. Cornice fracture lines.

They can easily be invisible from above, especially in mist. If in doubt, stay well back from any steep ridge or cliff edges. Cornices are formed by the wind, so if you know the direction the wind has been blowing from, you can determine where cornices are likely to be (on the lee side). A cornice doesn't break off vertically and directly above the edge of the cliff or ridge. The break line slants and can be well back from the actual edge. So don't venture too close, and if you see cracks in the snow near an edge, back off at once.

Rescue

As far as possible, ski tourers should be self-sufficient and able to deal with emergencies. There may come a time when an outside rescue has to be sought, however. It is important that the two people going for help (someone should go alone only if there is no alternative) have all the relevant information, including the specific location (with map reference if possible), the nature of the terrain and any features that can help identify the place, the nature of the injuries, the number of those involved, and the time of the accident. This should be written down. Those awaiting help should dig some kind of shelter and make sure everyone keeps warm and comfortable. Those going for help should contact the nearest ranger station or sheriff's office, who will then contact the local mountain rescue organization. Be prepared to take the rescue party back to the victims if possible. Most rescue teams are made up of local volunteers who rely on donations; if you need their services be as generous as you can afterward.

Insurance

In some areas rescue teams are volunteers; in others, such as the Alps, they are professional, and costs are high. Hospital treatment may be expensive anyway. Mountain rescue and medical insurance, which usually covers hospital costs, for organized tours abroad can usually be booked through the tour operator.

Clothing for the Snow

Twenty below and warmer is Hawaii-type weather; when the
wind isn't blowing, you can almost carry on in shirtsleeves.
Thirty below is perfect for skiing and dogsledding.
—**Will Steger,** North to the Pole

Unfortunately, a fair amount of gear has to be carried on anything longer than a short half-day tour close to civilization. Because of the potential severity of winter weather, even on day tours you should carry enough equipment to get you through an enforced night out. Your clothing is crucial. It needs to be adequate to cope with the worst blizzards and coldest temperatures while you are on the move and, in conjunction with your shelter and sleeping bag, while you are in camp. By choosing each item carefully you can keep the weight and bulk of your clothing to a minimum while still being prepared for all eventualities. The weight of each item is important; every extra ounce, whether on your body or on your back, reduces the feeling of freedom that nordic skiing gives, making you feel more like a beast of burden. If I find it hard to choose between two similar articles of clothing, I almost always go for the lighter one. Clothing also needs to be hard wearing and easy-care, plus low in bulk for carrying in the pack. Because skiing involves dynamic movement, clothing shouldn't be restrictive, so stretchy or loose-fitting garments are needed.

The Function of Clothing

Ski clothing must perform a difficult job. While on the move skiers generate a great deal of heat and often don't need to wear much clothing, but what they do wear must keep out snow and wind and at times rain and also allow for the speedy passage of body moisture from the skin to the outside air to keep them dry and comfortable.

Understanding your requirements can help in selecting the right garments for comfort in even the most severe storms. The aim is to stay both dry and warm, which requires achieving a balance between heat loss and heat production—not easy when you go in minutes from a strenuous, sweat-producing climb on a sheltered slope to sitting down in a cold breeze on the ridge above. It is your body heat that keeps you warm, so you should always don extra clothing to trap that heat as soon as you start to feel cool. If you let yourself get too cold, warming up again can be difficult.

Heat Loss

Heat is lost from the body in four ways: convection, conduction, evaporation, and radiation.

The air transfers heat from the body by convection, the main cause of heat loss. Wind increases convection, and windchill is a major winter hazard, so tightly woven, windproof clothing is essential.

Conduction is the transfer of heat by direct contact between two objects of different temperatures. Air is a poor conductor of heat, which is why fluffy clothing like pile or down that traps air in its fibers is very warm. It is the trapped air, in fact, that retains the body heat. Water, on the other hand, is a very good conductor of heat, which is why you chill quickly in wet clothing. To keep you dry while skiing, it isn't sufficient that your garments merely be made from waterproof fabric; they must also be designed to keep out snow, whether airborne or encountered in a fall. And once you are sealed into this "shell" clothing, so is your body moisture, so the material must breathe—let out moisture vapor. This property is far more important in cold-weather clothing than in summerwear; getting soaked in sweat can be very serious in winter. Wet clothing is cold clothing whether the cause is snow, rain, or sweat.

Your body creates moisture in order to keep you cool, counteracting the heat produced by exercise. Evaporation turns the moisture into vapor, a process that requires heat. If your skin is covered with sweat when you stop exercising, a large amount of heat is needed to evaporate the excessive moisture. This leads to after-exercise chill. To conserve heat you need clothing that transports the moisture away from the skin before it vaporizes.

Radiation is heat transfer between objects without any warming of the space between. Because an unobstructed route between the objects is required, clothing, especially shell clothing, prevents most radiation, and it is not something to be concerned about.

A combination of high-performance fabrics and careful design is needed to produce clothing that can cope adequately with the different forms of heat loss and the enormous variation in energy used (and therefore heat output) during a ski tour. The last twenty years has seen major developments in clothing fabrics, but even so it isn't possible to always be comfortable and dry. At times you will feel cold or damp. The important thing is to stop and put on extra clothing before you get too cold or too damp.

The Layer System

The best way to deal with the different clothing requirements is to have several layers of clothing rather than one or two thick garments. This system allows you to cope with widely varying conditions without either overheating or shivering. Though most of the layers may stay in the pack much of the time, the absolute minimum needed is four layers: a thin inner layer that transports moisture away from the body, an insulating midlayer, a windproof and snowproof outer layer, and a second, thicker insulating layer to wear during breaks or in extreme cold. I often carry six layers rather than four, which gives me more options for dealing with different conditions: the wicking inner layer, a lightweight windproof outer and a heavier waterproof outer, and two lightweight insulating layers, plus a thicker one for halts. Much of the time I ski in just a thin inner layer and a light windproof shell, carrying the rest for wearing at halts and in stormy weather.

The midlayer and outer layer of clothing should have plenty of adjustable openings so they can be easily vented to remove warm air, but you also need to be able to close all openings tightly to keep out wind and snow: spindrift—fine wind-driven snow—will find its way through the smallest gap, so closures should overlap and be easy to seal.

Base Layer (Underwear)

The main function of the first layer of clothing, in spite of its being known as thermal underwear, is to keep the skin dry rather than warm.

Damp clothing next to your skin will quickly make you feel cold when you stop skiing, because your heat output drops rapidly and the damp inner layer draws warmth from the body as it dries. To counter this effect you need clothing that will remove moisture from the skin as fast as possible and dry quickly.

Cotton soaks up perspiration and takes a long time to dry, so avoid it for next-to-the-skin wear. A cotton T-shirt might be nice to ski in on a warm spring day, but otherwise cotton inner clothing is countereffective.

Synthetic base-layer fabrics remove body moisture quickly by transporting or wicking it away from the skin: the heat of your body pushes the moisture through the fabric to the outside. If you sweat hard you will feel damp and clammy at times no matter what you are wearing, but because synthetic fabrics absorb little moisture and dry quickly you will soon feel dry.

Wool and silk are natural alternatives to synthetics. They work by absorbing moisture into their fibers and leaving the surface next to the skin dry. But when they become saturated they will feel damp and cold, and wool in particular is much slower drying than any synthetic. Even so, both are worth considering; I have skied for two weeks wearing the same thin wool shirt as a base layer with no problems. One advantage of wool is that, unlike some synthetics, it doesn't smell after many days of constant wear.

I prefer garments with turtle or polo necks to crew necks; they are much warmer and more versatile, keeping out drafts and preventing heat from escaping. Zippers, snaps, or buttons at the neck are helpful for ventilation on crewnecks and essential with high-neck garments. Close-fitting, stretchy garments help in trapping air and wicking moisture quickly and don't restrict movement. They also allow midlayers to fit easily over them. Seams should be flat-sewn, not raised, to avoid rubbing. Designs of long underwear vary little, but some companies do offer men's and women's versions. A close fit and an elasticized waist are the key features.

Once you have decided on the design and fabric you want, it is worth trying a garment on to check the fit, the comfort next to the skin, and the freedom of movement. Put on the layer you will wear over the underclothing—some combinations of fabrics won't slide over each other easily and can bind, restricting freedom of movement. Consider the quality of manufacture, looking for well-finished seams and neat stitching. A rough finish may rub against the skin. Finally, check the care instructions. Some materials are easier to wash and dry than others. All of them, by the way, pill slightly, especially expedition-weight fabrics. Turning them inside out before washing helps minimize this. On a hut-to-hut tour, garments can be rinsed out and dried overnight in the drying room or hung above a wood stove (not too close!), so there is never any need to carry more than a couple of tops. When camping in a tent I wear the same top throughout the trip (23 days is the longest so far) because drying even the thinnest top can be difficult. And when you are melting snow for all your water there won't be any to spare for washing clothes.

Base-layer garments usually come in two or three different weights of material, often graded lightweight, midweight, and expedition weight. The main choices in synthetic materials are polypropylene (polypro for short), polyester (brand names include Capilene, Polartec 100, Thermax, Coolmax, Thermastat, and more) and chlorofiber (Rhovyl/Modal and Damart). I have tried most of them and find it hard to choose among them. An interesting approach, too new at the time of writing for me to have tried it out, is Duofold's Vent-A-Layer innerwear. Made from du Pont's Thermastat, Vent-A-Layer garments have mesh vents under the arms and on the inner thighs to speed the passage of perspiration. Crew-neck top and long pants weigh 5 ounces (140 grams) each.

Whatever the fabric, the thinnest garments absorb less moisture, wick faster, and dry more quickly than the thicker ones. Except in really cold weather, thicker fabrics are better for wearing in camp or as a second layer. The thinnest garments are also, of course, the lightest and least bulky. Silk and Helly-Hansen Lifa Prolite polypropylene are the lightest, long-sleeved tops in these fabrics weighing only 3½ to 4½ ounces (100 to 150 grams). Expedition-weight garments can weigh up to 12 ounces (350 grains), as much as the lightest pile tops.

Midlayer (Warmwear)

The midlayer is the one that keeps you warm. While important, it is the one where compromises can most easily be made, so if you have to choose, go for good outer and base layers and make do with old wool or synthetic sweaters or thick shirts as warmwear. (Do not choose cotton or cotton-mix sweats, though; they soak up moisture like a sponge and take ages to dry). The advantages of specialist clothing have more to do with weight, durability, and bulk than with warmth.

WOOL

Wool, the traditional material for warmwear, is still popular with many people. It is comfortable, warm, and hard wearing but also absorbent, slow drying, and relatively heavy when compared with synthetics. I don't use wool shirts or sweaters for warmwear, preferring fleece and pile, which I think are more efficient. Many experienced skiers disagree with me. If you like wool, use it!

PILE AND FLEECE

Pile garments are my favorite midwear—they are warm, lightweight, extremely hard wearing, almost nonabsorbent, quick drying, breathable, comfortable, and easy to look after. Pile wicks away moisture almost as fast as base-layer garments and warms you quicker than anything else when worn next to the skin. If condensation forms inside your shell garment, a pile midlayer will keep it away from your inner layer. On several occasions my pile top, worn under a waterproof layer, has been quite damp on the outside but bone-dry inside. I have also found that you can keep dry in wet snow by wearing pile under a windproof nylon or polyester microfiber, or 65/35 cotton/nylon-mix shell, a combination that is comfortable and breathes very well.

No clear distinction is possible between fleece and pile, as many garmentmakers now call fabrics fleece that the fabric manufacturer, who should know, calls pile. Other companies, such as Patagonia and Helly-Hansen, still call their fabrics pile. In general, pile is a more open-weave, fluffy fabric than fleece, which is smoother and has a tighter weave. Since pile was the original name, I have used it to encompass fleece in the following discussion.

There are several different thicknesses and types of pile, giving a wide choice in the degree of warmth provided, and manufacturers often give advice on the intended use of their products. For example, Malden Mills, probably the major pile manufacturer and a company that researches new fabrics extensively, says their Polartec 200 is for "mild-to-cold conditions," while the thicker Polartec 300 is for "cold-to-extreme-cold conditions." Thin, tightly woven fabrics like Polartec 100M are the most wind resistant, though they are not as warm as thicker, more loosely knitted fabrics.

The lightest piles are probably the best for skiing. I find I overheat too quickly in heavier ones, although these are worth carrying to wear at halts, in camp, and when skiing in bitter weather. Lightweight pile garments shouldn't weigh more than 12 to 18 ounces/350 to 500 grams (and some are far less), while heavier ones can run to 21 to 25 ounces/600 to 700 grams. Anything more than that is too heavy for skiing.

The only drawback of most pile fabrics is their not being windproof. Windproof outers or linings or the new laminated pile fabrics can solve this problem; but you may overheat more easily in windproof pile, especially when wearing a waterproof jacket over the top. You also can't wear the pile and the windproof layer separately. An advantage of windproof pile is that you don't have to worry about getting it wet or covered in snow. Windproof pile garments are worth considering for skiing in extremely cold conditions and for wearing at stops and in camp, perhaps instead of a down top, in which case, buy a size that fits over your shell garments. It takes time, and a great deal of heat can be lost, if you have to take off your outer jacket, put on your pile top, and then put your jacket back on, and you may be tempted not to bother.

Windproof pile comes in four types: lined, shelled, reversible, and laminated. Because pile wicks better and is more comfortable next to the skin than smooth windproof fabrics are, I find lined pile the least comfortable. Shelled pile makes more sense. The best outers are lightweight, windproof, quick-drying nylons such as Supplex. Reversible pile, as the name suggests, can be worn either way around. Weights of these garments vary enormously, from 18 to 34 ounces (500 to 950 grams), depending on the type of pile and the type of windproof material.

The future almost certainly lies with laminated pile fabrics, which are barely any heavier than standard pile and just as pleasant to wear. These fabrics consist of a thin windproof membrane stuck between two layers of pile or between pile and a wicking base layer. The membranes are similar to those used in breathable waterproof garments and perform in much the same way. Laminated pile is very warm, much warmer than a nonwindproof pile top of the same weight. The breathability can be overtaxed when skiing hard, resulting, at times, in a great deal of condensation. This makes laminated pile better for use in extreme cold or at rest stops and in camp. The membranes also make them very water resistant, though they dry more slowly than standard pile when they do get wet. Although laminated piles can be worn as outerwear much of the time, they usually lack such essential features as hoods and aren't satisfactory replacements for fully specified shell garments. (For a pile garment that does work as outerwear, see the section on Freebird clothing on page 174.) Weights of laminated piles range from 21 to 25 ounces (600 to 700 grams).

Whatever the type of pile, the design is also important. Shirt, sweater, and jacket styles are all available. Whichever you choose, it needs to be close fitting in order to trap warm air efficiently and wick moisture away quickly. The warmest, weight for weight, are piles to which Lycra has been added to make them stretchy. To prevent cold air from being sucked in at the bottom, the garment should have an elastic hem or a drawcord. The broad, stretchy ribbing found on the cuffs and hem of many pile tops works well, but it does absorb moisture. It then feels cold and takes a long time to dry. The nonabsorbent and quick-drying elastic or Lycra binding now found on many garments is better. The use of such binding is often a sign that a garment is designed mainly for backcountry rather than street use. Windproof pile works better if there is ample opportunity for ventilation, so look for zippers in the armpit, adjustable cuffs, and drawcord hems.

INSULATED CLOTHING

Jackets insulated with polyester fill are popular for lift-served skiing, but most are too warm and not versatile enough for backcountry use. They are generally too bulky and heavy to carry in the pack; a windproof pile top is a better choice.

This is not to reject all insulated clothing, however. Down-filled tops are ideal warmwear for halts and in camp. Down is lighter than anything else for the warmth given and compresses much smaller than the alternatives. There are several very lightweight down tops available. The one I use is an over-the-head design that has a 6-ounce (180-gram) down fill and a total weight of just 17 ounces (480 grams)—lighter than most pile tops. It is large enough to pull on over a windproof top, so in stormy weather I don't lose heat by having to remove my outer layer before I can add insulation. I have never actually skied in a down top, but I know people who do when it is really cold.

An even lighter and less bulky garment is a sleeveless down vest, a versatile alternative to a sweater or jacket. A vest should be large enough to fit over your outer layer.

Overall, for backup insulation I suggest down tops for cold, dry conditions and windproof pile for wet cold.

Outer Layer (Shell)

The outer layer is crucial because it is the one that has to keep out the snow and wind. Care should be taken in its selection. Some breathable rain gear that works adequately in summer conditions fails in winter storms. Most of the materials available can cope with blizzards if the design is right, so a choice should not be made purely on the basis of the fabric.

Much of the time a fully waterproof garment won't be needed, windproof ones shedding dry snow just as well, but I have done enough skiing in the rain to always carry one. I usually wear a lightweight, single-thickness windproof top, which keeps me drier and more comfortable than any rain gear, even that made from the best breathable fabrics.

Condensation can occur inside any windproof shell garment, waterproof or not. I once went skiing on a dry, calm morning in a temperature of 20°F (–7°C) wearing a double 50/50 polyester/cotton windproof jacket. When I stopped after a few hours of zipping along a prepared track, I found a layer of ice on the inside of the jacket. I was wearing a light, polyester-filled jacket under the windproof, and the air between the two layers had become so cold that the moisture vapor from my body condensed on the chilled inner of the windproof and then froze. I skied the rest of the day without the windproof and stayed just as warm with no more condensation. The lesson is to wear only as much clothing as needed.

WINDPROOF SHELLS

Windproof shells need weigh no more than 7 to 14 ounces (200 to 400 grams), though fully specified jackets can be considerably heavier. The best fabrics are nylons and polyesters, especially the new microfibers, as they are lightweight, windproof, fast drying, low in bulk, breathable, water resistant, and comfortable. Simple designs keep the weight down. The main features to look for are a hood and large chest pockets.

An interesting development by W. L. Gore (the creators of Gore-Tex) is the XCR (extended comfort range) Windstopper membrane that can be laminated (glued) to a light nylon or polyester fabric to make a breathable, showerproof, quick-drying, comfortable, lightweight windproof material. When I first heard of it I wondered what the advantages over a simple nylon shell could be, but having used such a garment I am quite impressed. Working hard climbing breakable crust produced no condensation inside, and the laminated fabric felt warmer and more protective than an ordinary nylon top would. A simple design like Moonstone's over-the-head XCR

You'll need warm and windproof clothing in cold weather.

Windstopper wind shirt can be worn under a pile top or over one and weighs just 7 ounces (200 grams).

The traditional windproof material is 60/40 cloth, and, although heavier and slower drying than synthetics, garments in this cotton/nylon mixture are still worth considering. There are many similar materials, one example being Patagonia's Ventura Cloth (58 percent cotton/42 percent nylon).

Some lightly coated windproof garments are described as highly water resistant and promoted as ideal for spring skiing. In my experience they aren't, being much less breathable than noncoated windproof garments yet not fully waterproof. This sort of compromise doesn't work.

RAIN GEAR

Garments that are both windproof and waterproof are the standard for skiing—the best ones will keep out anything the weather can throw at you. Carrying rain gear in winter may seem unnecessary, but the weather can change with amazing speed, and wet snow can soak you just as quickly as rain. Freeze-thaw-freeze conditions can be particularly deadly if you are soaked through from melting snow when the temperature drops. I never tour without rain gear.

BREATHABLE MEMBRANES AND COATINGS. Fabrics should be moisture-vapor permeable, or breathable, to minimize condensation buildup. Breathability varies greatly, and a garment that passes enough moisture vapor to keep you dry during a gentle stroll in summer may leave you very wet if you use it for skiing.

Conventional breathable rain gear comes in two forms: coatings and membranes. Liquid silicone or polyurethane is applied to a base fabric to produce coated fabrics; membranes are ultrafine cling-film-like materials laminated to other fabrics. Coated fabrics are generally less breathable than membranes, though the best ones are almost as good.

Coatings and membranes can be either microporous or hydrophilic. Microporous material has millions of microscopic holes in it that are big enough for moisture vapor to pass through but too small for liquids to do so. Hydrophilic materials are more complex: they have chains of water-attracting (hydrophilic) molecules built into a close-woven, water-repelling material. Moisture vapor is conducted through the fabric along these molecules. Both microporous and hydrophilic fabrics require a variation in humidity (and therefore pressure) between the inside and outside to be effective, so the garments should be fairly close fitting. Because water vapor condenses on cold surfaces and the outer of a shell garment is usually cold, garments having the waterproof breathable component as the lining rather than the outer surface work best, as the breathable layer then stays warmer and drier. Thus the construction of a garment as well as its fabric is important.

Although there were many earlier attempts, the first waterproof breathable material that worked to any degree was the microporous polytetrafluorethylene (PTFE) membrane called Gore-Tex, first introduced in the late 1970s and still the market leader. Early Gore-Tex worked well but, having poor durability, stayed waterproof only for a short time. Gore-Tex is now a bicomponent fabric with an oleophobic (oil-hating) layer over the PTFE membrane that protects it from contamination. It seems much tougher, but I find it considerably less breathable. Still, it slightly outperforms all the coatings. Sympatex and Permatex are two hydrophilic membranes. They breathe well and, being made from polyester and polyurethane respectively, are very durable.

Large numbers of coatings are on the market, with many garmentmakers having their own versions and new ones appearing all the time. Established coatings include Ultrex, Entrant, HellyTech, Triple-Point, and REI Elements.

Coated garments are generally a single layer, though some have a loose lining. Membrane laminates are more complicated and here again construction is important. There are four ways in which a membrane can be incorporated into a garment.

A three-layer laminate is glued to both an outer and inner fabric, producing a stiff, durable material that doesn't breathe as well as any of the other laminates.

In a two-layer laminate the membrane is glued to just the outer fabric, giving a more flexible, more breathable material. Some form of loose lining is required to protect the membrane. Close-woven linings often inhibit breathability; mesh ones are better. This also applies to the linings sometimes found in coated garments.

Drop liners have the membrane suspended between separate outer and inner layers. Drop liners are very soft and comfortable and in theory highly breathable. In practice I have found that condensation forms quite readily on the inner lining of garments of this construction.

In my experience the most effective construction, though it is the least used, is the lining laminate, or liner-to-drop (LTD). This is a two-layer material in which the membrane, laminated to a light scrim fabric, is used as the lining. Because the membrane is on the inside, protected from the weather by the outer layer and kept warm by the air gap between the two layers, it breathes far better than any other construction. It is also softer and more comfortable.

NONBREATHABLE RAIN GEAR. Garments with PVC, polyurethane, or neoprene coatings will keep out snow and rain but will also keep in all body moisture. The result is sweat-soaked inner clothing. Their one advantage is low price. I wouldn't recommend one as a general ski jacket, but one could be carried as backup to a windproof top, being worn only in the worst weather.

DESIGN. Along with the fabric, the design of rain gear is an essential contributor to both breathability and waterproofness. The more ventilation a garment has, the fewer condensation problems there will be, so all closures and fastenings should be adjustable. Openings must also be protected against leakage, but no design can be 100 percent snowproof. Wind-driven sleet and spindrift will eventually find their way into any garment.

Seams, in particular, must be proofed in some way if they are not to leak. The most effective way of making them watertight is to heat-seal them with a special tape. All top-quality garments are finished in this manner; it is essential on those with membranes, as nothing else works.

The front zipper should be covered by a single or, preferably, a double waterproof flap closed with snaps or Velcro. Velcro is more weatherproof than snap fasteners but can ice up and be difficult to close in bad conditions. Snaps at the top and bottom help in lining up Velcro. A flap of material inside the top of the zipper acts as a chin guard and is worth looking for.

Hood design is important. In blizzards one with a stiffened peak helps to keep hail and driving snow off your ski glasses or goggles (a hat with a brim is even better). Skiing in a hood that restricts my peripheral vision upsets my balance, so I prefer one that allows me to see to the sides. Such hoods don't give quite as much protection, but again a peaked hat can help. A hood needs to be big enough for wearing warm headwear underneath. On some you can adjust the size. Whether the hood folds away into the collar or not is irrelevant, but the collar itself needs to be close fitting enough that snow cannot easily blow down it. Be sure, however, that you can zip it up fully over your warmwear.

Cuffs are important for ventilation and need to be adjustable. External Velcro closures are essentially standard, though snaps also work quite well. Internal closures are very difficult to adjust with gloves or mitts on or with cold fingers, and they usually prevent sleeves from being pulled down over gloves or mitts. They don't allow good ventilation and can cause your arms to overheat in warm weather or when skiing hard—I wouldn't consider a jacket with them.

Some garments have underarm "pit" zippers that are useful for ventilation purposes but do need to be covered with close-fitting flaps if they are not to admit spindrift.

A few pockets are useful, but large numbers of them simply add to the weight (and cost) of a jacket. Hem pockets, although almost standard, are usually covered by your pack hip belt and are thus not very useful. And if you can get anything into them it will then bounce around on your thighs and feel uncomfortable. Hem pockets are useful only for putting your hands in, so it is worth making sure you can do so comfortably. Some designs can be used only by those with double-jointed wrists! Large chest pockets are more practical. Pocket openings should have zippers and be covered by flaps, but you should still expect some snow penetration in a blizzard.

Drawcords need self-locking toggles if you are not to go crazy trying to untie frozen knots with numb fingers. Waist drawcords are useful for keeping wind and snow out when you are not wearing your pack, but they are not essential.

Finally, check the weight. Garments weighing much more than 28 ounces (800 grams) are unnecessarily heavy and will weigh down your pack; those under a pound (450 grams) are probably too light for winter use unless worn over a windproof top, but they could be fine for spring skiing.

Freebird Pertex/Pile Clothing:
An Alternative to the Layer System

Freebird clothing is made from polyester pile and Pertex nylon, a lightweight, quick-drying, hard-wearing combination that results in garments that are astonishingly warm for their weight and capable of coping with extremes of cold and wet weather.

The pile inner layer not only keeps you warm but also wicks away body moisture rapidly so there is always a dry layer next to the skin. The moisture then condenses on the inner surface of the Pertex and is absorbed by it before evaporating into the air.

Because both pile and Pertex are moisture-vapor permeable, garments made from them are condensation-free, resulting in a high level of comfort in wet, cold weather—when you stop skiing there is no after-exercise chill.

Pertex/pile keeps out both snow and rain. Dry snow and light rain are deflected by the pertex, while heavier rain and wet snow are absorbed by it before spreading out and evaporating. If the garments become saturated they will dry in minutes, and if they remain sodden they are still comfortable because the water trapped inside heats up—though this warmth won't last forever. Pile/Pertex is probably the only material that can truly be described as warm when wet.

To gain the most from Freebird clothing, it is important that it be used properly. This means wearing the basic garment, the over-the-head Mountain Shirt (weight: 25 ounces/700 grams), next to the skin and using the side and neck zippers for ventilation. If clothing is worn under the shirt it may cause overheating and absorb moisture, and other garments shouldn't be worn over the shirt because they will interfere with the evaporation of moisture from the Pertex. The only exception is when you are inactive in very cold or wet conditions, when another garment may be needed over the shirt. In most conditions, especially when actually skiing, the shirt is adequate on its own and replaces three layers of conventional clothing: underwear, warmwear, and shell.

I have found the Freebird Mountain Shirt excellent for skiing in stormy weather. It cuts down on the number and weight of garments carried, though I usually carry a thermal top for camp or hut wear and a second warm top to wear over the shirt at halts.

The Freebird bib pants (weight: 29 ounces/775 grams), while

very comfortable, are also very warm, too warm for me in still weather and in temperatures above 7°F (−12°C). However, those skiers who wear pile trousers or heavyweight long johns under windproof or waterproof shell pants even in mild weather may find the bibs a less-restrictive and easier-to-use alternative.

Legwear

As well as protecting you against the weather, your legwear should be roomy or stretchy enough to allow freedom of movement. There are a number of possibilities. The layer system again makes sense, though usually fewer layers are needed—often only one—than on the upper body. Thin long johns are the base layer, followed by a thicker midlayer, then a weatherproof shell. If the midlayer is windproof it may be all you need most of the time. The long johns can serve as backup for camp, and the shell can be used for severe storms or for camp backup.

The main choice in design is between bibs and ordinary pants. Bibs give good protection to the lower back and midriff and provide a better seal against snow entering your clothing, especially when you fall. However, you can overheat in bibs, and going to the toilet can be awkward, especially for women, and unpleasant in a blizzard if you have to remove other clothing before you can lower the pants. The solution to this problem is to choose garments with full-length side zippers and shoulder straps with both ends attached to the front of the garment so that the rear of the bibs can be lowered by undoing the zippers from the top without having to remove outer garments to unclip the shoulder straps. This design, first introduced by Patagonia, is called a drop seat.

If you go for pants rather than bibs, look for those with a high adjustable waist, which will be warmer and keep snow out better. Both bibs and pants may be knicker length or full length, though knickers seem to be rapidly disappearing. I have gone with the change. A decade ago I always wore knickers; now I rarely do, mainly because they are harder to find.

European ski tourers have long worn bibs (known as salopettes) made from thick, brushed, stretchy nylon; they are warm and windproof, shed snow quickly, dry rapidly, don't restrict movement, and are incredibly tough. They are very comfortable, too, but heavy at around 42 to 52 ounces/1,200 to 1,550 grams. Until breathable shell bibs came along I used them for most of the season, though I find them too warm for spring skiing. I have never yet worn other layers over or under them, but I have come close a couple of times. American equivalents seem hard to find. The nearest I have seen are Patagonia's Sporthosen, made from a blend of nylon, rayon, and spandex (weight: 11½ ounces/326 grams).

Breathable waterproof bibs or pants are the most popular leg-wear for ski touring. They can be layered over thin long johns or thicker fleece pants or both. Wearing waterproof outer legwear all the time means you cut down the weight in your pack. The best ones have full-length two-way side zippers for ventilation and a loose fit for freedom of movement. Anatomically shaped knees help. Again, it is worth checking that the seat can be lowered without having to remove other garments. Materials are the same as for shell jackets, with coated and laminated fabrics available. Reinforcement patches around the inner ankle are useful as protection against nicks from skis and bindings. Weights run from 21 to 42 ounces/600 to 1,200 grams.

If you're brave enough you can ski in shorts in the hot spring sun.

Pile legwear, although very warm, isn't windproof and needs to be used with a shell in all but the calmest conditions. Whenever I have tried shelled pile legwear, such as the Freebird bibs mentioned above, I have found it too warm. For me, medium or heavyweight base-layer pants worn under shell pants have always proved warm enough. Whichever you choose, a close fit is needed, and the stretchier the material the better in order not to restrict movement. In this respect Patagonia's Stretch Synchilla bibs and tights look excellent. They are light, too, at 18 and 12 ounces/510 and 240 grams respectively.

My own current choice for most of the season is waterproof breathable bibs worn over heavyweight base-layer pants. For late spring and early summer skiing I wear lightweight nylon microfiber pants over thin long johns, a combination I find windproof and weather resistant but not overwarm. Because microfiber isn't fully waterproof, though it does shed snow, I also carry lightweight rain pants.

In really warm weather you can ski in shorts, but I never have. I have seen too many bright "strawberries" on people's backsides where they have fallen on abrasive corn snow.

Hats

The heat loss from an unprotected head is considerable, so keeping your head warm is vital. The obvious and most popular headwear is a simple wool, fleece, or synthetic-fiber hat that can be pulled down over your ears when necessary. Peruvian-style hats with ear flaps are good. For most purposes, a hat, augmented by a jacket hood in storms, is all that is needed. The envelope-style hat is more likely to stay on your head than rounder hats when skiing downhill in a wind. This matters more than you may think. I have a very nice REI Ragg wool hat that I have given up wearing for skiing because the damn thing blows off all the time, and I am fed up with losing my balance as I grab it, or chasing it across the snow as it disappears into the distance. Stretchy fabrics stay on well, too; my current favorite ski hat is Patagonia's Stretch Synchilla Alpine hat (weight: 2 ounces/55 grams). A chin strap made of narrow cord is useful for preventing hats from blowing off, and it also enables you to flip the hat back off your head when you start to overheat but have it handy to pull on quickly when needed again.

I am loath to venture far with only one hat because its loss could be serious. I always carry two, the second one being a windproof, pile-lined peaked cap with ear flaps that can be worn in storms instead of a jacket hood, allowing for better peripheral vision. The peak helps keep wind-driven snow off my face and also shades it from the sun. It is a Lowe Mountain cap, made from Gore-Tex with a Polartec 200 lining (weight: 3½ ounces/100 grams). Current models have a Triple Point coated outer. Many others are available, of which the most interesting I have seen is Outdoor Research's A Hat For All Seasons, a Gore-Tex cap with a removable pile lining. In warm, sunny weather you can wear the cap, which is adjustable, without the lining as a sun hat.

Heavyweight balaclavas—which cover the head and neck, leaving just the face exposed—made from wool, pile, or expedition-weight base-layer fabrics are the standard wear for severe weather and do provide excellent protection. Many can be rolled up and worn as hats in less serious conditions. However, I find a peaked cap less restrictive and more comfortable to wear. If I need to keep my neck warm and block off heat loss at my throat, I wear a midweight polypro headover (weight: 2½ ounces/70 grams), a simple tube of material that is pulled over the head and worn around the neck like a scarf. If necessary it can also be worn as a balaclava or a hat and so is very versatile. Headovers, or neck gaiters, are also available in wool and pile.

Thus on most tours I carry three items of headwear: a warm hat, a windproof, pile-lined peaked cap, and a lightweight headover. In spring I leave one of these, usually the cap, behind and take instead a lighter hat to fend off the harsh sun. I have tried baseball-style caps, but they protect only your face. Now I wear a wide-brimmed canvas Tilley hat that shades my neck as well.

Headbands can be worn both to keep sweat off your face and to keep your ears warm—but I prefer a hat.

Gloves and Mitts

Cold hands can make skiing a miserable experience, so warm gloves or mitts are essential. They need not only to keep your hands warm but also to fend off wind and snow, allow moisture vapor to pass through, and let you fasten ski bindings, pack buckles, and zippers without having to take them off. And while skiing they shouldn't interfere with your pole handling.

No one pair of mitts or gloves will do everything, so a layer system is needed. For maximum dexterity, a thin pair of inner or liner gloves is best (weight: around 1 ounce/30 grams). They allow for the handling of items like bindings, tent poles, and cameras in extreme cold without your skin sticking to them. Polypro, Capilene, Thermax, thin wool, and silk all work well. In spring, liner gloves may be all you need, though I would never venture out without some thicker gloves or mitts as well. If you wear them regularly on their own they won't last long—a pair usually lasts me a couple of seasons at most. Those with sticky rubber strips or other coating on the palms and fingers grip poles best.

For real warmth and weather protection, thicker gloves or mitts are required. The choice is between a single pair that combines insulation and windproofness and two separate pairs that can be worn together or separately as required. The single is simpler and lighter and gives better dexterity but isn't so warm or versatile as the combination. A choice must also be made between gloves and mitts. Again, gloves give much better dexterity, but they aren't as warm as mitts nor as durable, being far more complex to make. If you suffer from cold hands, choose mitts. Warmth is the most important criterion.

Having tried many combinations, my preference is for two separate layers, and I prefer gloves to mitts because mitts impede pole swing to some extent. However, I have hands that warm up easily—if they didn't, I would use mitts. I have rejected single layers after several years of using alpine ski gloves made from Gore-Tex with Thinsulate insulation. They are windproof and snowproof and give good dexterity, but in bitter cold and strong winds they aren't warm enough, even when worn over liner gloves. Pile-lined nylon mitts are warmer but don't give the same dexterity. Two layers are warmer still, and you can wear just one of them in milder temperatures.

You can make up your own combination of gloves or mitts, but those designed to fit together are probably better, and many are now available. The materials for the warm layer are usually pile or wool. If you want to wear them on their own, as I do most of the time, wool is much more windproof. I have used Dachstein wool gloves and wool mitts (weight: 4 ounces/115 grams) and found them adequate in all but the worst weather. However, I have also found that they don't last long, usually splitting between the thumb and forefinger. This can be repaired with a leather patch, but I would rather have tougher gloves.

Most of the combinations available are mitts rather than gloves. The typical combination has removable pile inner mitts and waterproof breathable outers with high-friction grips on the palm and thumb. The best mitts are curved for comfort and to allow ski poles to be held without the palm creasing. They should be easy to adjust with one hand. Gloves with removable liners are less common, but good-looking ones are available from Black Diamond and Patagonia. The Black Diamond outer is cut on a curve, with palms made from a tough nonslip material called Keprotec that contains Kevlar. The rest of the outer is made from waterproof SealCoat, and the inner gloves are made from Retro-Pile sewn pile side in for warmth and comfort. The shockcord closures are easy to operate with one hand. They weigh 9½ ounces/270 grams per pair. They are the warmest gloves I have used—so warm, in fact, that I wear just the outer shells over liner gloves in mild weather.

Overmitts and gloves need to have easily adjusted wrist fastenings. Remember that you have to adjust the second one with a hand already encased in thick layers. This can be almost impossible when they have elasticized wrists. I have Lowe mitts with breathable waterproof fabric and simple Velcro straps that are easy to tighten. They also have a textured material on the palm and thumb that grips wet and icy items well. I used to use them occasionally with the Dachstein gloves but now prefer the Black Diamond combination.

Whatever combination of gloves or mitts you choose, carry a spare pair. Losing gloves does happen, usually because they blow away in the wind, and not being able to keep your hands warm would leave you in a desperate situation. If you tie wrist loops (often called idiot loops) to your gloves or mitts (some come with them) you can keep them attached to yourself when you take them off. If by some mischance you do end up without gloves, remember that you can pull socks over your hands—even dirty socks would be far better than nothing. Plastic bags or stuff sacks could be used, too.

Gloves tend to get wet frequently from both snow and sweat,

another reason for carrying spares. In warm spring sunshine, damp gloves can be dried by putting them on top of your ski poles when you stop for a break. But this doesn't work for most of the season; indeed, it can lead to their freezing, something even more likely if you leave them lying on the snow. The best way to dry gloves is to put them inside your warmwear. Even if they don't dry out fully they will at least be warm when you put them back on.

Socks

Thick socks are needed to keep your feet warm. The main criterion is that they fit well and that there be no folds or harsh seams that could cause blisters or sore spots. Most winter-weight socks contain at least some wool, though 100 percent synthetic ones are available. I find socks with a high wool content warmer than mostly synthetic ones and less likely to become sweat-soaked. However, those allergic to wool will need to seek out the thicker synthetic models. Socks come in a wide range of weights and thicknesses. The heaviest, weighing around 3½ to 5½ ounces/100 to 150 grams a pair, depending on make, are required for winter.

Overall, my preference is for traditional Ragg wool socks. They are warm and very durable, far more so in my experience than the new hi-tech socks with their complex constructions. They cost less, too, and can stand infrequent washing without matting down. If they have a little Lycra mixed in, Ragg socks keep their shape well and don't sag down around the ankles.

Thin wicking-fabric liner socks are worn under thick socks by some people, but my wide feet prohibit their use or my boots wouldn't fit, so I can't report on their effectiveness. Too many socks can restrict circulation and lead to cold rather than warm feet, so beware of cramming on as many socks as you can. If you suffer badly from cold feet you could try wearing vapor-barrier socks (described below) under your thick ones.

Knee-high stockings are useful for keeping your lower legs warm and are needed if you wear knickers, but generally calf-high socks are adequate.

Because feet don't usually overheat when skiing, socks don't get very sweaty—at least in my experience; if your feet sweat heavily you may disagree. I have found I can wear a pair of socks for several days without any loss in insulation or comfort, an advantage on camping trips, but I do like to keep a clean, dry pair for wearing in camp.

Vapor Barriers

All of the clothing described above is designed to speed the passage of moisture vapor from the skin to the outside air while preventing snow and wind from penetrating the layers. In most conditions this is the best way to keep warm and dry. However, there is an alternative that can be useful in extreme cold when it is difficult to wear enough clothes to keep warm without moisture building up and freezing inside the layers. A vapor barrier (VB) is a thin layer of non-breathable waterproof clothing worn close to the skin under your warmwear to prevent evaporative heat loss. It is extremely efficient, so efficient that I have found that when I wear VB clothing for skiing I overheat and start sweating heavily within a few minutes, however foul the weather.

VB garments are more useful in camp, especially as they are far lighter and less bulky than conventional clothing. I have found a VB top weighing just 3½ ounces/100 grams worn under a pile top to be as warm as a light down jacket worn over the pile. VB clothing can also be worn in your sleeping bag for extra warmth. Being thin and smooth-surfaced, VB isn't restrictive either, unlike bulkier clothing.

Special VB clothing is available, but a set of inexpensive lightweight, nonbreathable proofed nylon rain gear works almost as well. Ideally it should be worn next to the skin, but if, like me, you find it feels clammy, a thin synthetic base layer can be worn underneath. I rarely wear VB clothing, but I often carry it in case of emergency or colder-than-expected nights.

VBs work on the hands and feet too. For emergency use plastic bags will do, but if you are one of those who suffer from cold extremities, you may prefer more comfortable VB gloves and socks. Thin medical-type gloves work well on the hands, sliding easily into other gloves or mitts, while for the feet Black Diamond makes SealCoat VB socks. A pair weighs just 2 ounces/56 grams.

Spare Footwear

It is useful to carry spare footwear for camp and for wearing in huts and lodges. Trailing around in your ski boots leaving pools of melting snow behind won't make you popular! (Many huts have brushes outside for removing most of the snow. These should be used.) At the end of a long day your feet will probably welcome a change anyway. For huts, running shoes are the most popular choice, though slippers will do as well. You can pad around in stocking feet, but floors are often wet.

If your feet get really cold, insulated bootees are ideal for warming them up. I usually carry my REI Polarguard ones (weight: 12 ounces/315 grams) on camping trips. I prefer synthetic to down-filled ones because I don't have to worry about getting them wet. While bootees are fine in camp in soft snow, the soles, usually tough nylon, are very slippery, so on hard snow or steep slopes you need to take great care. Some form of insulation, usually a sewn-in footbed of closed-cell foam, is needed to prevent cold from penetrating from below.

Mukluks are an alternative that seems like a good idea for extreme cold and deep snow. These knee- or calf-high overboots are made from soft leather, leather and wool, or leather and canvas for dry cold, with rubberized lower sections and coated nylon uppers or a breathable waterproof fabric like Gore-Tex for damp conditions. They usually come with wool felt liners, but it would be worth getting them in a large size so you could add thick socks, pile sock liners, and insulated insoles when required. Many brands are available.

Using Clothing Efficiently

As with any other gear, just having good clothing isn't enough. The point of the layer system is to take off and put on garments whenever conditions change or you start to feel uncomfortable. If you fail to use your clothing properly you can still feel cold or get wet or even overheat. When skiing, go at a pace that doesn't cause you to sweat heavily. If you start sweating, stop and remove a layer. Thinking ahead can often prevent discomfort. When your route goes from sunshine to shadow, stop just before you leave the warmer air and don extra clothes rather than wait until you hit the cool shade and start to shiver. Similarly, when you stop, put on extra clothing immediately even though you may still feel warm. Don't wait until you start to cool down. By then you will have lost heat that it could take a long time to replace. If it is windy but you are climbing up a sheltered bowl or approaching the heights through the forest, again, stop before you come out into the full blast and put on your shell garments. Struggling into them in a gusting wind can be difficult and unpleasant, and you will lose a lot of heat in the process.

Load Carrying: Packs and Pulks

"You think your shoulders are sore now" he jabbed,
showing no sympathy, "wait until you add another sack
of food to your load."
— *Larry Rice,* Gathering Paradise:
Alaska Wilderness Journeys

Winter backpacking means heavy loads. The colder temperatures and stormier weather require heavier tents, heavier sleeping bags, more clothing, more fuel, and more food, apart from such items as waxes, skins, and snow shovels and at times ice axes and crampons. And on occasion you will probably end up carrying your skis, too. To make these loads as comfortable as possible, a top-quality pack is needed, and for really heavy multiday loads, consideration needs to be given to such alternatives as pulks.

Packs

For skiers setting off into the mountains with enough food and equipment to stay out for several days, the choice of pack is important from the point of view of both stability and comfort. A well-packed heavy load in a well-designed, properly fitted pack is difficult to ski with even when you are experienced. Skiing with a badly designed, heavily loaded pack, especially downhill, can be almost impossible.

A good pack should feel as though it has been glued to your

back. One that sways from side to side will make controlling your skis very difficult. Of the many packs designed to carry big loads, not all of them do so comfortably or with the stability needed for skiing.

A pack needs to be tough, too; you don't want to have to sit down in the snow to stitch up blown-out seams or replace broken buckles. Finally, in addition to being well designed and well made, a pack has to be fitted properly and packed correctly if it is to carry well.

Harness

The key to a comfortable and stable carry is the back system, particularly the hip belt. The combination of a flexible, semirigid frame and a well-padded, anatomically shaped belt means that most of the weight of a pack can be transferred from your relatively weak shoulders to your hips, which are strong and designed for load bearing.

A good hip belt will wrap around the hips snugly and have

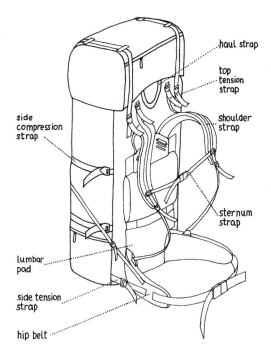

Figure 7-1. The suspension system of an internal-frame pack.

enough padding and rigidity not to deform under heavy loads. Most hip belts will carry loads up to 40 pounds/18kg comfortably, but few support heavier loads well. If you are likely to carry loads weighing more than that, as you are on winter camping trips of more than a few days, try on packs containing at least 55 pounds/25 kg and see how the hip belt feels. Many belts, I have found, twist under such weights and put painful pressure on the hip bones. The best belts have several layers of padding, soft on the inside, stiff on the outside.

For maximum stability, adjustable straps running from the sides of the pack to the hip belt are needed. These side-tension straps pull in the load around the hips and prevent it from swaying.

Shoulder straps should be padded, though they rarely carry much weight. Curved ones are more comfortable and less prone to distorting under load than straight ones. Shoulder pads with a shoulder-hugging S-shape greatly help stability and are also very comfortable. These straps follow the natural contours of your neck and shoulders, curving over the shoulders, then in toward the chest before cutting away under the armpits. Top-tension straps, running from the main shoulder straps up to the pack, are essential because they lift the load off the sensitive nerves on top of the shoulders while at the same time pulling the pack close in to the back.

A sternum strap pulls the shoulder straps inward and helps prevent the pack from swaying during descents. I rarely use mine otherwise, but it can make all the difference to controlled skiing with a top-heavy load, so I wouldn't use a pack that doesn't have one. Using a sternum strap on a pack that has an unintentional built-in wobble (as all too many do) can make it usable for skiing.

Frames

While many walkers still debate the relative virtues of external- and internal-frame packs, there is no question which are best for skiers. Rigid metal external frames carry the load too high for good balance and lurch from side to side at any sudden movement, making them essentially useless for skiing on anything other than flat groomed terrain. (However, Guy Sheridan, a very experienced wilderness ski tourer—see his book *Tales of a Cross-Country Skier*—uses a Norwegian Bergen external-frame pack with a pronounced curve that he finds very stable.) Flexible plastic external frames are better than metal ones but still not as stable as internal frames.

Soft packs with no frame at all are the most stable, as they hug the back tightly, but with loads above about 35 pounds/16kg some form of stiffening is needed to help transfer the weight from the shoulders to the hips. This is usually just two malleable parallel aluminum-alloy stays. Variations include stays made from carbon fiber and flexible plastic frame sheets for extra support. All seem to work well as long as they are the right size.

Fitting

Numerous back systems are available, many of them adjustable, some fixed in length. Most work well as long as they are fitted properly, but many people don't bother; in part this is the fault of the packmakers, as the fitting instructions supplied with packs are often brief and unclear. Knowledgeable store assistants should be able to ensure your pack is the correct fit, but those who buy mail order or from a store with unhelpful staff will have to fit their packs themselves. Different packs adjust in different ways, so a single set of instructions isn't possible, but there are some basic rules to follow.

Most top-quality adjustable packs are available with two or more sizes of frame, including ones designed for women. Fixed-back-length packs come in as many as five sizes. An overtall frame will wobble, and a too short one will prevent you from carrying the weight on your hips, so it is worth taking some time to find the right size. To do so, measure the distance between the top of your shoulders and a point level with the top of your hip bones. If this distance is more than 20 inches/50cm you need a large frame, 27 inches/70cm or more in length. If it is between 18 and 20 inches/45 and 50cm, a medium frame of around 25 inches/65cm will be best. Less than 18 inches/45cm and you need a short frame, under 25 inches/65cm.

These are only approximate measurements—the way packmakers measure both packs and back lengths varies, which can present problems if you buy mail order (as I know from experience, having had to return a pack that was too long). If you order the wrong size pack, do exchange it. Using a pack with a sophisticated back system that doesn't fit is like wearing quality boots that are the wrong size.

Malleable frames need to be bent to the shape of your back. Makers often recommend removing the frame stays from the pack and bending them over your knee. I have never managed to do this with any success and find it much easier to simply allow the frame to conform to my back during the first few days' use. This process can be speeded up by using the pack with all the straps tightened firmly to force the frame to bend to your shape.

Once you have selected a pack with roughly the right frame size, load at least 30 pounds/14kg into it and loosen all the adjustment straps. Then put the pack on and fasten the hip belt so that the top of it is about an inch (2cm) above the top of your hipbone. The padded part of the hip belt should extend around in front of each hipbone by about 2 inches (5cm). Once the hip belt is taking the weight, tighten the side-tension straps to pull the load in around your hips for better stability. Each time you put the pack on, these straps should be loosened first or the hip belt won't wrap around your hips properly.

With the hip belt fastened, adjust the back length so the shoulder straps sit correctly—they should curl over your shoulders and attach to the back of the pack or the adjustment system about 1 to 2 inches (3 to 5cm) below your shoulders. The top-tension straps should then rise off the front of your shoulders at an angle of about 45 degrees.

The top of the frame should now be 2 to 4 inches (5 to 10cm) above the top of your shoulders. If it is less you need a larger frame; if more, a shorter one.

This will give you the basic fit. In use the pack will be more comfortable if you adjust it according to the terrain, shifting the weight between shoulders and hips. On the flat you can slacken off the shoulder straps and top-tension straps and carry virtually all the weight on your hips. On descents, tighten them up again for a closer fit and better balance. Experiment with a new pack until you know what works best for you in different sorts of terrain. If your shoulders or hips start to ache, don't ignore the pain, adjust the harness until the pressure abates. Similarly, if your pack is lurching around as you ski, stop and tighten the straps until it feels more stable. Not making adjustments makes having a sophisticated heavy-load-carrying system pointless.

Pack Bags

Compared with the harness system, the style of pack bag is relatively unimportant. Some people like a simple, cavernous single-compartment sack, others prefer as many compartments as possible. In general, whatever the design, the load should be carried close to the body for maximum stability. If you choose a pack with side pockets, make sure they are fitted high enough to allow you to swing your arms. Packs with fixed side pockets should have slots behind them for sliding skis into. Packs without side pockets almost always have side-compression straps that can be pulled in around the load to hold it steady and will also hold skis when you have to carry them. Straps are needed for snow shovels, ice axes, and crampons, too. I like packs with plenty of straps to secure my load in place, whatever the size, so it doesn't shift about while I am skiing. Rear pockets are useful for carrying light items you need quick access to, such as hats and gloves, but carrying heavy items in them can affect the balance of a pack.

Easy access to the contents is essential. You should be able to unfasten straps and zippers with mittened hands—that means large zippers with tags on the pullers and click-fastened buckles that don't need threading. Two-compartment pack bags are much better for access than single-compartment ones. Similarly, front or side zippers that give access to the main compartment are very useful; they enable you to get at gear that isn't at the top of the pack without having to unload other items into the snow. Lids should be large so they will easily cover the biggest load. Detachable, extendible ones that rise upward as the load grows are better than lids that tip backward, restricting head movement.

Lots of compartments and pockets means lots of zippers, and zippers are a potential source of failure. I like large chunky zippers, especially on the lower compartment, and I avoid lightweight ones. Coil zippers, unlike toothed ones, are self-repairing. Lower compartments should have vertical straps running over the zipper to take some of the strain and to act as a backup. Safety pins will do for a makeshift repair if a zipper does fail; they can also be used as replacement pullers. Sometimes the backing of zippers tears away from the pack or the teeth tear away from the backing material—then a needle and thread are needed for repair. If a coil zipper won't hold the two halves of the zipper together it may have widened, in which case squeezing it carefully with pliers or a mole wrench may restore it to working order.

My own preference is for a two-compartment sack with front or side-access zippers to the top compartment, an extendible, detachable lid with a large pocket, a rear pocket or pockets, and detachable side pockets. I use the side pockets only for really massive loads. I also like large packs: small packs, stuffed to bursting and with gear dangling off the outside, are uncomfortable to carry, lack stability, and are hard to pack and unpack. Buy a pack big enough for the largest loads you think you might carry. You don't have to fill it. For hut-to-hut touring, a pack with a capacity of at least 3,500 cubic inches (60 liters) is needed. For ski backpacking, 6,000 cubic inches (100 liters) isn't too much. My favorite packs, the Gregory Cassin and the Dana Designs Astralplane, have capacities of 7,000 cubic inches (115 liters) without side pockets.

People with short backs (who aren't necessarily short people) will find that larger packs won't fit them properly. On extended trips they may have to strap gear outside their packs. In a group, those with bigger packs can carry the bulkier communal items, leaving smaller ones for small packs. If you do have to attach gear to the outside, start by lashing items such as tent poles or a foam pad to the side-compression straps. If you still don't have enough room, soft items such as sleeping bags, clothing, or the tent can be strapped on as well, in stuff sacks that are waterproof or lined with plastic bags. Items attached to the outside should be compressed as much as possible and strapped down tightly. What you don't want is gear flapping around in the wind or catching on branches. Side pockets can also be used to extend the capacity of a pack and keep gear in order.

Most pack bags are made of proofed nylon, which is hard wearing and abrasion resistant but can't be counted on to be waterproof—the inner coating doesn't usually last very long, and it is punctured by stitches. Waterproof pack liners or stuff sacks are essential, especially for items such as down-filled sleeping bags and clothing. Pack covers aren't practical because you may need to carry snow shovels, ice axes, crampons, and even skis on the outside of your pack. The most water-resistant packs I have found are the New Zealand–made Macpacs. They are made from a polyester/cotton fabric that absorbs the waterproofing solution rather than being coated with it, which means it won't crack or peel off and can't be punctured. I still keep my down gear in waterproof bags, but I have noticed very little water penetration in my Macpac Cascade pack.

Weight

I don't think weight is a major consideration with packs. Comfort and durability are far more important. My Gregory Cassin weighs 6 pounds 6 ounces/3kg (about the average for this size pack) and is worth every bit of it. Smaller packs, 3,500 to 4,000 cubic inches (60 to 65 liters), weigh slightly less, around 4 to 5½ pounds/1.8 to 2.5kg. The difference in weight depends more on the materials than the size. Heavier packs are usually made from tougher materials and have more padding in the shoulder straps and hip belts and chunkier zippers and straps. A frame adds weight too.

Choices

There are many good brands of pack. What fits one person best may not be ideal for another, so there is no such thing as a "best" pack—just the best for you. As with boots, try on several styles in the store before making a final decision. Women, in particular, may have problems finding a pack that fits well, as most packs are designed for men—calling them unisex is simply an attempt to sell them to women. However, many companies do now offer women's packs with different-shaped hip belts and shoulder straps, and they are worth seeking out.

When you try a pack, think of how you would pack your gear and how accessible it would be as well as how comfortable the back system is. Walk around the store and, if you are not too self-conscious, drop into a telemark position to see how the pack feels. It is worth taking time over the decision. A good pack should last for years and can make all the difference to the success of a tour. There is little satisfaction in fighting a load all the way and ending a day with aching shoulders and sore hips.

Packing

When skiing you need to keep your center of gravity low for maximum stability, so the heaviest gear shouldn't be packed at the top of the pack, as it is for walking. The weight needs to be as close to your back as possible to prevent the pack from pulling you backward. To enable the pack to snug around my hips I load the lower compartment with soft items such as sleeping bag and spare clothing. I pack heavy, relatively low-bulk items such as stove, fuel, food, repair kit, and flashlight batteries close to my back at the bottom of the upper compartment, putting lighter and bulkier items like the tent and the bivy bag higher up and to the outside. At the top of the pack and in the lid pocket (and the rear pockets if any) I keep items I might need during the day, such as rain gear, warm top, first-aid kit, wax kit, climbing skins, sunscreen, hats, gloves, and camera and film. Once I have packed I push the load down hard, then cinch tight all the straps to pull in the load as close as possible. If anything can move inside the pack it will upset the balance. On the outside of the pack I strap the shovel, plus the ice ax and crampons if I have them with me, and also my closed-cell foam pad so that it is available as a seat at stops. If I am camping I carry my Therm-a-Rest mattress inside the lower compartment.

Finally, balance is so important when skiing that if your pack wobbles or feels lopsided you should always stop and repack it.

Skiing with a Heavy Pack

On long camping tours there is no avoiding a big pack unless the terrain is suitable for using a pulk (described below), and there is no escaping the fact that a heavy load slows you down and affects your balance. The rewards are in the freedom being self-sufficient gives and the opportunity to explore areas otherwise inaccessible.

There are a few ways to make skiing with a heavy pack more bearable. It is much easier to put your skis on first, then your pack. When you fall, take your pack off before you try to regain your feet—it is almost impossible to get up in deep, soft snow it you don't. Turns that don't involve much unweighting, like wedges and telemarks, are easier and far less tiring than those that require a lot of up and down movement. To minimize the chance of the pack throwing you off balance, keep your upper body still. Skiers who lean into turns will fall often when carrying a big load unless they alter their style. Keeping your poles low and not using them quite so much for propulsion helps keep the weight off your shoulders when striding along the trail. Don't worry about a loss of speed—with a heavy load you won't be zipping along anyway.

A well-packed heavy load in a well-designed, properly fitted pack is essential when skiing downhill.

Pulks

On long expeditions into remote areas where supplies for several weeks are needed, small lightweight pulks or sledges are often used. The main difference between the two is that sledges ride on long runners, while pulks sit directly on the snow (though they may have narrow guide runners on the base). A waterproof cover fits tightly over the load. Twin or single shafts (the latter better for maneuvering apparently) link the pulk to a shoulder or waist harness.

I have never used a pulk, but those who have say that hauling a heavy load is much, much easier than carrying it on your back, especially over flat and undulating terrain. Loads you couldn't lift can be hauled on a pulk in comparative comfort. I have seen 200 to 220 pounds/90 to 100kg quoted as a perfectly feasible weight. With truly massive loads you could haul a sled and carry a pack as well.

Being specialty gear, pulks are not that readily available. Most commercial pulks are quite expensive. For occasional use a plastic child's toboggan can be adapted, using strong lines (such as 5 to 7mm polypropylene rope) to attach it either to your pack if you are carrying one or to a waist belt. A cover could be made for the sled, or you could lash on a large, strong waterproof bag, threading the straps through holes drilled in the side of the sled. These holes could also be used for the haul ropes. The disadvantage of this system is the lack of rigid traces between you and the sled, giving much less control and necessitating care that the sled doesn't catch up with you on downhills. One remedy is to slip hollow tubes of plastic, such as small-diameter PVC pipe, over the haul lines. I have adapted a small plastic sledge in this way but have not used it on a serious trip.

Purpose-designed sleds are usually made from fiberglass and resin laminates, though wood, plastic, and, for maximum performance and low weight, Kevlar and carbon-fiber models are available. Snowsled, a British company, supplied sleds for Will Steger's international transantarctic expedition as well as to the National Science Foundation's Antarctic program and many other polar expeditions and scientific programs. For general ski touring, Snowsled's Trail pulk looks very useful. It is 3¾ feet/1.14 meters long, weighs 11 pounds/5kg, and has a payload capacity of 90 pounds/40kg. It is made of fiberglass with polyethylene runners and has a hauling shaft that fits inside the pulk for easy carrying. Other features are a padded waist harness and a proofed nylon cover with a full-length zipper. Next up in size is the 4-foot/1.22-meter, 19-pound/8.5kg Standard pulk. It has a payload capacity of 188 pounds/85kg, more than most people are ever likely to need.

Hip Packs

Hip packs, also known as waist bags or fanny packs, are useful for carrying small items such as sunscreen, lip salve, gloves, hat, maps, and compass that may be needed frequently during the day. I use a hip pack on camping trips, wearing it in front of me, when my pack is so heavy that I don't want to take it off every time I need something small.

Daypacks

You can use your large pack for day tours, when one base is used for several nights, tightening down all the straps to maintain stability. For day trips from home or forays from a roadhead, many people prefer to use a smaller pack for smaller loads. I find one with a capacity of 2,500 to 3,000 cubic inches (40 to 50 liters) adequate. Chest and waist straps are still needed to aid stability, as are side straps for carrying skis when walking. Padded backs are useful for comfort but aren't essential.

Shelter and Warmth

*One gains nothing worth having on mountains without
paying for it; beyond the snowline minor hardships will always
be met in a small tent. . . . In the end they are far
outweighed by the joys of dwelling for a space on snowfields
close to the sky, where the dawn and sunset come like armadas
in slow and solemn grace, and the very air has a beauty,
which we call purity.*
—W. H. Murray, Mountaineering in Scotland

Many people believe that winter camping must be an uncomfortable, unpleasant, and above all, very cold experience. And so it can be, if you are ill-equipped and inexperienced. However, with the right skills and good equipment, snow camping can greatly heighten the enjoyment of a ski tour. By camping you can explore those mountain and wilderness areas, by far the majority, where there are no huts, deciding where you want to spend the night rather than having to reach a specific place each night. Even the most primitive huts cut you off from the mountains, separate you from the world you have come to be part of. By camping you stay in the wilderness throughout your trip, aware of every change in the wind or the temperature, attuned to every nuance of the winter landscape.

Camping in winter isn't as easy as camping in summer, and you will have to carry more weight, but the rewards are far greater. In many areas you can camp where you like, not having to use specified backcountry campgrounds as is required in summer. Even heavily used campsites can look pristine and perfect in winter, the bare ground, fire rings, flattened vegetation, and other signs of use and abuse hidden under a purifying blanket of snow.

The winter camper does have responsibilities. Just as in summer, minimum-impact camping should be practiced, with as little sign of your presence left behind as possible. Rubbish hidden in the snow will reappear come spring, so take everything away with you.

Snow camping has practical as well as aesthetic advantages. There are no mosquitoes or other biting insects, a great boon. Bears will be hibernating, so you can dispense with the hassle of hanging your food and cooking well away from your tent. The first bears may emerge quite early in spring, though, so it is best to be cautious. If you use the same tent year-round, wash and air it thoroughly after the winter season to ensure that all food smells are banished. If you camp regularly in the snow it could be worthwhile having two tents, one for summer and one for winter.

Tents

A tent for winter camping must be able to withstand strong winds and shed snow easily, and it should be easy to pitch with gloves on in a blizzard. Plenty of room is needed, as you may spend a long time inside, as much as eighteen hours a day during the long nights of midwinter and perhaps several days at a time in a prolonged storm. These are not times when you want to be squeezed into a tiny bivouac tent. In addition to generous living space, a winter tent should have a large vestibule for storing damp gear and cooking safely under cover. If packs are left outside, which they may have to be if your tent is small, take out items you need, then stand the packs upright so they don't become totally buried if it snows. In strong winds it is a good idea to anchor them with ice axes or skis through the haul loops.

Unfortunately, the strongest, roomiest tents are also, not surprisingly, the heaviest. Even so, a stable tent with ample space for two needn't weigh much more than 8 pounds/4½kg; many weigh much less. If you intend moving on every day, then the weight of your tent is very important. However, if your aim is to set up base camps to tour from, then you may decide that extra space is more valuable than saving weight and choose a bigger, heavier tent.

Features

In general, tents need to have many guying points and a strong pole system. Steep-walled tents shed snow easily and are roomier inside. A heavy snowfall can quickly flatten tents with flat and gently sloping roofs.

Double-skin tents are less prone to condensation than single-skin ones, even when the latter are made from breathable waterproof fabrics, and the air trapped between the two layers makes them warmer. After the severe problems with condensation and cold that two of my party had with a breathable single-skin tent on the Columbia Icefield (see Chapter 10), I wouldn't use a single-skin tent for winter trips of more than a few nights. All lightweight tents are made from nylon these days, the rain fly coated, the inner uncoated. Nylon has replaced cotton, the only fabric available until a few decades ago, because cotton absorbs condensation and takes a long time to dry, and if it freezes it becomes very stiff and difficult to pack. Even when dry, cotton is much heavier than nylon.

Poles should be shockcord linked to make handling them easier in bad weather. Aluminum alloy is generally considered stronger than fiberglass, but some well-regarded mountain tents do come with fiberglass poles. Check the pitching instructions on geodesic and dome tents to see how the poles should fit together. In some designs it is important for stability that the poles stress against each other correctly. Usually this just means having one set of poles running over another. As a hedge against high winds or heavy snow loads, you may want to weave the poles of a geodesic tent as you put them in—a trick tried and tested by mountaineers. You slide in the first set of poles as usual. Then, when you put in the third pole, go under the first pole you encounter and over the second. For the fourth pole, go over the first and under the second. Those who have done it tell me weaving takes no extra time, and makes a latticework that strengthens the tent. Be forewarned that I have never used a tent whose poles require weaving, and it doesn't sound like something I would like to try in a blizzard. If you have a tent like this, practice well.

Entrances at each end of the tent provide ventilation and ensure that you always have one entrance protected from the weather. The entrances can be left open at the top in all but the worst weather to create a flow-through of air. Door zippers must open from the top down for this, which is also useful for getting in and out of the tent when snow has built up around the edges.

Vestibules are essential for safe cooking under cover. If there are two vestibules, you can use one for cooking and one for gear storage.

Some tents come with protected ventilators above the flysheet doors that allow good airflow even when the doors are shut, while excluding blown snow. They make tents safer, lessening the risk of asphyxiation, and are well worth seeking out.

Designs

Tent designs suitable for snow camping include geodesic domes, tunnel tents, and traditional A-pole ridge tents—but not the domes in which the poles cross at the tent apex; they tend to deform badly in high winds and sag in heavy snowfalls. In general, the more poles there are and the more often they cross each other the less unsupported fabric there is to catch the wind and therefore the more stable the tent—which is why geodesic domes and variations are regarded the best for winter mountain use. Those who camp mostly in the forest can get by with less storm-resistant tents.

If weight is crucial, then tunnel tents are the best choice. They are not quite as stable as geodesics, but good ones will stand up to most storms, and they are much lighter and easier to pitch despite not being freestanding. I have used the North Face Westwind three-pole tunnel tent extensively, including on the Canadian Rockies ski tour described in Chapter 10. At a weight of 6 pounds/3.4kg it is just light enough to carry on short solo trips but roomy enough for two to survive several days inside in a prolonged storm.

The most stable tent I have ever used is the Wild Country Quasar. It has a stretched geodesic shape, combining the curved roof of a geodesic with the rectangular floor of a tunnel. The rectangular floor makes it easier to pitch than square- or round-floored domes when you need to squeeze the tent onto a small platform. At 8 pounds 14 ounces/4kg it is not light, but it feels very secure in strong winds, and it has masses of living room and two large vestibules. Full geodesics weigh even more and are perhaps better suited to base camps than tours when you move on every day. The North Face VE25 is the standard. It weighs a hefty 11 pounds/5kg but sleeps three. A tent I haven't used that has a very good reputation is Sierra

Designs' Stretch Dome with expedition fly. (*Backpacker* magazine's December 1992 issue rated it the best in a field test of four-season tents.) It sleeps two to three and weighs 9 pounds/4.1kg.

All these tents are for two or three people. The solo ski tourer has less choice, having either to carry the weight of a two-person tent or sacrifice a degree of stability. I have used the North Face Westwind as a solo unit despite the weight, but unless the forecast is for really windy weather I usually take my single-hoop Phoenix Phreeranger tent that I use for summer backpacking, which weighs only 4 pounds/1.8kg, or else I take the roomier and only slightly heavier 4¼-pound/2kg Swedish-made Hilleberg Nallo 2, a two-hoop tunnel tent. Hilleberg tents, the best-made I have come across, are well suited to winter camping, being designed for the cold, windswept mountains of Sweden. They are not available in the United States to the best of my knowledge (see Appendix C for address).

Much lighter than any of the tents just mentioned, yet big enough for three people, is the Black Diamond Megamid, an interesting minimal shelter. It is a single-skin pyramid tarp tent made from proofed ripstop nylon, with just a single upright pole and no groundsheet. Its floor is 81 square feet (24 square meters), and it is 5 feet 7 inches (170cm) high in the center, yet it weighs just 3 pounds 6½ ounces/1,525 grams. It is pitched with only four stakes, so it can be up in seconds. It can be dug into the snow for wind protection, and of course you can cook safely inside. Condensation dripping on your sleeping bag could be a problem, but using breathable bivy bags, often carried in winter anyway, would solve it. Nothing else offers nearly as much room as the Megamid for so little weight. It is also less than half the cost of most domes.

Check over any tent before buying. Look for neat, straight stitching, reinforced corners and guy-line attachment points, two-way zippers on the flysheet door (for ventilation), and seam-free, tray-shaped groundsheets. Imagine pitching the tent in a storm in the dark at the end of a long, hard day. Could you do it with mitts on? You may have to!

Running a Winter Camp

Good group organization is essential when camping in the snow. Deciding in advance who will stamp out the tent platforms, who will pitch the tent, who will hold it down in a wind, who will set up the stove and start melting snow or go to collect water if available, and in what order these and other tasks should be done will make setting up camp much quicker than if no plans are made. Even when alone, think out what needs doing and what order you will do it in. Decide where gear will go and make sure none is cast aside on the snow, where it could soon disappear.

Pitching

It is not enough for comfortable snow camping that you have a good tent; you also need to know how to use it to the best advantage. To start with, care has to be taken with the choice and preparation of the campsite. If any shelter, such as trees, cliffs, or banks, is available it should be used, as long as there is no danger from avalanches. For warmth, remember that cold air sinks. Valley bottoms, basin floors, meadows, and lakes will be chillier than the surrounding slopes or forest.

Camping on deep snow has little effect on the landscape, so you can camp anywhere without worrying too much about harming

When possible it is better to camp on dry ground.

the environment; but one point is worth thinking about: if there are signs of much animal activity in an area, particularly in forested areas, it is best to camp elsewhere. Wildlife has a hard enough time surviving the winter without being disturbed by people.

Thin snow cover is a different matter. Camping on it will com-

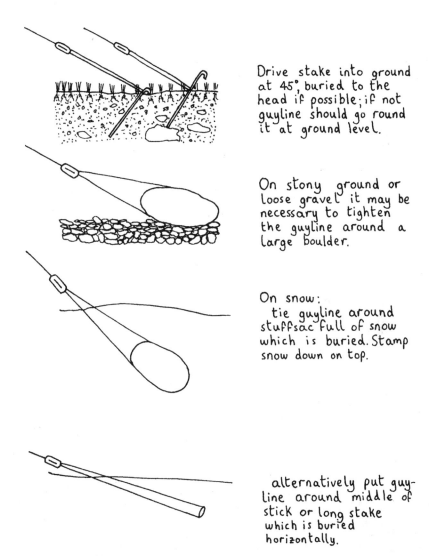

Drive stake into ground at 45°, buried to the head if possible; if not guyline should go round it at ground level.

On stony ground or loose gravel it may be necessary to tighten the guyline around a large boulder.

On snow:
tie guyline around stuffsac full of snow which is buried. Stamp snow down on top.

alternatively put guy-line around middle of stick or long stake which is buried horizontally.

Figure 8-1. Staking out a tent.

press the snow, causing it to take longer to melt, thus shortening the growing time for the plants below. Bare ground may be saturated with snowmelt and even more easily damaged, so greater care must be taken in spring camping. Choose sites where you know that the terrain below the snow can stand compression, such as vegetation-free areas of gravel and stones or, in the forest, conifer needles. Alternatively, climb up to areas of deeper snow or drop down to find dry areas in the valley.

If the snow cover is very thin and the ground below is suitable for low-impact camping, it is often worth shoveling the snow away before pitching the tent. This isn't practical in deep snow, and unless you can find an area of hard snow, a flat platform must be stamped out. It is easiest to do this with your skis on. Remember to make the platform much bigger than your tent so there is room for guy lines and for walking around the tent. The platform should be smoothed flat and, if possible, left to harden before you pitch the tent, otherwise you will find the floor rather lumpy.

Main guys and staking points can be anchored securely with skis, ski poles, and ice axes. Large curved or T-shaped stakes designed to hold in soft snow are available but tend to be heavy. Nonetheless, carrying half a dozen on long ski-camping tours is probably worthwhile, especially if you intend to make day tours from a base camp and thus can't use your skis and poles to stake out the tent. The lightest I have found are Black Diamond's T-stakes. They weigh about an ounce and a half (40 grams) each. Stakes can be buried horizontally with guy lines tied around the middle, then stamped down in the snow. Once the temperature drops below zero they will freeze into place and you will probably need to hack them out (carefully!) with a shovel or ice ax in the morning. Tie short guy lines to the staking points of your tent before a tour or else carry plenty of cord and add them when necessary. An alternative to burying stakes is to fill stuff sacks with snow, attach the guy lines, and bury them. If there are trees or large boulders near the site, it is worth running a line out to them for added security.

If your tent has snow valances—ground-level flaps running around the edge of the flysheet—then pitching is much easier: you just pile snow on them. However, valances severely limit ventilation and are a nuisance when not camping on snow, so overall I don't recommend them. If your tent doesn't have valances, stability in

Protect your tent from high winds with a wall of snow blocks.

high winds can be improved by heaping snow against the edges of the tent.

When the wind is really strong and a sheltered site isn't available, a wall of snow blocks can be built as a windbreak. However, drifting may occur on the leeward side and bury your tent, which can also happen if you dig a pit to pitch your tent in—this happened to me at a camp high on the vast Columbia Icefield in the Canadian Rockies (see Chapter 10). We dug our two tunnel tents into the snow, leaving a gap between them and the back wall of the pit. However, a storm kept us trapped for four nights instead of the one we had intended spending. During the worst night we had to dig the tents out every few hours to prevent their collapsing under the weight of snow. I have since learned that one solution to this problem is to build two walls, a high one some 15 feet (5 meters) or so away from the tent and a smaller one half that distance. I haven't tried it myself, but those who have tell me it works and that any drifting occurs between the two walls. If you build only one wall, pitch your tent the same number of feet in front of it as the wall is high so that snow buildup will occur between the tent and the wall.

If snow builds up around the tent someone has to go out and shovel it away. Do this as often and as carefully as possible—it is easy to damage the tent with the shovel blade. Snow pressing on the walls could cut out ventilation when cooking and lead to asphyxiation, and so could a collapsed tent. Tents with ventilators are a help.

A pit about a foot (30cm) deep dug right in front of the tent can make getting out much easier; you can sit with your feet in it while you put on boots and clothing and then simply stand up to leave the tent. Such pits work best in tents without vestibules. If your tent has two vestibules, a pit can be dug in one of them, leaving the other for gear storage and cooking. An alternative is to dig a pit outside the vestibule and use a large stuff sack or other item as a seat while you put your boots on. If you do dig a pit, don't forget it is there when leaving the tent after dark!

All walls and pits should be dismantled and filled in when you leave a camp, so other visitors will not be aware you have been there.

Ventilation and Condensation

Dampness is a major enemy when snow camping because drying out wet gear is almost always difficult and often impossible, so you need to be careful to keep snow out of the inner tent. A light brush or whisk is useful for brushing snow off clothing and for removing the snow that inevitably finds its way inside despite the best precautions. Wet clothes should be left in the vestibule or even outside, preferably in a plastic bag or stuff sack. Don't leave boots outside; they will freeze. Instead, brush off the snow, then store them inside the tent in a waterproof bag. If it is really cold I wrap the bag in spare clothing to help keep the boots from freezing. Some people put their boots in their sleeping bag, but I have never fancied doing this, my sleeping bag being close fitting.

When cooking in the vestibule, as much ventilation as possible is needed to prevent steam from condensing on the flysheet and dripping back onto you and your gear. Ideally, cooking should always be done with the flysheet doors wide open. If this isn't possible you should at least leave the top section of the zipper undone. In severe storms even this may not be possible, and cooking with the doors shut may be the only option. Then all you can do is try to minimize the inevitable condensation by keeping lids on your pans and, when you have finished cooking, leaving the stove running for a few minutes to dry out the air a little.

Wet, often dripping, flysheet walls are almost unavoidable in calm conditions, another reason for having a roomy tent in which you can keep well clear of the sides. It is also a reason for using either a sleeping bag with a water-resistant shell or an overbag or bivy bag made of waterproof breathable fabric inside the tent. A small sponge is useful for wiping up drips and condensation.

Bivy Bags

If someone is injured or you have to spend an unintended night out, a bivy (bivouac) bag or sack (sometimes called an emergency bag or overbag) is the best and quickest way to gain protection from the weather. Even if you are able to dig a snow shelter, a bivy bag is useful for keeping your sleeping bag or clothing dry, and it can serve the same purpose in a damp tent. And when the stars shine and the wind dies and you decide to sleep under the vast winter sky ringed by shining peaks, a bivy bag can add several degrees of warmth to your sleeping bag, keep off stray breezes, and protect it from frost. Bivouac bags are so useful that I always carry one.

Bivy bags made from breathable waterproof fabrics such as Gore-Tex perform best; nonbreathable ones will leave your sleeping bag wet with condensation if you spend a night in one. There are various styles and weights, the most basic designs weighing the least. Those with nonbreathable coated-nylon bases are adequate but can result in considerably more condensation than ones made entirely from the breathable fabric, especially if you roll over during the night so the nonbreathable section is above you. Some form of hood is needed with a zippered or drawcord-fastened closure. While you can seal yourself entirely into a microporous-fabric bag such as one made of Gore-Tex, you must not enclose your head in one made of hydrophilic fabric because it isn't possible to breathe through these fabrics (although they pass moisture, they don't allow air to enter— see Chapter 6 for details of how these materials work). However, hydrophilic bags are cheaper and lighter than Gore-Tex, some weighing as little as 13 ounces/350 grams. Gore-Tex bags start at around 20 ounces/550 grams for the simplest designs. There is also growing evidence that hydrophilic bags work better than microporous ones in really cold temperatures, around 0°F/–18°C.

Double bags are available, which could be useful in emergencies when two people warm each other, but single ones can be used for solo trips without having to carry the extra weight and as sleeping-bag covers for extra warmth. The main thing is to ensure that your sleeping bag will fit easily inside. Roomy ones can also be used for storing clothing, boots, and even water bottles overnight.

I wouldn't risk damaging an expensive breathable bivy bag by using it as the roof of a snow trench (described later), so I carry a tarp, plastic tube tent, or plastic bivy bag in country where such shelters are feasible.

Tarps

Not all ski campers spend their time above timberline. If you camp regularly in forests, a tarp may be all you need for shelter. Using a tarp saves on weight and makes ventilation easy. They are also worth carrying on day tours in forested country for making emergency shelters or even just to use as a wind shelter. They are not as warm as tents, so a warmer sleeping bag and more clothing will probably be needed. Nylon tarps are the lightest, rectangular ones from companies like Campmor and Outdoor Products weighing from 10 to 50 ounces/300 to 1,400 grams for sizes ranging from 5 by 7 feet (1.5 by 2.1 meters) to 12 by 16 feet (3.6 by 4.8 meters). Moss Tents produces a sophisticated ripstop-nylon tarp called the Parawing, which has "hyperbolic paraboloid compound curves" to aid the shedding of wind and snow. Parawings come in two sizes, of which the smaller looks the best for ski touring. It measures 8½ by 8½ feet (2.6 by 2.6 meters) and weighs 28 ounces (795 grams). Whatever the style of tarp, you will need a few stakes and some cord for tying it to trees.

Tarps are used in winter in exactly the same way as in summer, only your ingenuity and available anchoring points limiting the shapes of shelter you can construct. Steeper-roofed constructions are better if snowfall is likely, and it is advisable not to erect the tarp under branches bearing particularly heavy burdens of snow in case it falls and crushes your shelter.

Groundsheets

If you use a tarp you will need a groundsheet, which is also useful in the snow shelters discussed next. A bivy bag will protect your sleeping bag, but it won't provide a place to put other items. Nylon tarps can be used as groundsheets, but the thin fabric isn't very durable and may not be sufficiently water resistant under pressure to prevent snowmelt from coming through.

I have found the best groundsheets to be the laminated sheets of aluminized polyethylene, polyester, and fiberglass sold under the names Sportsman's Blanket (17 ounces/500 grams) and Allweather Blanket (12 ounces/340 grams). They measure around 4 by 6½ feet (1.2 by 2 meters), big enough for one person. They are very durable but crack at the seams if always folded the same way. Rolling them up is a better idea.

Avoid the thin silver space blankets often promoted for survival use. The material tears easily and is very difficult to handle in a wind. A bivy bag is much better for emergency use and a tougher material for a wind shelter or groundsheet.

Snow Shelters

High winds and blizzards can make tent use difficult or even impossible at times, so winter campers need to know how to dig snow shelters; even hut users may need one in an emergency.

Snow shelters aren't just for emergency use. Snow is an excellent insulator, and a snow shelter is warmer than a tent. A nice roomy one can make an excellent base for day tours, and they are better than a tent in snowy or blustery weather because they are absolutely quiet and still inside. Small ones can even be dug for lunch shelters in stormy weather. I once spent 36 comfortable hours in a snow-hole in the Cairngorm Mountains in Scotland while a blizzard raged outside. Skiing was impossible and camping would have been very difficult and unpleasant.

Snow shelters range from basic trenches and slots to complex igloos. The possibilities are limited only by your imagination, snow being a very malleable substance.

In an emergency anything from pans and mugs to ice axes can be used to dig a shelter, but it is much quicker and easier to use a snow shovel (see Chapter 9) or, in hard snow or ice, a snow saw. A shovel should always be carried, but I would only bother with a saw if I set out with the intention of sleeping in the snow.

Practice building snow shelters so that if you have to dig one in a storm you will know what to do. A good time to practice is when the weather prevents your going far from a hut or base; practicing in bad weather will demonstrate the difference a shelter makes to your comfort.

Snow-Holes

The type of shelter you build depends in part on its intended purpose and in part on the nature of the terrain and the amount and whereabouts of the snow. If you want a shelter for the night or to use as a base, then a snow-hole or snow cave is the best choice. In areas where deep snow is available only on banks and slopes it may be the only feasible type to build.

To make a snow-hole you need a suitable bank of snow—at least 6 feet (2 meters) deep and preferably much deeper. The steeper the angle the better. Such banks are often found beside streams and on the lee sides of bowls. Before you start digging check to see if there is any avalanche danger from above. Digging is hot work, so

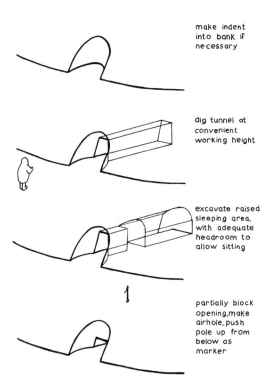

make indent
into bank if
necessary

dig tunnel at
convenient
working height

excavate raised
sleeping area,
with adequate
headroom to
allow sitting

partially block
opening, make
airhole, push
pole up from
below as
marker

Figure 8-2. Stages in excavation of a snow-hole.

Digging a snow-hole is best done wearing waterproof garments.

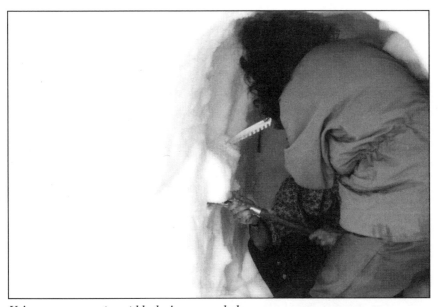

Using a snow saw to cut blocks in a snow-hole.

strip off warmwear, but wear waterproofs to protect your inner layers from getting wet. If you start partway up the slope you can throw the snow downhill, which is easier than piling it up.

Start the snow-hole by digging straight into the bank at about head height. If you have two shovels, two entrances can be started about 6 feet (2 meters) apart. Dig in for about 4 feet (1.2 meters), then start to clear an area on either side at about waist height. Dig upward rather than down, but make sure there is at least a foot (30cm) of snow for the roof or there will be danger of its collapsing. The aim is to produce sleeping platforms with a trench between them for cold air to sink into. If the snow is very hard, a snow saw will speed things up, but it is not essential. Don't try to dig out or lift too much snow at once. Lightweight snow shovels can be broken.

How big you make the snow-hole depends on how many it must sleep and how ambitious you are feeling. Several holes can be linked by short passages for a large group. The sleeping platforms should be high enough for you to sit up comfortably, and the roof should be smoothed and rounded to minimize dripping. While one person is digging out the hole, someone else can be removing the

Sealing the entrance to a snow-hole.

Note how the original large entrance to this snow-hole has been reduced to keep warmth in and snow out.

snow from the entrance. Snow can be thrown onto a tarp or other smooth sheet of nylon or plastic and then hauled outside. A shelf can be dug out between the platforms for use as a kitchen. A tarp or even the tent if you are carrying one can be used as a groundsheet. Niches can be cut in the walls to store small items, but be careful to keep track of everything. Gear trodden into the floor can be hard to find. Don't leave your boots in the cold trench—they will freeze hard.

Once the hole is dug and no more snow has to be removed, stop up most of the entrance with snow blocks. If you have one, a spare tarp can be used to cover the entrance to help prevent its filling up with snow. Having the floor of the hole sloping down to the entrance is the best way to prevent snow and cold air from entering. If you started with two entrances, fill one in completely. Occasionally you may hit rock or earth at the bottom or back of your hole. All you can do then is try again farther along the bank or adapt the hole to accommodate it.

Ventilation is very important, so as backup to the entrance (which may drift over in a storm), poke a hole in the roof with a ski pole. If you leave the pole poking out of the hole you can easily

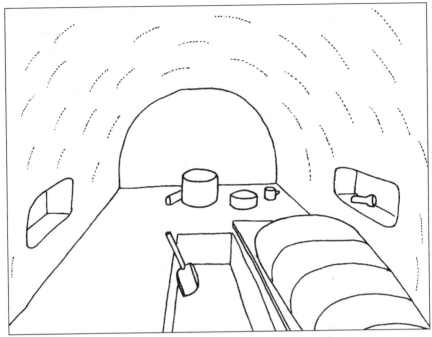

Figure 8-3. Sleeping benches and cooking area inside a snow-hole.

Snow-holes can be surprisingly cozy.

make sure the hole stays clear of snow. It will also act as a marker so that no one skis over your roof (don't investigate a ski pole sticking out of the snow; it probably marks someone's roof) and to help you locate your snow-hole. Keep a shovel handy inside the hole. Snow-holes are very stable, but the entrances can get blocked with snow very quickly.

Snow Trenches

A good snow-hole will take at least a couple of hours to build, so it isn't really a practical proposition in an emergency. However, a slot or sentry box big enough for one person to get out of the wind can be shoveled out in a matter of minutes. It can always be enlarged if you decide to stay put. But the best emergency shelter is a snow trench or snow grave, which can be built very quickly (seven minutes is the fastest I have heard of) and will shelter two people. At least 5 vertical feet (1½ meters) of reasonably level snow is required, so this is a technique for places where the snow falls heavily and lies deep.

Start by digging a slot about shoulder width and a little shorter

Dig a snow trench shoulder width and a little shorter than your skis and use the snow to build a wall at the windward end.

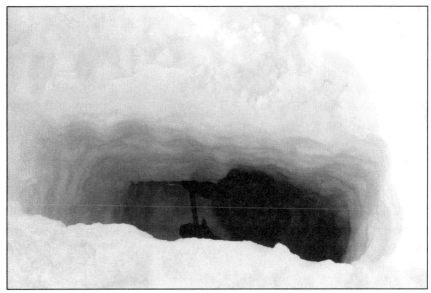

Dig out the sides at the bottom of the trench to make room for your legs.

Lay ski poles across the trench.

Put a pair of skis in a bivy bag and lay the bag over the trench.

Snug and warm in a snow trench.

than your skis. While one person digs, another can build a wall around the windward end with the excavated snow. Dig straight down until the trench is 4 to 5 feet (1.2 to 1.5 meters) deep. There will now be room for two people to sit in the trench. Insulating mats can be used as the floor. To roof it, lay two ski poles across the trench, then slide a pair of skis into a plastic tube tent, bivy bag, or folded-over tarp (the open sides can be tied together with cord—don't worry about bunching of the material, it doesn't matter) and lay this bundle across the poles. Use snow to hold the ends down. You can get in and out of the trench by lifting one corner of the roof and sliding in. If this is only a temporary shelter while you lunch or rest out of the wind, no more needs to be done. However, if you are going to spend more than a few hours in your trench, perhaps even the night, dig out the sides at the bottom to make slots you can slide your legs into so you can lie down.

The size of the trench is determined by the size of your tube tent or folded tarp; about 3 feet by 7 (0.9 to 2.1 meters) is adequate. If you have a tarp for the roof you can dig a bigger trench and stretch the tarp out, weighing down each side with snow and perhaps using upright poles or skis as roof supports from inside. Such a large trench will hold more people than the grave type, but the roof is much more vulnerable to collapse by snow. A small trench will be warmer than a big one, too, and quicker to dig. Overall, if your need is to get out of the wind quickly, several snow graves are better than one large trench. If it looks like your stay will be prolonged, a more solid roof can be put on a snow grave by using snow blocks to make an A-frame-style roof.

When you leave a snow trench, fill it in and stamp the snow down. Apart from leaving as little sign of your presence as possible, this also ensures that other skiers won't have an accident by skiing into it.

If there isn't enough snow for digging a trench or cave, you can still make a shelter by piling up a huge heap of snow, compressing it as you go to help set the snow, leaving it to set, and then tunneling into it. I have never done this, but apparently it works well.

Natural Shelters

Where possible use the terrain to help you build emergency shelters. Big snow scoops often occur under the roots of fallen trees, under steep riverbanks, and around large trees and big boulders where the snow has melted or been blown away by the wind. These can be quickly dug out to make lunch shelters and even roofed with tarps or tent flysheets for longer stays.

Sleeping Bags

There is nothing worse than shivering through the long hours of a frosty night between two pieces of flimsy material laughingly described as a sleeping bag. Once you have suffered such an experience, as I did a few times when I began winter camping, a decent sleeping bag becomes a very important piece of gear.

A sleeping bag is essential on camping tours and at huts that provide little more than a roof over your head. It is advisable to carry a sleeping bag on all hut-to-hut tours anyway in case of a shortage of bedding. Even on day tours it would be useful in the event of injury or an unexpected overnight stay, though some people prefer merely to take extra clothing. Certainly in a group it is worth taking one or two sleeping bags along.

A three-season bag can be upgraded for winter by using a second, lighter-weight bag either inside or over it. The result will be bulkier and heavier than a single winter bag but less expensive and more versatile: the lightest bag can be used in midsummer, the three-season bag in autumn and winter, and both together in winter. If your three-season bag is down filled, its warmth could be increased with a pile or synthetic outer bag that would also add protection against damp. The outer bag must be roomy enough not to compress the fill of your inner bag, or some of the benefits will be lost. The North Face makes a bag specially designed for this purpose, the Expedition System overbag. It has a 3M Liteloft synthetic fill and a Gore-Tex outer, weighs 2 pounds 8 ounces/1,300 grams, and North Face says it adds about 18°F/10°C to the temperature rating of your bag. A large hood, covered zippers, and Velcro tabs enable you to seal yourself inside when it is really cold or when bivouacking in a storm.

Feathered Friends offers a down overbag with 14 ounces/400 grams fill in the top two-thirds and a pocket for a foam pad as the base. The total weight is 2 pounds 8 ounces/1,125 grams. It is available with or without a Gore-Tex shell and with or without a hood. Overbags such as these can be used alone in summer. Feathered Friends also offers the Rock Wren liner bag, with 10 ounces/280 grams of down fill, sewn-through seams, and a total weight of 1 pound 8 ounces/680 grams. Again, there is an optional Gore-Tex shell, though it seems unnecessary in a liner bag. The Rock Wren also has arm openings so you can stay in the bag while cooking or reading and a drawstring-closed foot so you can turn it into what is effectively a giant, extra-long down coat.

For regular winter campers a fully specified cold-weather sleeping bag is probably the best choice, being lighter, less bulky, and more comfortable than two separate bags. Nothing beats snuggling into a luxurious thick sleeping bag on a chilly night after a day spent battling through a winter storm. But how do you decide which of the many on the market is the right one?

Insulation

The insulating material is a key factor. The choice is between down, polyester, and pile.

DOWN. Down has the best warmth-to-weight ratio, the lowest bulk when packed, and is very durable (lasting at least three times as long as polyester, according to one manufacturer who uses both types of fill). I also find that down bags can be used comfortably over a much wider temperature range than polyester ones. Down is soft and molds around the body better than synthetics, making it both warmer and more comfortable. Down's only apparent disadvantages are the high price and the lack of resistance to moisture—it loses virtually all warmth when wet, absorbs masses of water, and takes ages to dry. However, the initial cost is offset by the long life, and keeping a bag dry isn't the problem many people think it is, as long as you take a few basic precautions. I have never yet had a down bag get more than slightly damp. A waterproof stuff sack ensures that the bag stays dry in the pack. I use Black Diamond SealCoat stuff sacks; they have taped seams and really are fully waterproof. When your snow-hole or tent is dripping with condensation, a water-resistant outer shell or a waterproof, breathable bivy bag or overbag will keep the down dry. I prefer a bivy bag because it can be carried separately on day and hut tours in case of an enforced bivouac.

SYNTHETIC FILLS. Polyester bags are far less expensive to buy than down, retain some of their insulation when wet, and dry much faster. However, they are also heavier and bulkier, though compression stuff sacks (provided with some models) can help to reduce them to pack-size proportions. They also have a much shorter life, no more than four or five years according to one reputable maker. For those who camp only occasionally in winter and then mostly on roadside campgrounds with perhaps the odd short foray into the hills, polyester bags are fine, but for those to whom weight and bulk are important I still recommend down. There are many types of polyester fill, some better than others, with Quallofil and Polarguard the best regarded. 3M's Liteloft, Albany International's Primaloft and Microloft, all three introduced in the early 1990s, look as though they might be the closest imitation of down, the ultimate goal of synthetic-fill designers. They are reportedly longer lasting, too.

PILE. Although no U.S. manufacturer makes pile bags, British-made Freebird ones are available and do have enough advantages to be worth considering. As we know from its use in clothing, pile is warm when wet, nonabsorbent, quick drying, incredibly durable, and inexpensive. When covered with a Pertex nylon shell, as are Freebird bags, it is also windproof and snowproof. Compared with down, however, it is much bulkier and heavier for equivalent warmth. Pile bags are ideal for snow-holes, damp cabins, and bivouacs, as you don't have to worry about keeping them dry. I have used the Freebird Superbag in wet, cold conditions around freezing point and found it very good. Freebird pile bags are designed to be used with Freebird pile clothing (see Chapter 6). The combination works very well.

Fit and Shape

Although not as important as the insulation, the design of a sleeping bag does affect the performance. For winter-camping bags the hooded, tapered "mummy" shape is standard. Hoods should be big enough to tighten around your face, leaving just a small air hole to breathe through, while the foot of a bag should be circular and well stuffed with fill. Flat-sewn footpieces will cause cold feet. Shoulder baffles are useful but not essential. Side zippers, almost standard these days, need good insulated baffles behind them. Single baffles should be attached above, not below, the zipper, but double baffles are better. Two sets of full-length zippers are also a good safeguard, providing a better seal against the cold and backup in case one zipper breaks. These are sometimes found on bags for extremely cold conditions, below –10°F/–23°C.

The closest-fitting bags are the most efficient in terms of warmth. A too-large bag will have much cold, dead air space that your body has to heat. A bag that is too tight can feel restrictive and lose heat where you push against the sides. Consequently, many bags come in two sizes. A smaller bag with less fill may prove warmer than a larger bag. A camper once told me that he had exchanged his winter-rated down sleeping bag for the same maker's three-season bag because it was too large. He found he slept warmer in the lighter but closer-fitting bag. If possible it is best to get into a bag before buying to see how closely it fits and how comfortable it feels.

Shell Materials

Shell and lining materials are usually tightly woven nylons that are lightweight, hard wearing, windproof, quick drying, and feel pleasant next to the skin. Bags are available with waterproof, breathable shells made from materials such as Gore-Tex, but they aren't fully waterproof because the seams can't be taped, and they are much more expensive. Nor can you use the Gore-Tex shell separately from the bag. Overall, a bivy bag is a better bet.

Construction

Construction methods also affect the warmth of a bag. Sewn-through or single-layer construction, in which the inner and outer are sewn together at intervals to create oval tubes to contain the fill, is the simplest method of making a sleeping bag. It is used for the lightest down and synthetic bags but isn't suitable for winter-weight ones because of the considerable heat loss through the seams.

In down bags the construction to look for is box or slant-wall, in which strips of material are sewn between the inner and outer shells to create four-sided channels that have no cold spots and allow the down to expand (loft) fully. V-baffles create triangular compartments and are sometimes used for sections of a bag where warmth is critical, such as over the chest, but they are heavier than box or slant-wall construction. The channels themselves usually run straight across the bag, though they may be zigzagged, and on some bags there are short vertical or radial channels over the chest to ensure that the down stays in place. Side baffles are needed to prevent most of the down from shifting to one half of the bag. A few bags purposely exclude side baffles so you can move the down where you want it to cope with varying temperatures, but I am dubious and worry that the down might shift of its own accord. I am also wary of bags with differential fill, in which most of the fill is in the top half of the bag on the basis that the stuff underneath you gets crushed anyway and so isn't very effective. I often wake up with the bottom of the bag above me, so I would rather have the fill evenly distributed.

Double-layer construction, used mainly in synthetic bags, consists of two or sometimes three sewn-through layers inside each other with the stitch lines offset to minimize heat loss. Lighter and considered more efficient is diagonal-layer or shingle construction, in which batting of polyester fiber is angled over itself to cut out cold spots before being sewn to the inner and the outer.

Warmth and Weight

Makers give sleeping bags temperature or season ratings, but there is no consistent standard, and they should be taken as rough guidelines only. Furthermore, some people sleep cold, others warm. If, like me, you are one of the lucky second group you can use a lighter sleeping bag than colder sleepers, who might well need a bag rated for lower temperatures than they expect to encounter. Other factors, such as tiredness, humidity, food intake, type of shelter, and clothing worn can affect how warm you feel. What you sleep on is particularly important, and most manufacturers rate their bags on the assumption that an insulating mat will be used.

While the warmest three-season sleeping bags can be used in winter with the addition of clothing, if you intend camping regularly, a bag intended for bitterly cold temperatures is far better. These are often called four-season sleeping bags—an inaccurate description, as any bag that will keep you warm at +5°F/–15°C is likely to be far too hot at +65°F/+18°C. Three-season would be a better name, the seasons being autumn, winter, and spring.

Years of testing sleeping bags have shown me that down bags are usually rated conservatively, which is to say that I can sleep warm in them in colder temperatures than they are rated for, but that polyester bags often have very optimistic claims made for them, so optimistic that I wonder just where the makers get their figures. I have had some very cold nights in polyester bags.

I particularly remember one unpleasant bivouac in a synthetic-fill bag rated to –2°F/–20°C. The night was calm and clear. The temperature when I climbed into the bag was +27°F/–3°C, and I started out sleeping in a long-sleeved, midweight polyester shirt and lightweight polypro bottoms. I also slid the sleeping bag into a Gore-Tex bivy bag in case of heavy frost. An expedition-weight closed-cell foam mat was under the bag. After a few hours I awoke feeling chilly. I added a lightweight fleece shirt and thick wool socks and slowly drifted back to sleep, only to awake cold again a few hours later. I pulled out the down sweater that was acting as my pillow and wrapped it around my knees and backside, and dozed fitfully until dawn. The overnight low was 0°F/–18°C. My own estimate is that the bag wasn't suitable for temperatures below +25°F/–4°C. That was an extreme case, but I would be wary of synthetic bags that claim to be as warm as down bags of the same weight.

How warm a bag you need depends on many factors. As a warm sleeper I can sleep naked comfortably in a bag with a fill of 16 to 20 ounces (450 to 575 grams) of down in temperatures down to +24°F/–5°C. Wearing thermal underwear I can use such a bag easily to +14°F/–10°C. Adding pile clothing would probably keep me warm at +5°F/–15°C, though I haven't tried it. I have, though, bivouacked comfortably on snow at –2°F/–20°C in a bag with a down fill of 28 ounces (800 grams) wearing just a short-sleeved thin shirt, thin long johns, and wool socks.

For most uses and most people, bags with 28 to 32 ounces (800 to 900 grams) of down fill should be adequate. Cold sleepers and those planning on camping in temperatures below 0°F/–18°C should consider bags with 35 ounces (1,000 grams) and more. Such bags are very warm. Those with around 39 ounces (1,100 grams) of fill are rated down to –24°F/–32°C. At the same time, down bags have a wide temperature range. I have used a 39-ounce-fill bag at +44°F/+7°C and not been too hot. Having more fill than you need doesn't mean you will be uncomfortable at night, but you will be carrying more weight than necessary. While huts with wood-burning stoves are generally warmer than tents or unheated huts, they can still be very cold if they have not been used for several days. I have stayed in a Norwegian hut during a cold spell when the outside temperature was down to 0°F/–18°C, which was so chilly that the temperature in the dormitories didn't rise above +24°F/–5°C the first night despite the stove. Those who had brought very light bags to save weight found it hard to keep warm. I slept comfortably in a bag with 32 ounces (900 grams) of down fill.

Some models are lighter than others, but, roughly, a bag with 20 to 24 ounces (570 to 670 grams) of down fill will weigh 40 to 52 ounces (1,140 to 1,500 grams) in total; one with 28 to 35 ounces (800 to 1,000 grams) of fill will weigh 55 to 60 ounces (1,500 to 1,700 grams); and one with 35 ounces (1,100 grams) plus of fill will weigh 65 to 80 ounces (1,800 to 2,250 grams).

Polyester bags weigh at least a third more than down for the same warmth. I must admit I use them only when I am sent one to test.

Pile bags are not really comparable with the other types, as they are designed to be used with clothing. The one I usually use, the Freebird Superbag, weighs 64 ounces (1,800 grams). The warmer 4S outer and inner combination weighs 95 ounces (2,700 grams) for the medium size and 112 ounces (3,175 grams) for the large and has kept me warm without clothing down to +24°F/–5°C.

Vapor Barriers

Much warmth can be gained for little extra weight by using a vapor barrier (VB) liner in your sleeping bag. A VB liner is a coated inner bag that prevents heat loss through evaporation by preventing body moisture from escaping, which in turn prevents it from forming. A VB liner also helps keep your bag dry because it keeps body moisture out of the fill, especially useful if you have a down bag. Losing less moisture also means you will wake less thirsty, saving time needed for melting snow in the morning, and making dehydration less likely. VB liners feel most comfortable if you wear thin synthetic underwear. They work best in dry, cold conditions. The North Face, which makes a good VB liner weighing 7 ounces (200 grams), recommends it for use in constant temperatures of +14°F/–10°C or below.

VB clothing used for the same purpose (see Chapter 6) is a more versatile choice than a liner. I have found my VB clothing very effective for sleeping in, and it allows me to use a lighter bag.

Insulating Mats

Whatever type of sleeping bag you use, a good insulating mat is essential for sleeping on snow and frozen ground and is often needed in the more basic huts where mattresses may be absent or limited in number.

Without a good insulating mat, ground cold will penetrate even the thickest sleeping bag. Standard closed-cell foam mats aren't all the same, and only some are suitable for winter camping. Look for ones designated "four-season" or "expedition." They should be a half to 1 inch (10 to 25mm) thick and will weigh 9 to 12 ounces (250 to 350 grams). Both three-quarter and full-length models are available. Unless you are tall, over 5 feet 10 inches, the shorter one should be adequate if you use clothing for a pillow and under your feet. For those who feel the cold, two mats are useful.

I carry a closed-cell foam mat, strapped outside the pack so it is easily available, on all but the shortest day tours, both for use as a seat during stops and in case of a bivouac. Small sit mats are adequate, and some packs come with removable ones as back padding, but I prefer a longer mat for a combined seat and back rest that would also be better in the event of an enforced bivouac.

For camping there is a much better alternative to a closed-cell foam mat in Cascade Designs's Therm-a-Rest self-inflating mat (there are other self-inflating mats around, but Cascade Designs was first and their mats are still the lightest and best). The Therm-a-Rest has a proofed nylon cover and an open-cell foam inner that sucks in air and expands when the valve is opened. It comes in two thicknesses, 1 and 1½ inches (2.5 and 3.8cm), and two lengths, 47 and 72 inches (119 and 183cm). The thinnest, shortest one, called the Ultra-Lite, weighs 1 pound 1 ounce (500 grams). I use it year-round and have found it far more comfortable than a standard closed-cell foam mat and perfectly warm when sleeping on snow at 0°F/–18°C. Compared with an ordinary foam mat the bulk is very small, and it can be folded up and carried inside the pack, where it is well protected from damage—but not very accessible, so I also carry a small closed-cell foam sit mat, which is less vulnerable than the Therm-a-Rest, to use as a seat during the day.

Keeping Warm at Night

How to use a sleeping bag may seem obvious, but there are a few points to observe that will help you keep warm. First, your bag must be kept dry unless it is pile, and even pile bags are more comfortable dry.

Down bags should be taken out of their stuff sacks and shaken out before you use them to enable them to loft fully. Because bags retain rather than create heat, it is better to get into one when you are warm rather than wait until you are cold. In severe cold I treat my sleeping bag as an article of clothing and sit or lie in the tent in it with the collar or hood drawcord drawn tight across my chest and under my arms to prevent its sliding down. Before you get in the bag (ideally, as soon as you make camp) you should remove damp clothing and replace it with dry items. If your outer clothing is dry but your innermost layer is damp it may be enough simply to put on an extra warm layer.

Occasionally you may wake in the night feeling cold. If you haven't already done so, pull the hood drawcords tight and do up the side zipper fully. Next don extra clothing. If still cold eat something sweet and high in calories or even get up and make a hot drink. If it is the part of you touching the ground that feels cold, your insulating mat may be inadequate. Putting clothing and even your pack under you can help. If you do wake in the night feeling cold, the one thing you shouldn't do is nothing. Shivering through a sleepless night is not fun or good preparation for the next day's skiing. If you repeatedly have cold nights you probably need a warmer sleeping bag or a vapor barrier lining or suit of clothing and perhaps a thicker insulating mat.

Living in the Snow

*It sounds so lovely, a warming, flaming campfire in the raven
black night of the high arctic latitudes. And it is lovely,
but only for a while, for the heat of it scorches your skin and
almost roasts one side of your body, while the frost jabs its
icy darts into the other.*
—*Ejnar Mikkelsen,* Mirage in the Arctic

Winter camping is about more than keeping warm and dry in your
tent and sleeping bag. Much more time is spent in camp in winter
than in summer, so the other aspects of camp life—cooking, relaxing,
entertainment—take on a greater importance.

Campfires

Not so long ago winter travelers relied on fires for cooking and keeping warm. In his book *Dangerous River,* R. M. Patterson tells the story
of a solo snowshoe journey he made in the Nahanni River region of
the Mackenzie Mountains in northwestern Canada in the 1920s. To
keep warm at night he would make a big fire to sleep next to, with a
pile of wood at hand. Every couple of hours the fire would die down,
and he would wake up cold and put more wood on it, then sleep for
another few hours.

This style of winter living was fine in the days when few people
ventured far into the wilderness, but today it causes too much damage, destroying trees and leaving unsightly scars. Efficient use of
modern lightweight clothing, tents, and sleeping bags is the best way
to keep warm, and a portable stove is the best way to cook.

That said, it is a good idea to know how to light a fire in winter when necessary, especially if you travel regularly in forested areas. Many huts have wood stoves, and there isn't always dry kindling and logs available. A fire lit at the mouth of a tarp erected as a lean-to (raise the back off the ground to allow a draught so it doesn't fill with smoke) provides a surprising amount of warmth and is a good way of restoring morale to a cold, tired party. A fire can also be used for drying wet clothing, but be careful—if you place items too close they may melt. Protect sleeping bags and down-filled jackets from sparks.

If you can't light a fire without leaving a trace, then don't light a fire at all except in an emergency. In some places it is possible to have a fire without leaving a scar. Shingle banks by rivers are ideal—they will be swept clean come snowmelt. Driftwood is usually plentiful, and you are not depriving the land of needed nutrients by burning it.

Don't light fires around timberline unless absolutely essential; trees grow slowly there, and every bit of dead wood is needed to replenish the soil. Furthermore, if the snow is deep the only wood available will be the tree branches. Never light a fire if it means damaging live trees. Even burning snags can spoil the appearance of an area, making it look used. If there is snow-free ground on which you can light a fire, do so only if it is bare of vegetation. Fires shouldn't be lit in popular areas where summer visitation is high; keep them for little-visited places where any scar you do inadvertently make won't be seen and using up fuelwood won't have as much effect.

If you do decide or need to light a fire on snow, a couple of points should be kept in mind. First, look up. The heat of your fire will rise. If the branches above are loaded with snow it will melt and slide off, probably dousing your fire. In Jack London's short story "To Build a Fire," a trapper who is cold and wet makes a fire in order to survive. Numb with cold he struggles desperately to get the fire lit, using all his matches in the process. Then, just as the fire has finally caught and is beginning to warm him, snow from the branches above crashes down and smothers it, ending his chances of survival. Probably your life won't depend on your fire, but it would be frustrating to have it extinguished.

The snow *below* your fire matters, too. Light the fire directly on it, and it will slowly sink out of sight. Instead, make a platform of fairly substantial, preferably wet, logs and build the fire on top. It will take quite a while for the heat to percolate downward. For kindling, use scraps of paper topped with bits of dry birch bark (not stripped from trees) and small twigs. A candle, if you can spare one, lit in the center will help, too.

If you carry stove fuel, sprinkle a small amount on the wood before you light it, then touch it with a match held at arm's length. I don't recommend using fuel, but I know it is a common practice. Be especially careful with white gas, which is explosive and will flare high in the air when lit. What you must never do—something I saw done in a refuge hut only a week or so before writing this—is stick a lit butane/propane stove (or any stove for that matter) into smoldering wet wood in an attempt to light it. The cartridge is quite likely to explode. On that occasion I leapt up and offered to help light the fire even though it seemed a futile task, the only fuel available being green wood brought down by a recent storm. Fortunately, the person using his stove as a flamethrower let my companion and me take over. An hour or so later my companion got the fire lit.

Wood for a fire should be gathered from the ground and never snapped off trees, whether live or dead. Winter storms usually bring down trees, as do avalanches, so unless the snow is deep there is usually fuel to be found. Collect only wood that can burn easily, leaving large logs and branches where they are. Hacking at wood with ice axes, which I have seen done, is fairly ineffective and a good way to ruin the ax.

All wood should be burned to ash and the ash scattered widely so there will be little trace of your fire when the snow melts.

Stoves

Being able to produce hot food and drink quickly is essential in winter, so a good stove is a necessity. Although it is to be avoided if at all possible, melting snow is often the only way to obtain water. As much heat is needed to produce a given quantity of water from snow as is needed to bring the same amount of water to boiling point, so a fuel-efficient stove is a good idea, especially for long tours. Melting snow is easier and quicker in a big pot than a small one, so good stability is required. Reliability is paramount, and far more important than weight or bulk, as melted snow could be your only supply of water for days at a time. The failure of your stove could be a major problem. Stove choice is an emotional matter for many people, so I am aware that some of what I have to say may provoke disagreement.

Four fuels are available: butane/propane gas in pressurized cartridges, kerosene, white gas or an equivalent such as Coleman fuel, and denatured alcohol or methylated spirits. Alcohol, more commonly used in Europe than the United States, is suitable for short camping trips but has disadvantages that discourage my using it on long trips. If you usually cook in the tent vestibule, however, note that alcohol is the safest fuel. Whichever fuel you choose, you will need more than twice the amount in winter that you require in summer. I plan on a quarter pint of kerosene or white gas per person per day, twice that much for alcohol, and a minimum of one standard-size (7 to 9 fluid ounces/198 to 250 grams) butane/propane cartridge for each person for each two days.

Butane/Propane Stoves

Butane/propane stoves (forget pure butane; the mixture is far superior, especially for below-freezing temperatures) are the simplest stoves to use and the easiest to control. They work fine when the car-

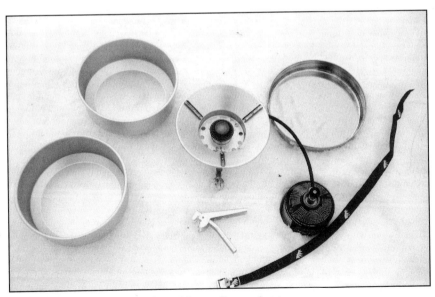

A butane/propane storm cooker with an alloy cook set.

tridge is full, but as it empties the pressure inside drops and the heat output lessens. I have found that the colder it is the quicker the flame weakens and the more time you have to spend warming the cartridge with your hands. For snow melting and long-term use I would rather have a steady flame. Stoves that attach to the cartridge via a tube are far more stable than those that screw directly in and can also be fully surrounded by a wind shield (essential in stormy weather) for greatest efficiency and fuel conservation.

Despite the advent of the butane/propane mixture, I still think that cartridge stoves are best suited to three-season use. However, if you carry a stove for the occasional brew-up or possible emergency, the lighter weight is an advantage.

Most screw-in stoves will fit most resealable cartridges. The odd one out here is Camping Gaz, whose cartridges have a different fitting. They also make stoves that clamp onto a cartridge that can't then be removed until it is empty, making for an awkward shape to pack. I would always go for a stove that can be separated from the cartridge for packing.

White Gas and Kerosene Stoves

For maximum heat output unaffected by temperature, kerosene and white gas are the fuels to choose even though the stoves that run on them are the most complex and hardest to use. Because much cooking in winter is done under the tent flysheet, kerosene is the safest choice; it is harder to light than white gas and won't ignite if spilled. However, for the same reasons it is more difficult to use and messy, as it doesn't evaporate when spilled and leaves long-lasting greasy stains. If you can get it, deodorized or purified kerosene is cleaner than the standard sort. A separate fuel such as alcohol or solid-fuel tablets may be needed to preheat (prime) the stove. The standard kerosene stove is the Optimus OOL Camper, a solid and dependable cooker that works well. For groups it is fine. For solo or duo use it is a bit on the heavy side at 39 ounces (1kg). It is also far more difficult to use than the more modern multifuel stoves.

White gas is easier to light than kerosene, though it still needs priming. It is also cleaner, evaporating fairly quickly if spilled, but it is also far more volatile and explosive. Overall, it is not a fuel to choose for using in the tent and certainly shouldn't be considered by anyone inexperienced in stove use. Automobile gasoline can be used with white gas stoves, but this isn't advisable; it clogs the jets and fuel lines. Unleaded gas, in particular, should be avoided because it has additives that block up stoves quickly. (Note that Coleman makes two Peak 1 stoves specially designed for unleaded gas.)

Multifuel Stoves

To avoid having to choose in advance between kerosene and white gas, you could buy a stove that will run on either. This is particularly important if you travel abroad, as white gas is very hard to find outside North America, while kerosene is very common. It is sometimes claimed that multifuel stoves, needing to work with two or more fuels, are bound to be less efficient because they can't be as finely tuned. MSR's figures for their two versions of the WhisperLite give a very slight efficiency advantage for the white gas model over the multifuel one used with white gas. However, the figures also show that the multifuel is more efficient when used with kerosene than the single-fuel white gas version. Overall, while the theory sounds logical, I don't think single-fuel stoves are actually superior to multifuel ones, especially as the most efficient stove I know runs on more types of fuel than any other.

The MSR X-GK II runs on several different fuels.

If you are really unsure what fuel may be available, then the stove to go for is the MSR X-GK II, which is designed to run on kerosene, white gas, gasoline, diesel, white spirits, jet fuel, and more. The X-GK comes with an efficient wind shield and is lightweight at 14 ounces (400 grams), fuel efficient, very stable, simple to use, and easily maintained in the field. It comes with a pump that plugs into a fuel bottle and burns very hot, ideal for melting snow. It is also easily field maintainable; I always carry the tiny 2-ounce (56-gram) maintenance kit, though I have rarely used it. It is very simple to convert the X-GK from one fuel to another by changing the tiny jet. All in all, I would say it is the best stove available for winter camping even when you always use white gas.

Alcohol Stoves

Alcohol is the least popular stove fuel in the United States, and alcohol stoves often receive poor reviews in the outdoor magazines. Users, however, are often more pleased with them. After *Backpacker* gave an alcohol stove a bad review they received many letters from satisfied owners.

The only real objection to alcohol is that it is not a hot fuel, roughly twice as much being needed for the same heat output as other fuels. Consequently, the weight of fuel becomes excessive on long tours where snow has to be melted. Alcohol is fine for short trips. (It is the same as the alcohol found in liquor, by the way, but with some nasty substances added to discourage swigging it.) You might find fuel alcohol listed as wood alcohol, rubbing alcohol, and marine stove fuel.

Alcohol stoves work well in the cold and in stormy weather, despite what some people claim. They are the standard expedition stoves in Sweden and Norway, where the winters are long and bitter. Four of us once used one to make hot drinks in appalling weather in the Norwegian mountains while sheltering behind a small boulder. The water was boiling by the time we had gotten our mugs ready. Other stoves might not even have been fully alight by then. Some probably wouldn't have worked at all.

Another big plus with alcohol stoves is their reliability; having no moving parts, they are nearly indestructible. They are also very safe because the fuel isn't pressurized and so are ideal for cooking in a tent vestibule and for people who feel nervous about stoves (not an

An alcohol-burning stove with a stainless steel cook set.

unjustified feeling; stoves are potentially dangerous). Although alcohol blackens the outside of pans—don't scrub this off, it speeds up heat absorption—it is otherwise a clean fuel, evaporating quickly if spilled, without leaving greasy stains.

The best alcohol stoves come with effective rigid wind shields, pan sets, and small brass burners. Several brands are available, Trangia being the best known. The only real danger comes when refilling the stove after it has gone out during use; the flame is very difficult to see, making it hard to discern whether it has, indeed, gone out. To avoid igniting your fuel bottle, pour a little alcohol into the burner cover and tip it into the stove. If the cover catches fire simply drop it into the burner well. At worst you might singe your fingers.

Stove Safety

All stoves are potentially dangerous and need to be handled carefully. Read the instructions thoroughly and practice at home before taking a stove on a tour. You need to be able to operate it safely when cold and tired and with numb hands.

When using a stove in a tent vestibule (use one inside the inner tent only if absolutely essential) make sure there is adequate ventilation: all stoves give off deadly carbon monoxide that is odorless and won't be noticed. Also ensure that nothing flammable is within touching or melting distance—provide a clear space of at least a foot in all directions. Kerosene and white gas stoves often flare during lighting. They should be lit outside and then brought in under the flysheet. Refilling a stove or changing a cartridge should be done outside, too. Take care not to spill fuel and be sure there are no naked flames such as burning candles nearby. Afterward, ensure that fuel tank and fuel bottle caps are screwed down tight before you light the stove.

Stove Accessories

Special aluminum bottles are needed for carrying liquid fuels. Quart/liter ones weigh around 6 ounces (150 grams). On really long trips gallon cans are a better choice.

Protecting your stove flame from the wind is essential, so if an adequate wind shield isn't provided you should buy or make one. MSR's foil wind shield is lightweight (1¾ ounces/50 grams) and excellent for low-profile stoves, while taller folding aluminum shields (8 ounces/225 grams and upward) are available for tall stoves from manufacturers such as Coghlan's. Be careful with stoves that have the fuel tank or cartridge situated directly under or next to the burner. They shouldn't be fully surrounded by a wind shield because they could overheat and explode.

On long trips or with large groups MSR's XPD Heat Exchanger is worth its weight of 7 ounces (200 grams). This corrugated metal circle fits around the pans and the burner and directs heat up the sides of the pan, thereby reducing boiling time. MSR claims a 25 percent increase in stove efficiency. Those who have used it regularly say it saves its weight in fuel in four days when used for cooking for two, quicker for larger groups. It won't fit pans less than 6 inches (15cm) in diameter, but although designed for MSR stoves, it can be used with other models.

A base is needed for your stove to prevent its melting down into the snow. The blade of a snow shovel can be used or a small square of closed-cell foam or heavy-duty aluminum foil.

If you have one of the small pumpless Optimus stoves like the 123R Climber (the old Svea) or the 8R Hunter, Optimus offers a minipump that vastly improves their performance in cold weather. But you have to be careful not to overpressurize the tank, which could cause the safety valve to blow, shooting out a jet of flame and liquid fuel (for this reason always point the safety valve away from yourself and the inner tent).

When the purity of your fuel can't be guaranteed, a small filter funnel can ensure that you aren't constantly cleaning your stove.

Carrying a small pricker for cleaning stove jets is also necessary unless you have a model that has a self-cleaning wire. Even if your fuel is clean, food spills can block the jet. If you forget your pricker, improvise. I was once careless enough to let soup boil over on my MSR WhisperLite Internationale, which I was running on kerosene. The flame sputtered and went out. Unable to find my repair kit, I tried needles and safety pins, but they were far too thick. Not far from my camp was a small hut that I had seen two people enter earlier, so I made my way there through the dark. Neither of the two figures lying in their sleeping bags had a jet pricker. I rummaged through the detritus in the corners of the window sill in the vain hope that previous users had left behind a pricker or something else of use. As I was leaving the hut unrewarded and convinced my trip was over, a voice called out, "Try a toothbrush bristle." Back at the tent I cut off a tiny fragment of nylon, holding it carefully between two cold fingers, and inserted it into the jet. It went in; once again the stove worked; and my trip was saved. I now carry two jet prickers, each in a different place.

Matches and Lighters

The best stove in the world is useless if you can't light it. Matches weigh virtually nothing, so I carry plenty in plastic bags in several places in my pack. Strike-anywhere wooden ones are best, though book matches are fine as spares. I carry mine in the original boxes, but waterproof plastic and metal match safes are available. Some come with a double sleeve, the inside one containing the matches, the outside one with a striker inside. Before purchasing any match safe, be sure you can open it with cold, numb fingers.

Cigarette lighters are also worth carrying—the spark alone can light white gas or butane/propane (but not alcohol or kerosene). I keep a lighter in a plastic bag, and if it is butane fuel I put it in a warm pocket before use. A refillable gasoline lighter like the classic Zippo works better. I also carry a canister of windproof, waterproof matches in my repair kit in case of emergency.

Kitchen Utensils

The same pans you use in summer will do in winter, though for snow melting it is useful to have a large pan as well. Quart pans are the minimum size needed for cooking for two. A pair should be ample; more is just extra weight. A stainless steel set complete with lid and pot lifter shouldn't weigh more than 26 ounces (750 grams). Although aluminum is lighter and conducts heat more quickly than stainless steel, it is also more likely to burn, easier to dent, scratchable, and harder to clean. Cheap ones can taint food. Good cook sets are available in both aluminum and stainless steel, so the choice is a personal one. I don't think nonstick pans are worth bothering with; they are too difficult to look after in the wilds, and you have to carry a plastic or wooden spoon to use with them.

The best pans are fairly wide and shallow. Tall ones are unstable, hard to clean, and tend to burn the food at the bottom while the top is still lukewarm. Close-fitting lids speed up cooking time and make for efficient fuel use.

Pot lifters are needed for pans that don't have handles, and some form of cotton cloth such as a bandanna is useful for holding the hot handles of those that do. Be careful of using gloves if they are made of synthetic fabric—they could melt if the metal of the pan is very hot. Plastic plates, mugs, and spoons are warmer than metal, though this isn't a major consideration. Insulated mugs keep liquids hot longer.

Small items are easily lost, so take care not to put them down in the snow. Brightly colored items are easier to find if you do mislay something. White plastic spoons are disastrous! Strips of bright-colored sticky tape can be used to mark items, making it less likely you will lose them.

Water Bottles and Vacuum Flasks

Snow-covered country can be as arid as any desert, and you can dehydrate just as fast, especially under a hot sun. Drinking plenty of liquids is important but easy to neglect. Some of the thirstiest days I have ever had have been when skiing. Drink plenty at breakfast, more than you would in summer unless you are prepared to carry a lot of liquid with you. A vacuum flask or insulated bottle is much better than ordinary water bottles, which can easily freeze in your pack, and a hot drink is very welcome in bitterly cold weather. Standard plastic-and-glass flasks are adequate until they break—which in my experience happens often and usually before I have touched the contents. Stainless steel flasks will withstand endless mistreatment. Each time mine gets another dent I think, There would have gone another glass flask. If the dents get too big, so the inner and outer layers touch, then heat will be lost and your drink will be warm rather than hot, so you should still look after these flasks. There are now many stainless steel flasks available that weigh little more than plastic ones, but some are very heavy, so check the weight before you buy. A pint (half-liter) flask is the smallest to consider. It shouldn't weigh more than 15 to 20 ounces (425 to 550 grams). Many people prefer a quart size despite the extra weight (around 24 ounces/680 grams) and bulk. Wide-mouthed flasks can be used for thick soups and even stews as well as drinks.

Water bottles are less useful except in spring, when they are less likely to freeze. You may find streams and open water to drink from then, too. If you tie a length of cord to your water bottle you can easily lower it into lakes and creeks to fill without getting your hands wet or venturing onto unstable ice or banks of overhanging snow. If there isn't any open water, bottles can be half filled with snow and put inside your pack, where movement may eventually cause the snow to melt if the temperature isn't too low. Don't pack the bottle tight with snow. If it can't move it probably won't melt.

Dehydration is most likely in spring. On hot days I like to carry both a pint-size vacuum flask and a quart-size water bottle. Keeping your water bottle buried inside the pack and wrapped in clothing makes freezing of the contents much less likely than if you carry it in an outside pocket. If the lid freezes on, warming the bottle inside your jacket is the quickest way to thaw it out. Wrapping a water bottle in an insulated sleeve made from closed-cell foam (available commercially but easy to make from foam and duct tape) will even keep liquids reasonably warm, as was demonstrated by someone on a tour, much to my surprise. A large collapsible water container is useful in camp for storing melted snow or for hauling water if there is a source nearby.

Water purification may be necessary in some areas. Filters, purifying tablets, or simply bringing water to a rolling boil for two to three minutes are all methods of dealing with contaminated water. Snow, as long as it is white and you are careful where you collect it, is generally pure.

Food

The type and amount of food you eat is determined by how much you are prepared to carry. If you really want something, take it. In winter there is no problem with food going bad; anything perishable can be stored in the snow in camp. On long tours the weight of your food can become a problem, especially for small groups. Larger groups who split the weight of tents and cooking gear and who may carry only two stoves between four or six people can manage heavier loads.

Nordic skiing is arduous, especially when you are carrying a heavy load, so you will burn a lot of energy, which you will need more calories than usual to replenish. The amount needed varies enormously between individuals—somewhere between 3,500 and 5,000 calories should be about right. When planning food as a group make sure you are confident there are enough calories. It is better to increase the communal amount than have people taking private supplies—unless they are prepared to share. One person's munching away on a hidden store of goodies while another's stomach rumbles as they sit out a storm is not conducive to good group feeling.

Fats have twice as many calories for equal weight as carbohydrates or protein, so carrying more fats will increase calories without adding too much weight to your load. Dollops of margarine can be added to your evening meal or even your breakfast porridge. Carbohydrates provide energy more quickly and are more easily digested, though, so don't rely too heavily on fats.

Carbohydrates come in two forms: simple and complex. Simple carbohydrates are digested so quickly that they can provide a rush of energy. Unfortunately, it may be followed by a slump soon afterward. Sugar is a simple carbohydrate, and while it is worth having a few sugar-based snacks along in case quick energy is required, they shouldn't make up much of your food. The energy provided by complex carbohydrates is released more slowly and steadily, making them the best for sustained skiing.

Cooking Time

When snow has to be melted for cooking you don't want to spend additional time waiting to eat, so foods that cook quickly are preferable. The best need merely to be mixed with boiling water, and they save on stove fuel, too. However, meals that need to be set aside for five or ten minutes after adding hot water will cool rapidly, so you need to either wrap the pan in warm clothing or put it back on the stove to reheat before eating.

Alternatively, on long winter evenings when you have plenty of time, it is nice to have a luxury meal that takes longer to cook.

Breakfast

On long camping tours where all food has to be carried, I stick to relatively lightweight breakfast foods such as oatmeal, muesli, or granola. They are quick and easy to prepare—important when you want to be skiing early—especially if you premix them with dried milk and sugar. If you are going to eat them hot, soaking cereals overnight speeds up cooking time. I plan on eating 4 to 5 ounces (110 to 140 grams) of cereal a day.

Fried foods aren't ideal for breakfast because they take longer to digest than carbohydrates. They are also more complicated and messy to prepare. In huts this may not be too much of a problem; when camping it can be a real hassle.

You should have plenty of liquids at breakfast, so carry lots of tea, coffee, fruit crystals, or other favorite drinks. They will improve the flat taste of melted snow. High-calorie drinks such as chocolate make sense, but I must admit I like my coffee at breakfast.

Lunch

It is possible for some people, myself included, to ski all day without eating and not run out of energy, if they are fit and have a good breakfast. This isn't a good idea, and I am not suggesting anyone should go out for the day without food, but it is good to know that it is not absolutely essential. You need food to keep warm as well as for energy. Even if you don't think you are likely to eat it, carrying some food, maybe just a small bag of trail mix, is a good idea on even a short tour just in case you are out longer than intended.

On day tours when weight is no problem you can take whatever you like. Cereals, made up largely of carbohydrates, such as bread, crackers, cookies, and granola bars, are all excellent for keeping you going. Trail mix is also good for snacking, and the fructose sugar contained in dried fruits provides slower-release energy than does refined sugar. Some foods, like bread and even candy bars, can freeze, so keep them inside the pack and not in an outer pocket. If your sandwich or chocolate does freeze, stuff it down your jacket to thaw before eating it—otherwise you risk a cold mouth and broken teeth. I don't recommend chopping up chocolate bars with an ice ax (I've seen it done!).

For a number of reasons, a succession of snacks is better than one long lunch stop. A steady supply of calories for energy and warmth is more easily provided by several small meals than one big one. And your body takes longer to digest a larger amount of food, so you should really rest for a while before you continue skiing—fine when you are relaxing on a summit in the sunshine, not so attractive when you are huddled behind a boulder in a blizzard.

My own choices for lunch foods are cheese and jam on bread or crackers, trail mix and granola and cereal bars. I particularly like Bear Valley MealPack bars, which are lightweight (around 3½ ounces/100 grams), packed with calories (400 or so per bar), and delicious. They can be bought through Alpineaire or REI (see Appendix C for addresses) if your local health-food or outdoor store doesn't stock them.

If you are ski camping you will always have your cooking gear with you and can stop and make a hot meal whenever you want. I rarely do; in bad weather I want to reach the next campsite as soon as possible, and in good weather I don't feel the need for hot food during the day. "Instant" soups or meals are the best if you do like to get the stove out during the day.

Dinner

To keep weight down on all but the shortest tour, dried foods will be needed for your evening meal. Packet soups plus dehydrated or freeze-dried meals based on pasta, quick-cooking rice, or instant potatoes are standard. Supermarkets can provide all that you need either in the form of complete meal mixes or as separate ingredients.

Check cooking times though; some are long. Check amounts, too; some are small, with few calories. Specialist freeze-dried backpacking meals are more expensive, but they are often easier to prepare, higher in energy, and contain fewer additives than supermarket brands. Of the ones I have tried I like Alpineaire the best.

Seasonings and condiments can make dried dinners more palatable, while dried milk can be added to just about anything for flavoring and extra calories. Cheese and margarine are good for this, too. I carry plenty of hot drink mixes—coffee, tea, cocoa—plus instant pudding for extra calories every couple of nights.

Weight

A diet based on the foods I have described and providing around 4,000 calories a day works out to about 2¼ pounds (1kg) of dry weight per day. If this menu seems a little basic and you would rather have some fresh foods, take them by all means. Just remember you have to carry them.

Despite my admonitions, the most important thing about the food you carry is that you enjoy eating it. So whether it is tomatoes or tagliatelle, if you like it, take it.

Emergency Food

Rather than carry anything specially designated as emergency food, I simply carry more than I think I will possibly want to eat. On day tours this means a large bag of trail mix or an extra couple of cereal bars. On camping trips it means enough food for an extra day out.

Carrying Food

Repackaging food can save a lot of weight and make organizing cooking easier, especially on long trips and with large groups. Food can be split into daily rations to ensure that you don't eat too much of something too early in a trip. Clear plastic bags (self-locking are best) make it easy to see what is what, but make sure you label similar-looking items such as potato powder and dried milk. Heavy items such as sugar should be double bagged for safety. Cooking instructions can be put in the bags with the food or written on the outside with an indelible pen.

The Kitchen in Action

In bad weather you will probably cook from inside your sleeping bag, setting up the stove in the tent vestibule. If you have more than one tent you can pitch them with the doors close together for joint cooking. We did that on the Columbia Icefield, melting snow on one stove and cooking and boiling water on the other. We produced hot food and drink more quickly than if each tent had cooked separately. If you are melting snow in the vestibule, heap lots of snow just outside so you don't run out. Make sure you collect clean white snow well away from your designated toilet area. Pink snow is contaminated with algae that will upset your stomach, and yellow snow should definitely be avoided. If you are melting snow near where another party has previously camped, go some distance—at least a hundred yards—away to collect snow and check it carefully. You don't know where previous visitors have dumped their wastewater or taken a pee.

In good weather it is much pleasanter to site your kitchen outside. In deep snow you can create as lavish a dining and cooking area

By pitching tents close together, chores like snow melting can be shared.

as you like by digging into a bank or even straight down. One of the best kitchens I can remember was at a site just above timberline in Banff National Park in the Canadian Rockies. We dug a narrow trench and cut a seat into the back of it that we lined with our insulating mats so we could sit comfortably while we cooked and ate. A small grove of stunted trees helped cut the breeze, while before us we had superb views of the peaks around Citadel Pass. In a cold wind you can dig deeper. As with other snow structures, fill in and disguise kitchen sites when you leave so the area looks as untouched as possible for future visitors.

If at all possible, use fresh water rather than melted snow. It saves time and fuel and a lot of hard work. I would rather spend an hour going to collect water than melt snow if I have the choice. There is a knack to melting snow. Don't pack a pan full of snow, then put it on the stove. If you do the snow will burn! This may sound ridiculous but it is true, and anyone who has tasted water tainted with scorched snow will know how unpalatable it is. Instead, start with a little water, if you have any, in the bottom of the pan and add small amounts of snow gradually, or put a very little snow in the pan, turn the heat down and keep stirring until it has melted. Keep adding snow until you have filled all your available containers. This is where two stoves are useful: one can be used for melting snow, the other for cooking.

Flasks can be used to store warm water overnight. Water frozen inside plastic bottles is useless, so store them inside the tent wrapped in spare clothing or stuff sacks. If you dare, you could keep them in your sleeping bag. This sounds chilly to me, with the added risk of spillage, so I have never done it. Pans of water can be left to freeze overnight and then placed on the stove to thaw (ice won't burn). I often tip my breakfast cereal into a pan of water the night before, then thaw and cook it in one step the next morning. Snow insulates well, so water will (apparently) stay liquid if full pans and bottles are buried a foot or so down. I must admit that I have never tried it. If I did I would mark the spot well so I could locate it easily the next morning even if it had snowed heavily during the night.

Wastewater should be poured into the snow at least a hundred yards from streams or lakes (use your map to determine their location if you can't tell from the terrain itself). Use the same spot throughout your camp, and cover it over with fresh snow when you leave. Only water should be disposed of. Food scraps, including liquid oils and fats (which will solidify when cold), should be carried out. Otherwise they will attract animals when they reappear in the spring (if not immediately) and help teach them to raid campsites. All empty food packets and other litter should be packed out, of course. Check before you leave for half-buried scraps—come summer they will reappear if not picked up. These same strictures apply in areas of permanent snow. Leave the area as you would like to find it: pristine.

Gear for Safety and Comfort

Snow Shovel

A snow shovel is absolutely essential. If you are caught in a blizzard and are unable to reach safety because of injury or exhaustion, digging in for the night may be the only way to survive. A snow shovel is also necessary if you have to dig someone out of an avalanche. Apart from these emergency uses, for which, hopefully, you will never have need of it, a snow shovel can be used for clearing away snow from the doors of shelter huts, leveling platforms for tents, digging wind shelters for lunch stops, digging snow-holes and snow trenches, burrowing down through the snow in search of water, and as a heat-resistant stand for a stove. I never go skiing without my shovel.

There are several lightweight models with detachable handles available. Weights are in the range of 25 to 30 ounces/700 to 850 grams. Metal blades are stronger and better for cutting through hard snow and ice than plastic ones. The weak link is the connection between the blade and the handle; check that it is strong and secure. No lightweight shovel can be very strong, so don't try to lift huge masses of snow, especially wet snow, with it if you want it to last. If the original rivets at the connection do start to rip out, as they did on mine after much use, they can be drilled out and replaced with pop rivets.

Of the many shovels on the market, the Voilé is one of the best. It has a larger-than-average blade (10 by 11 inches/25 by 27cm), a quick-release handle with the choice of two grips, and a weight of 25 ounces/710 grams. Black Diamond's Mountaineering shovel, smaller and lighter at 19½ ounces/560 grams, is another high-quality model.

There should be at least one shovel for each two members of a group. If there are only two of you, each should have a shovel, for security in case of breakage and lest the one with the shovel gets caught in an avalanche.

Light

Winter nights are long and dark. Even in the spring you will need some form of light in camp. A headlamp is essential for camping tours and in case you get caught out after dark. A hand-held flash-light is nearly useless while skiing and difficult to use when pitching the tent or cooking in the dark. Of the many headlamps available, the Petzl Zoom is recognized as one of the best. It has a battery box on the back of the head, a strap that goes over the head as well as around it, and a swivel lamp with a beam that is adjustable from spot to flood. It weighs 5 ounces (140 grams) without the battery. I have used one for more than 10 years and find it tough, efficient, and comfortable. The standard design, with a flat 4.5-volt MN 1203 alka-line battery (which also weighs 5 ounces/140 grams), is fine for most needs. For prolonged use in extreme cold it might be worth getting an accessory called the Kangaroo Pouch that can be worn inside the clothes to keep the battery warm. A spare battery and bulb should always be carried. If flat batteries are hard to find, an adapter for three AA batteries is available that fits inside the battery box. With batteries it weighs 2½ ounces (70 grams).

An alternative that looks good, especially for extreme cold, is Black Diamond's Forty Below headlamp; it works off a lithium D-cell that lasts up to 20 hours when it really is 40 below. Like the Petzl, it also has a swivel lamp and flood-to-spot adjustable beam plus an adapter for four AA cells. It weighs 6 ounces (168 grams), with another 3 ounces (84 grams) for the D-cell.

While a headlamp is essential, batteries are heavy and ineffi-cient in the cold, so it is worth having some candles along as well. A candle creates a surprising amount of warmth as well as light and can be used to dry out condensation. A pan lid or the blade of a snow shovel can be used as a stand, but a candle lantern, which can be hung from the roof of a tent, is safer and more effective. Because it is windproof, a candle lantern can be used outside as well. Lanterns that take thick stearin candles give more light than those that take only tiny night light candles. Such lanterns weigh around 4 ounces (110 grams).

Naked candles are better in snow-holes because the flame will reflect off the walls to give a wonderful sparkling light. Niches can be cut in the walls for them at whatever height you want, so safety isn't a problem.

White gas, kerosene, and butane/propane cartridge lanterns give out tremendously bright light and a lot of heat. Most are heavy, but it could be worth carrying one in a large group where weight can be shared or if sleds are being used. There are a few lightweight cartridge lanterns around, such as the Camping Gaz Lumogaz 470 lantern, which weighs 9½ ounces (275 grams) and is adjustable up to 80 watts. It gives 6 hours of continuous light with the 9-ounce (270-gram) CV270 butane/propane cartridge and 13 hours with the 19-ounce CV470 cartridge. The Bleuet 470HP stove can be run off the same cartridges (but not at the same time).

Signaling Aids

A headlamp can be used for signaling in an emergency but isn't much use unless it is dark. Many people carry a whistle as well. Six blasts or flashes followed by a pause, then six more, is the international distress signal. Plastic whistles are best, since metal ones can stick to your lips in extreme cold; the louder the better. The Storm Whistle from the All-Weather Whistle Company of St. Louis is claimed to be one of the loudest available, reaching almost 95 decibels and is audible even under water. Don't blow it unless you have to!

Alternatives, perhaps worth taking on long tours in remote country, are flares and lightweight strobe flashers. I have never carried either.

Bright colors, especially orange, can help attract attention. I like to have at least one eyeball-searing item in my pack, usually a plastic bivy bag.

In forested country probably the best way to attract attention is with a large fire of green wood that makes lots of smoke. Ideally, three fires should be lit in the form of a triangle, an internationally recognized distress signal. Plenty of matches, including waterproof and windproof ones, should be carried for lighting fires, along with a cigarette lighter and some form of starter such as a candle or a chemical fire starter. Keep matches well sealed in plastic bags. See the beginning of this chapter for details on lighting fires in winter.

Avalanche Beacon

To have much chance of surviving an avalanche, a buried person has to be found quickly, but locating a victim can be difficult. To improve your chances it is sensible to use an avalanche beacon in country where avalanches are likely. These small battery-operated devices can be used both to receive and send signals. They should be set in transmit mode and worn under clothes so they are unlikely to be ripped off in an avalanche. Everybody in the party should have compatible beacons and have practiced using them. See the section on avalanches in Chapter 5 for more information.

First-Aid Kit

Injuries do occur and you should be prepared to deal with them at least temporarily. A basic first-aid kit will cover most eventualities. You can put one together yourself, packing it in a plastic box or tough nylon pouch, or buy one ready-made. Carry a first-aid booklet, too. The following is the contents of my kit:

Sterile ambulance dressing: major bleeding
Sterile lint dressing x 2: severe bleeding
Band-Aids, assorted sizes: minor cuts
Second Skin: blisters
Antiseptic wipes: cleaning cuts and blisters
Triangular bandage: arm fracture/shoulder dislocation
Safety pins x 4
Elastic bandage x 2: ankle/knee sprains, compression for
    severe bleeding, holding dressings in place
Sterile dressing: burns
Painkillers (ibuprofen/aspirin)
Blunt/sharp nurse's scissors

This is adequate for most tours, but on a long tour in a very remote area you might want to carry extra items such as antibiotics and prescription-strength painkillers. Groups could carry splints and other items as well.

If you regularly go on long ski tours, it would be a good idea to take a first-aid course or at least study one of the books on the subject, such as James A. Wilkerson's *Medicine for Mountaineering*.

Ice Ax

In deep snow and cold temperatures, ice tools are rarely needed unless mountaineering climbs are your goal or crevassed glaciers have to be crossed. However, where there is less snow cover and the climate is warmer, ice and hard-packed snow are more likely, and an ice ax and crampons (discussed next) may be needed. I take them on tours if I suspect there may be ice on my route or if I am skiing in a high mountain area unfamiliar to me. Usually I don't carry them, preferring to turn back and find another route if I meet problems rather than carry the extra weight.

Choosing an ice ax may seem a daunting task when faced with a rack of fearsome weaponry in your local outdoor store, but there are actually only a few designs suitable for the skier (most axes being for the iced-cliff and frozen-waterfall climber). Axes for gentler terrain are usually designated "walking" or "general mountaineering" axes and look disappointingly innocuous compared with some of the climbers' tools.

The head of a good basic ice ax should have a gently curved pick with a few teeth at its end and a broad adz for cutting steps (and digging snow shelters in emergency if your shovel breaks or has been left behind). (Steeply inclined or "banana"-shaped picks are for ice climbing, as are axes with hammer heads rather than adzes.) The other end of the shaft will sport a rounded spike. Ice ax heads may be made from either a single piece of steel or two pieces welded together. The latter, while apparently not strong enough for serious climbing, are cheaper than the former and perfectly adequate for ski-touring use. Shafts may be of wood, fiberglass, or metal. Metal is the strongest and lightest but cold to hold. A rubber hand grip alleviates this and is worth looking for. An ice ax needn't be heavy or expensive. Most weigh between 18 and 28 ounces/500 and 800 grams.

Two contentious aspects of ice-ax selection are its length and whether it should be fitted with a wrist sling. Generally the recommended length is that which leaves the spike an inch or so above the ground when the ax is held by the side at arm's length. For most people this means somewhere between 60 and 80cm (axes are always measured in centimeters). There are those who argue that those

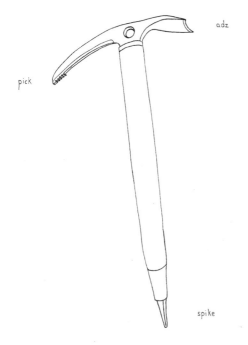

Figure 9-1. Be sure to choose an ice ax that is suitable for skiers.

lengths are too long, making using the ax on steep slopes and for self-arrest difficult. Such people, and they include experienced mountaineering instructors, recommend much shorter axes. I have used both 55 and 70cm axes extensively, and I feel much more secure with the longer ax because it can be used without the need for bending low over it.

Some axes come fitted with sliding wrist loops, and all axes have holes in the head for fitting a wrist sling if required. The arguments in favor of a wrist loop are that it makes losing the ax unlikely if you drop it, you can pull on it to take some of the strain off your wrist, and the ax can be suspended from your wrist when scrambling. The arguments against a wrist loop are that it is awkward to move from wrist to wrist when you change direction and that if you let go of the ax in a fall and it is still attached by the wrist loop it could do you an injury. I use a sling, mainly to take strain off my wrist, but I am not convinced that one is really necessary and I do find it awkward to constantly switch from hand to hand when zigzagging up or down a slope. I would definitely suggest using one if you have never used an ax before; you can always discard it when you are familiar enough with your ax to be unlikely to drop it.

Just having an ice ax isn't enough in itself. It is not a magic talisman. Every winter I am surprised at how many people I meet on tricky terrain with their axes strapped to the back of their packs. I suspect there is some element of false bravery operating, whereby nobody wants to be the first to admit to feeling more secure with ice ax in hand. This is silly. Just think how you would feel as the rescue team approached to pick you up from the bottom of a slope you wouldn't have fallen down if your ax had been in hand—that is, if you are still able to think at all. I work on a simple principle. If I am on terrain too icy or steep for skis or where the snow is too patchy for them, and I think a slip could take me very far or be at all dangerous, then I remove my ax from my pack and carry it in my hand however unlikely such a slide might be. What other people do is up to them.

Using an ice ax is quite simple. By pushing the shaft into the snow—on the uphill side if you are traversing, above or below you if ascending or descending—you have a third point of contact to help with balance. If you do slip, putting your weight onto the ax will

Carrying an ice ax between pack and shoulders. . . .

. . . gives you quick access to it.

push it farther into the snow and probably stop your slide before it has really started. If short sections of ice or hard snow have to be crossed, the adz can be used for cutting steps. For longer stretches of ice, crampons should be worn.

How you should hold the ax is another matter of debate. The most comfortable position is with the pick pointing forward; the hand can then rest on the wide flat top of the adz. You are also less likely to impale yourself on the pick if you stumble. However, to effect a speedy self-arrest the pick should be pointing backward. I carry my ax like this if I think a fall is possible.

When you are not using your ax it can be carried on the back of the pack using the straps provided, but that means you have to take your pack off when you need it. I strap my ax that way only on long approaches to the snow or when I don't expect to need it. Otherwise I slide it down my back between the pack shoulder straps to make it easily accessible. Ice axes are potentially dangerous implements, and care should be taken when carrying one. Rubber covers for the head and spike are a good idea, especially when transporting the ax to and from the mountains.

SELF-ARREST

The main reason for using an ice ax rather than a ski pole for assistance on dangerous terrain is so that you can stop a slide if one occurs. A fall that might result in no more than muddy trouser knees in summer could mean a high-speed collision with boulders lying far below when the grassy slope is covered with ice or hard snow. To self-arrest you use the pick of the ice ax, backed up by your body weight, to stop the slide.

Ideally self-arrest should be learned on a course at a mountaineering school or from an experienced friend. Once the basics are mastered they should then be practiced and practiced until they become second nature. In a real incident there won't be time to think about what to do. The aim is always to stop as quickly as possible. That cliff may not be far away.

To practice self-arrest, find a slope of hard snow with a good safe run-out so that if you fail to stop yourself you are in no danger. Make sure you have no loose bits of clothing, such as a scarf, that the ax could catch on. Practice without crampons, since these can catch in the snow and are potentially dangerous. Wear gloves, a hat, and shell clothing.

Start by lying on your back with your feet downhill and push yourself off down the slope. Hold the ax diagonally across your body with your lower hand on the shaft near the spike and the upper hand over the head, with the pick pointing away from you. Once you have picked up a little speed, roll sideways toward the head of

Self-Arrest—A feetfirst slide on your back (beginning at left): Bring the ax into the self-arrest position across the body, with one hand over the adz and the other around the lower shaft. Roll sideways onto the pick and insert it into the snow. Do not roll toward the side where the spike is; the spike may catch in the snow and cause the ax to be ripped from your hands. Tuck the adz into your shoulder and use your body weight to apply pressure to the pick until you come to a stop.

    Not pictured: For a feetfirst slide on your stomach: As above, except that you are already on your stomach.

    For a headfirst slide on your back: Plant the pick next to your body and, as you rotate around the pick, flip onto your stomach and bring the ax under your body. Apply pressure as above.

    For a headfirst slide on your stomach: Plant the pick down-slope of your head and out to the ax-head side, then pivot around the pick until your feet are pointing downhill and you can apply pressure as above. Do not let the ax get away from you as you are pivoting.

the ax and onto the pick, tucking the adz in just above your shoulder so you can use your shoulder and chest to push down on the shaft. Arching your back exerts extra pressure. Holding the ax far above your head will prevent the use of your body weight to help force the pick into the snow and may lead to its being ripped out of your hands. Make sure your lower hand is close to the spike so it doesn't swing below and stab you in the thigh, and don't roll toward the spike or it may catch in the snow. Pulling up with your lower hand keeps the spike out of the snow and helps you arch your back. Your feet and knees can be used as extra brakes, unless you are wearing crampons (which you shouldn't do when practicing), in which case you will need to keep your feet off the snow so the crampon points don't catch and flip you over onto your back.

Because you may fall in any position, you should also practice self-arrest when sliding headfirst both on your back and on your front. The self-arrest position is exactly the same as described above. The problem is how to get into it.

To arrest from a headfirst slide on your back, first grasp the ax with both hands, then place the pick off to the side into the snow so you can pivot around it until your feet are downhill and you can then stop. As you pivot you'll find you'll roll onto your stomach.

Face-down headfirst slides are harder to stop. Again, you first need to grasp the ax with both hands and place the pick off to the side and pivot around it. As your legs swing downhill, however, the ax will end up above your head. To prevent its being snatched from your hands you have to remove the pick from the snow, again pull the ax into the correct position close to your shoulder, then push the pick back into the snow.

With both sorts of headfirst fall, make sure you place the pick to the side on which it lies. Bringing it across your body is *not* a good idea; it could lead to injury or to the spike's catching in the snow. It also takes more time, and speed of recovery is very important.

Crampons

When you need an ice ax you probably also need crampons. Indeed, when you have to walk across flat areas of ice, as is sometimes necessary if the number of rocks sticking out makes skiing dangerous (to the skis if not to you), crampons are more useful than an ice ax. If I carry one I also carry the other.

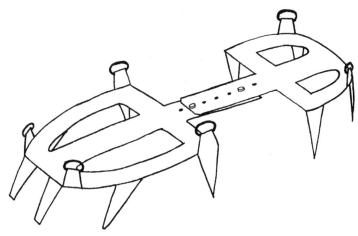

Figure 9-2. Full-length crampons are a necessity for traversing icy terrain that can't be skied.

As with ice axes, specialist ice-climbing crampons are not needed for general use. The major difference between ice-climbing and general-purpose crampons is that the former are laterally rigid. Such crampons can't be easily fitted to ski-touring boots (or if they can they are likely to fall off), as they are designed for specialist mountaineering boots with fully rigid soles. Look, instead, for hinged or flexible crampons that bend in the middle. The number of points doesn't matter unless you also intend doing some serious snow and ice climbing (which will require separate climbing boots), but full-length crampons are required—instep ones are useless on anything but very gentle slopes. Weights range from 21 ounces/600 grams to over 35 ounces/1,000 grams. "Walking" or "ski mountaineering" crampons are much lighter than fully specified climbing crampons and are perfectly adequate for ski touring. Most of the time they will be in the pack, and there is no point in carrying more weight than necessary.

Many crampons come with step-in bindings, which are much easier to use than straps; unfortunately, they won't fit ski-touring boots—whether three-pin or NNNBC. The protruding toepiece is the problem on the former, the lack of a welt on the latter, so nordic skiers still have to put up with fiddling with frozen straps with numb fingers. Smooth neoprene-coated nylon straps are the best because

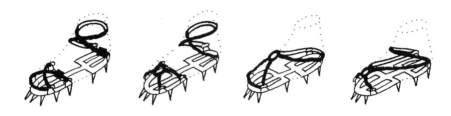

Figure 9-3.Whichever way you choose to strap on your crampons, ensure a good fit to your boots. Loose, ill-fitting crampons can be a nuisance and a danger.

they remain flexible when very cold but, unlike leather, don't stretch. There are several different methods of strapping on crampons (see Figure 9-3). They all work, but they should be practiced at home so when you have to put your crampons on in a blizzard you can do it relatively quickly.

Crampons that keep falling off are a real nuisance and can be dangerous, so it is important that they fit your boots properly. Although most crampons are adjustable, it is still best to take your

Four-part crampon straps.

Flexible, or hinged, crampons.

boots to the store when you buy a set. That way you can be shown how the straps work and how to fit them. If you use supergaiters, have them on the boots; they can affect the fit. To check the fit fix the crampon to the boot but don't fasten the straps, then pick up the boot and shake it. The crampon should stay on. An alternative method is to pick up the crampon with the boot attached and hold it upside down. If the crampon fits, the boot won't fall off.

Walking in crampons is fairly simple, but there are a couple of points to keep in mind. The first is to ensure that you keep your legs well apart. It is easy to trip over your crampons and fall flat on your face or catch a side point in your gaiters or trousers and rip them or even gash your leg. For maximum security on slopes you need to put your foot down flat so that all the points are in contact with the snow or ice. If your crampons have front points you can kick them into the snow and balance on them. This, however, is getting into the realm of climbing rather than occasional use for crossing patches of ice.

Carrying crampons is awkward. All those sharp points can easily get tangled up with other gear. Rubber spike protectors are available, but they are prone to tangling themselves and often make matters worse. I prefer to use a large Cordura nylon detachable pack pocket with a full-length side zipper that can be tucked inside the pack without danger to other items of gear. Most packs come with straps or patches for carrying crampons on the outside, the best place when they are likely to be needed often.

Rope, Harness, and Slings

Technical mountaineering gear is needed only if crevassed glaciers are to be crossed or alpine climbs are to be attempted. It is important to know how to use such equipment before you venture onto dangerous ground, but it comes under the heading of mountaineering rather than nordic touring, and this isn't the place to go into equipment selection or use. A good mountaineering textbook will give all the details.

Snowshoes

On long tours into remote country it could be worthwhile to carry a pair of snowshoes as a backup in case of ski breakage. I can think of a couple of occasions when I wish I had done so. Walking in deep, soft snow can be impossible and skiing very difficult. Snowshoes can also be useful for packing a trail for skiers to follow. And if you find you simply cannot come to grips with skiing technique, snowshoes offer an alternative way of getting about in the winter wilderness. I used a pair of Sherpa Sno-Claw Featherweights (weight 3.3 pounds/1,500 grams) on the John Muir Trail one spring before I took up skiing, and while slower than the skis some of my companions were using, they actually proved more versatile in thick forest because of their shorter length. Large ones also float better on soft, deep snow than skis do. In some far northern areas where the snow is usually soft and "bottomless," snowshoes could well be a better choice than skis.

Modern aluminum and nylon modified-bearpaw snowshoes are reasonably lightweight and small in bulk (as little as 2 pounds/865 grams for a pair of 8-by-25-inch/21-by-64cm Redfeather Redtails), making it possible to lash a pair to your pack (but remember that bigger ones float better on soft snow). If you are using a sledge, taking along snowshoes is even easier. You can use them with any boots, including mukluks, and you can get by without poles—I had none in the High Sierras—though poles help a great deal, especially when you are carrying a big pack. Snowshoes with bindings that pivot downward make climbing slopes easier, while those with metal teeth underneath will grip on ice and hard snow. In the Sierras I was surprised at the type of terrain I could cross in snowshoes even with a mammoth 100-pound/45kg pack (yes, I should have had a sledge as well). I even kept them on when fording streams, something I wouldn't do in skis.

There are quite a few brands of new-style snowshoes around, but if the romantic image of snowshoes appeals to you, bringing to mind trappers slipping softly through the snow-covered woods of the Yukon, you can still get traditional wood snowshoes. For the same flotation they will be bigger and heavier than modern styles, however. If you carry a pair for group use, make sure they have bindings that don't have to be adjusted for different-size boots.

For those who are interested in learning more, there is a good book on the subject by Gene Prater called *Snowshoeing.*

Sunscreen

Skiers are particularly prone to sunburn because they are exposed not only to direct sunlight but also to sunlight reflecting off the snow. Sunburn is caused by exposure to ultraviolet radiation. So, unfortunately, is skin cancer. It is now known that various man-made pollutants in the upper atmosphere, CFCs being the most notorious, are damaging the layer of ozone that protects the earth from much of the sun's ultralight radiation. Early in the 1990s a 20 percent thinning of the ozone layer was discovered in the northern hemisphere. This is at present only seasonal, but the problem is expected to worsen in the next few years, with perhaps an actual hole appearing like the one that has already appeared over the Antarctic, leading to increasing numbers of skin-cancer cases. Protecting your skin against the sun is now very important whether you burn easily or not. It should be noted that ultraviolet radiation can still be a danger on overcast days, especially those with high, thin cirrus clouds. Two-thirds of the day's ultraviolet radiation occurs during the middle four hours, making that a critical time to protect yourself.

To minimize the chances of suffering sunburn, a good sunscreen should be used on exposed skin in all but heavily overcast weather, even if you think burning is unlikely and even if you are wearing a sun hat. Water-resistant sunscreens are the best for skiers; they won't run off with your sweat as you slog uphill. All sunscreens have a sun protection factor (SPF) number. The higher it is, the more protection. SPFs of 15 and above give virtually total protection and are recommended for people whose skin burns easily and for skiing at high altitudes where ultraviolet radiation is stronger (it increases by 4 percent in intensity for every 1,000 feet/300 meters of altitude). Creams with SPFs of 8 to 12 applied at least twice a day are probably adequate for most people. All exposed skin should be covered. Because of the reflected light, make sure you put sunscreen under your chin, behind your ears, and in your nostrils. Sunscreen can stain clothing, so care should be taken not to slop it everywhere. Cream is preferable to liquid for this reason, though the latter is just as effective and usually cheaper.

Burned lips are especially painful and may erupt into cold sores. Although sunscreen can be applied to the lips, many brands leave an unpleasant taste and wash off quickly. Lipsticklike tubes of lip salve work much better.

Sunglasses

Sunglasses are essential to prevent snow blindness, which can occur in hazy as well as bright light. I found this out the hard way on a solo circumnavigation of the Hardangerjokul ice cap in Norway when I spent a day skiing over undulating featureless terrain in fine mist. The visibility was very poor and the navigation difficult, so I spent the day straining to see what lay ahead. I didn't wear sunglasses or ski goggles, and by the evening my eyes were very sore and itchy and I was seeing double. I was lucky that it was the last day of my tour, for I wouldn't have been able to continue; the condition lasted for several days. But I did not suffer complete snow blindness, a very painful affliction (see page 145).

Specialist glasses are needed, as many inexpensive drugstore-quality glasses won't cut out ultraviolet light. Look for glasses labeled "special-purpose" and avoid those labeled "cosmetic." Of the many types of lenses available, gray or brown ones render colors accurately and are best for most uses; glass lenses are scratch resistant, but plastic ones weigh less. Glacier glasses with side shields, though popular, are needed only for high-altitude travel, and I find they fog up easily. I have used ordinary glasses without side shields up to 15,000 feet/5,000 meters without problems. Wrap-around glasses with large lenses, often sold for mountain biking, are a good compromise. They provide almost the same protection as side shields but are much less prone to fogging. Antifog agents may help if you do have a fogging problem.

If your glasses don't come with a neck cord it is best to add one so you don't lose them in a fall. Croakies, Chums, and Eye-Ties all work. They are also useful for keeping your glasses around your neck when you take them off—pushing glasses up onto your head is a good way to have them fall off. In case you do lose a pair, carrying spares is a good idea. I carry ski goggles as my backup.

Clip-on dark lenses are available for those who wear glasses, but all the people I have spoken to say that prescription sunglasses or contact lenses with ordinary sunglasses are much better.

Ski Goggles

Ski goggles are an alternative to glasses, though they are a little restricting and more prone to condensation. I carry a pair as a spare in case of breakage or loss of my sunglasses and to wear in the worst blizzards, especially when skiing straight into a storm, when they give more protection than any glasses. Double-lens models suffer less from condensation than single ones. Yellow lenses give the clearest visibility in flat light or mist.

Repair Kit

A few basic items are needed in case gear needs repairing. The most useful are strips of sticky-backed ripstop nylon, which can be used for patching tears in any nylon item, from the tent flysheet to the sleeping bag. The manufacturers' repair kits for the Therm-a-Rest mattress and MSR stoves should be carried if these items are used. A needle and thread come in handy, too. I carry the Black Diamond Expedition sewing kit, which contains a sewing awl, two buttons, two safety pins, a cotter pin (for rethreading drawcords), two needles, and several weights of strong thread, all packed with instructions into a neat leather pouch. The total weight is only 1½ ounces/40 grams, yet with this kit you can repair everything from packs to socks. I keep all these items in a zippered stuff sack along with the repair items for ski gear described in Chapter 2.

Health and Hygiene

Injury rather than illness is the main concern in winter, but that doesn't mean that basic hygiene should be neglected. The paucity of water and the cold temperatures usually hold washing to an absolute minimum. However, all skiers should wash their hands after going to the toilet and before they handle food. This is especially important when communal cooking is undertaken. If water is at a premium, antiseptic wipes can be used. They are also nice for washing one's face, and they can help prevent chapped skin.

The key aim when siting a toilet is to make sure that it is at least several hundred yards away from any water source. If you are not sure where these lie, check your map. Choose a spot where it is unlikely anyone will want to camp, stop for lunch, or dig a snow-hole; stay away from obvious ski routes, sheltered flat areas, and the base of steep banks. Whether you should bury feces or leave it on the surface where it will decay faster depends on whether anyone else is likely to come that way. In popular areas bury, in remote ones don't. In deep seasonal snow buried feces will reappear come spring, so you need to think about where it will lie. In thin or patchy snow, shallow cat holes should be scraped or dug in bare earth or gravel in often-visited areas.

Toilet paper is another problem. It lasts far longer than feces and shouldn't be left to decorate the wilderness. If possible, burn it, as long as there is no fire danger: sparks and bits of burning paper blown off by the wind could set dry bushes and trees on fire, so just because the ground is snow covered doesn't mean burning paper is safe. When you can't burn toilet paper, seal it in a plastic bag and pack it out to a waste bin or a hut with a wood stove or fireplace. To avoid this problem don't use toilet paper. Snow is much better.

Leaving the tent for a pee in the middle of the night in a blizzard or even in just very cold temperatures is not pleasant. The solution is a pee bottle. It should have a wide mouth and be very clearly marked so no one mistakes it for a water bottle. In the morning it can be emptied out at the toilet site. Sani-Femme, Lady J, and Freshette make devices that enable women to use pee bottles easily.

Chairs

Chairs are not something I had ever considered carrying into the wilderness at any time of the year until the early 1990s, when several kits appeared on the market that enable you to turn your sleeping mat into a comfortable seat. To my surprise, when I tried one I found it excellent. I have a Cascade Designs Therm-a-Rest'R chair kit that weighs just 10 ounces/284 grams and rolls up small. It is made of nylon with composite side stays. I carry it on the outside of my pack rolled up with my mat already in it. At first I took it only on camping trips, but now I find it coming along on day tours more and more often.

Entertainment

At some point, every winter camper ends up sitting out a storm in a tent, snow-hole, or hut. The longest I have spent on one site is four days, only one of which was spent skiing. For such occasions, and for long winter evenings, some form of entertainment is a good idea, unless your companions are really sparkling conversationalists. Books are my favorites, though cards are less antisocial. Some people like to listen to personal stereos or radios. I don't, but I occasionally carry one for listening to weather forecasts. If you do use a radio, always use headphones or earpieces. Others may be there for the silence. I always take some form of entertainment. Nothing is worse than sitting watching snow fall day after day, and working out on the map all the places you could ski in if only it were clear gets depressing after a while.

Another way of passing the time is to keep a diary of your tour. I carry a small hard-backed notebook and a few pens, kept with other papers in a zip-around proofed nylon case, and I try to write something every day. I am always surprised at how many people keep no record of their trip.

A Ski Tour in the Canadian Rockies

The purpose of the information gathered in this book is to help you plan and carry out successful wilderness ski tours. At times the details of equipment and techniques—from types of ski to stove fuel, technical clothing to snow shovels, from how to dig a snow-hole to bushwhacking on skis, from turns for powder snow to stream crossings—may seem to overwhelm the whole point, which, after all, is to go skiing. Departing from this emphasis on the functional, this final chapter tells the story of one ski adventure, a tour that didn't work out exactly as intended. Mistakes were made and plans changed, but there were wonderful and exciting moments, too. I hope this story gives a taste of the opportunities that learning ski touring makes possible.

> It should be emphasized that the Columbia Icefield . . . contains many regions of huge crevasse fields. In the spring, these snow-covered crevasse fields can be very difficult to perceive. Roped travel with complete glacier-travel and winter-camping equipment and a strong, self-reliant party is essential. This is advanced ski mountaineering.

Unfortunately, we did not read these words or the other advice in Kunelius and Biederman's guidebook *Ski Trails in the Canadian Rockies* until after our 10-day epic on the largest ice field in the Rocky Mountains, the 200-square-mile Columbia Icefield from which meltwater runs to the Atlantic, Pacific, and Arctic oceans and which is notorious for poor weather. The four of us, Scott Steiner and Clyde Soles from Colorado, Todd Seniff from Vermont, and myself from

Britain, intended to cross the ice cap, then head south across the series of ice fields that runs along the Continental Divide, the watershed of North America, to Kicking Horse Pass, west of Lake Louise in Alberta, Canada. This was already our second plan, the first, to make a continuous six-week ski tour through the heart of the Rockies from Banff to Jasper, Alberta, having been abandoned because of the lack of snow at low levels following a warmer-than-usual winter.

Where snow did lie it was soft, sugary in texture, and knee to waist deep. One tussle with this depth hoar, as it is called, during an attempt to place a food cache near the headwaters of the Alexandra River had revealed that attempting to travel far in it was simply unrealistic. It took an exhausting hour to wade—ski is the wrong word—just a few hundred yards.

We still needed to plant a cache, however, so we turned to the permanent snows of the glaciers and ice fields and a route in via the Athabasca Glacier, whose toe almost reaches the Icefield Parkway, a spectacular road that runs through Banff and Jasper national parks. Over its five-mile length the Athabasca Glacier rises more than 3,000 feet, most of it in the upper third, which is compressed into three icefalls. We reached only the second of these before we were forced by driving spindrift, strong winds, and poor visibility to dump our loads on the crevassed shelf below, where we hoped we could find them again, and escape back to the road. The day trip was good practice in roped skiing, something we had done little of before, and glacier travel. We wore climbers' sit harnesses clipped to chest harnesses made from slings and had prussik loops tied to the main rope in case of a fall into a crevasse. We all wore avalanche beacons under our clothes. Going up roped, with skins on our skis, was easy; coming back down was a little more problematic!

If we had read what Kunelius and Biederman had to say about the route up the Athabasca we might have thought twice about using it:

> The Athabasca Glacier offers little in the way of easy travel. . . . The lower section is liberally covered with millwells, some very wide and deep. Travel directly through the icefalls has become extremely difficult . . . , many accidents adding to their reputation. Some mountaineers prefer a route that hugs the edge of the glacier, which lessens some of the crevasse problems but severely exposes one to the snow and ice avalanches pouring off the cliffs of Snow Dome.

We could see small slurries sliding constantly down the over-hanging glaciers and vertical snowfields that line the Athabasca, and we decided to stay well out in the center. The snow being firm and easy to ski, we returned from our cache-laying convinced the Athabasca Glacier was the key to the problem of access to the ice fields. We decided to use it as a route onto the Columbia Icefield, then explore northward from a base camp, perhaps climbing some peaks en route, before picking up our food cache and continuing our journey southward, where the bulk of our route lay. It was the only way we could see to reach the main ice fields without a long and difficult approach through the depth hoar in the forests.

Having left our cache on the Athabasca Glacier, two days later we were back again, heavily laden with winter camping gear and 10 days' food. The weather forecast was inconclusive: a little snow, maybe some cloud, definitely unsettled, could clear. . . . We went anyway, glad to be setting off at last. We found a way through the crevasses and icefalls without too much difficulty, though we had to cross some wide and deep, open crevasses by way of snow bridges. They were quite solid, but we approached them carefully and crossed one at a time. The flat shelves between the icefalls were more danger-ous because the crevasses were hidden. On several occasions one of us broke through, only our skis and the tension from the rope pre-venting a fall into the depths below.

A last steep climb took us under the impressive towering cliffs and hanging glaciers of Snow Dome and onto the vast plateau of the Columbia Icefield. Across the whiteness rose the distant peak of Mount Columbia, highest in the region. At 9,900 feet we decided to make our first camp.

As we were now exposed to the full blast of a bitter, snow-laced wind, we dug a large pit to shelter the tents on the lower slopes of Snow Dome. The work kept us warm, and in the tents the tempera-ture rose to a reasonably comfortable +26°F. "Tomorrow probably heading for Columbia," I wrote in my journal. But it wasn't to be— we were to stay on this site for the next four nights; building a snow shelter would have made sense for such a long stay.

Dawn saw snow falling and the tents half buried. Todd and I dug them out. The visibility was nil. Moving on would be dangerous and difficult, so we settled into the tiny tents for the day—reading, brewing hot drinks, playing cards, writing in our journals, poring over maps, trying not to eat too much of our precious food, and taking turns digging out the tents.

This chore involved a long struggle to put on shell clothing and boots. Then it was up with the flysheet zipper and the sudden brutal shock of the white wind and the desolate reality that lay beyond the doorway. At the edge of our pit a half-buried huddle of packs, skis, ropes, fuel cans, and other detritus protruded from the snow. Around the tents snow had piled up several feet, while cornices had built up on the sides of the pit. Farther afield all was white and flat, the land and sky united. No horizon, no solidity, just the fading away of a pale, insubstantial haze. The tents cleared of snow, an even more lengthy struggle ensued to get back in without bringing too much snow along. The snowfall kept up all day.

That night we dug out the tents at 9:00 P.M., then 1:00 A.M., then again at six, taking a good hour to clear the snow each time. I was the first one out at daybreak, and as the gray light slowly spread I caught occasional glimpses of the black edges of cliffs high on Snow Dome and, far above, whirling tatters of cloud. A short excursion enabled Todd and me to work out a way of navigating in the whiteout with a system of hand signals between the second person on the rope—who held the compass—and the leader, who could be stopped only by a tug on the rope. I was surprised to find that we couldn't manage more than 30 yards or so in a straight line. After an hour we turned and followed our almost-buried tracks back to the snow-besieged camp. We concluded that with great care we could travel safely in these conditions, albeit very slowly.

Back at the camp Scott and Clyde, bored with lying in the tents, had begun to dig a snow cave in the back wall of the tent pit. Todd and I joined in, and several hours later we had a large roomy cave in the making—when disaster struck. I saw the center of the roof start to sag as Scott scythed his shovel through a section to smooth it out. Then the roof broke into slabs and collapsed. I was closest to the entrance and dived for it, managing to get an arm and then my head out before the falling roof trapped me. Fortunately, Clyde had gone to the tents to brew a hot drink. I yelled to him and he heaved me out. We immediately began digging for the others. Scott freed himself by simply pushing his head upward until he broke through. Nobody was hurt. Further digging eventually recovered Scott's hat and shovel, the only missing items. We were puzzled by the collapse because the roof had been about four feet thick. We could only think that the fresh snow hadn't consolidated properly. None of us had tried to dig a cave on a flat surface before, being used to digging into steep banks. In retrospect, we should have heaped up a huge mound of snow, left it to settle, then dug into it, the best way to build a shelter on flat snow unless you are skilled at igloo construction.

Blue skies, sun, and some views gave us hope for the next day. In the evening the wind dropped and moonlight spread over the pale snow.

Day three on the ice field dawned with a weak sun filtering through the murk. We seized the opportunity to retrieve our food cache from below the icefall and then climb the 11,500-foot Snow Dome in the afternoon. As we descended to our food dump, a steady stream of small but noisy avalanches poured off the slopes of Snow Dome; we stayed out in the middle of the glacier, taking great care on the steeper slopes. Crevasses visible on the way up three days earlier were now hidden, and we broke through the thin crusts of several; again we would have disappeared into them if we hadn't been on skis and roped together. A party of four were ascending the glacier under the walls of Snow Dome—they were the only people we were to see during our 10-day crossing of the Columbia. The wheeling and diving black shapes of several ravens marked our food cache, but none of the bags had been damaged.

The cache retrieved, we began our climb up Snow Dome, a long arduous slog on skins into an increasingly bitter wind. Wearing stretch bibs, a midweight base layer, windproof synthetic-filled sweater, Sympatex shell jacket, polyester ski hat, polypro headover, gloves, and overmitts I still felt cold. To the west rose Mount Columbia, steep and grim; far below were the tiny dots of the four other skiers building an igloo. The misty summit came and went in a blur of cold, and we were soon enjoying the descent, through wind crust at first but then good, new powder. Roped skiing was difficult, with all of us taking unexpected falls when the rope suddenly went tight. Halfway down we unroped, hoping our speed would carry us over any hidden crevasses. We all reached camp safely; either our tactic had worked, or there were no crevasses.

That night the storm returned, the howling wind keeping us

awake, but the next morning we decided to move on anyway and spent the day moving cautiously and slowly southward over the heart of the ice field toward the Castleguard Glacier. I broke trail all day, seeing very little, not even my skis most of the time, eventually finding myself on steep, slabby slopes that felt very insecure. I traversed downward away from them, to be suddenly confronted with a deep, black chasm that loomed out of the whiteout. Retreat seemed the only option, and we climbed back up to the flat plateau and pitched camp in the now-familiar howling wind. The expedition was in the balance; the growing feeling that we had to get off the ice field was set against our continuing desire to progress south.

Three more days of frustration tipped the balance decisively toward escaping the ice fields. We spent the first day in the tents again as the storm raged on, trying to keep warm and prevent our clothing and sleeping bags from becoming any damper. Only at 9:30 in the evening did the clouds lift to gradually reveal a serrated mountain horizon ringing our white plain. The clearance was but a prelude to a stronger blast of storm, and we slept badly as a ferocious wind rattled the battered tents. Spindrift piled up between the inner and outer, further shrinking our limited living space. At dawn we choked down a hasty breakfast of granola bars and packed up, unable to face another day in our damp bags.

We skied west and descended toward what we thought was the Castleguard Glacier. As we started down a steep, narrow icefall hemmed in by towering, unstable-looking walls and seracs I had an uncomfortable feeling that we had gone wrong. When we dropped below the clouds an open, flat-bottomed valley appeared that didn't accord with the map. A thousand-foot-plus drop-off finally stopped us. We were too far to the west and descending the wrong glacier. The canyon below was that of Bryce Creek, not the Castleguard River. We slowly climbed back up to the plateau to camp yet again in the storm. This was our third camp on the ice field but our seventh night. Our eighth would be spent there, too.

Another long, tedious day in the tents. The wind whistled and whipped past. Several feet of fresh snow fell. Not once did the clouds lift. In our double-skinned tent, although everything was damp, we did manage to reach a temperature of +70°F. Todd came over from his Gore-Tex tent to say that he and Clyde couldn't get warm and their down sleeping bags, although Gore-Tex covered, were soaked. He had shivered the previous night away. Escaping from the ice field was becoming urgent.

We woke to stillness. No wind, no snow. Outside, the skies cleared slowly and Snow Dome appeared across the ice field. Descending the Castleguard Glacier under the ramparts of Castleguard Peak took us through a complex but beautiful icefall with many open crevasses and long, curving snow bridges. Then easy downhill running took us off the glacier, through a barely ski-width corridor under an overhanging curl of snow that we skied quickly but one at a time, and into a steep-sided, narrow canyon overhung by slopes that looked ready to avalanche any minute. We had no choice but to thread a way down this gorge. Our relief was great when we reached the safety of the forest and had only arduous bushwhacking in depth hoar to contend with. That night we camped on a gravel bar in the center of the Castleguard River valley and lit a campfire to dry our gear. The view, with Watchman Peak towering above us, its hanging glaciers green in the evening light, was spectacular, but we all knew before we discussed it that, for now, we had had enough.

Sun, snow showers, and superb scenery were the backdrop to a day of very hard bushwhacking in the forest as we descended the banks of the river canyon above a series of gorges. Camp that night was on a superb site on another gravel bank by the Alexandra River. High above, a ring of peaks, cirques, and glaciers dominated the forest. But there was nowhere to pitch the tents, the gravel being too soft to hold stakes, so we bivouacked under the stars. The temperature fell to +24°F.

Our southward route lay across the Alexandra and back up onto the ice fields, but our hearts weren't in it anymore. A cloudy dawn settled the matter. Up there the wind would still be howling, the snow blowing, the visibility nil. We headed for the road. The ski out was mostly on good snow in superb scenery, though we did have to walk a few sections and ford many ankle-deep streams. In the final disaster of the trip, one of Todd's skis snapped in half and he was forced to posthole through the deep snow. They were heavy-duty telemark models that were brand-new at the start of the trip. At least we weren't still up on the ice field. That evening we reached the Icefields Parkway. Our crossing of the Columbia Icefield had taken 11 days.

The battering had taken its toll. Our plan for a continuous route was one casualty. Now, half the party—Clyde and Scott—decided they had had enough and were returning home. Todd and I elected to stay and try to retrieve something from the dreams that had been blown away on the Columbia. When I had first researched the area after Scott's original proposal for a ski tour there I had been enthused by pictures and descriptions of Mount Assiniboine and was determined to visit it. So now I put forward a plan to Todd and, two days after coming down from the Columbia, we dumped our spare gear in the Banff bus station and caught the bus to the Sunshine alpine ski area. The storm we encountered on the ice field had been general, and much new snow had fallen—good news for us: it was now late April and the season was coming to an end.

The classic ski tour from Sunshine to Lake Magog at the foot of Assiniboine is often done in one day when there is a good, hard trail in place. It took us three and a half. On the first afternoon we made good progress across the glorious skiing terrain of the Sunshine Meadows to make camp on a superb site in the shelter of a few wind-stunted firs below the squat block of Citadel Peak. The great pyramid of Assiniboine itself appeared once in the distance, briefly towering over the surrounding peaks.

Light snow fell during the night, but even so we expected to make good progress the next day. But 10 minutes after leaving camp the cable binding ripped out of one of Todd's skis—his second pair of the trip, borrowed from Scott after the demise of his first set during the retreat from the Columbia. Under the binding we saw a pincushion of holes where other bindings had been screwed on. Although we could have effected a makeshift repair, it seemed unwise to continue farther into the wilderness with damaged skis.

When we had finished cursing, we came up with a plan: without skis we sank deep into the snow, making foot travel impossible. Todd, the faster skier, would set off back to Sunshine on my skis with his broken pair strapped to his empty pack. He left me sitting on a foam mat beside a mound of gear with a tarp slung behind two ski poles as a windbreak. Four hours later he returned with a pair of rental skis.

We pushed on late in the day, with the snow softening rapidly. We reached Citadel Pass quickly, then easy running took us down the first part of the descent to Golden Valley. This was avalanche territory, and we crossed some old avalanche debris, but despite being soft the snow seemed well consolidated and stable. Once the slopes steepened and we were in the forest, we encountered soft sugar snow that was very difficult to ski through. In the deep forest of the valley bottom the snow was so soft and deep that we switched to walking. A few hundred yards of desperate postholing and we decided skiing was easier after all. A few more hundred yards and skiing again seemed impossible. It was skis on, skis off, skis on, skis off over endless little knolls for what seemed hours. We both fell over frequently, becoming sodden from the wet snow. To add to the frustrations, it began to rain. We headed for Policeman's Meadows where, we had heard, there was a trapper's cabin left open for casual use. We didn't fancy trying to camp in the wet, deep snow in the forest. The last mile and a half took two hours, and we were soaked to the skin and exhausted as we struggled across the meadows in the fading daylight to the welcoming cabin from whose chimney streamed a column of smoke.

The dark, low-roofed cabin felt luxurious. Warmth welled from the hot woodstove, stoked up from the plentiful supply of logs by Jari, the skier already in residence. As we stripped off our wet gear and donned warm clothes he told us he had flown in the previous afternoon on one of the thrice-weekly helicopters to Assiniboine Provincial Park and had spent the day skiing down to the cabin. It had taken him seven hours. He had intended skiing down to the nearest road the next day, where he had a lift arranged, but he was worried by the state of the snow in the forest, a worry that the tale of our struggle did nothing to alleviate.

He was right to be concerned. We spent the next day relaxing while the storm blew over and the skies cleared, hoping a cold night would ensue and harden the snow. Jari set off to descend to the Simpson River. We weren't surprised when he returned at 3:30 P.M., having failed to make any real progress. Deep, soft snow had soon stopped him in the forest. Then he had tried to cross Citadel Pass but had been driven back by strong winds.

A clear sky and a hard frost saw us off to an early start the following morning for Lake Magog on snow that had changed radically, now being firm and easy to ski. Jari was with us, hoping to have the park ranger at Assiniboine radio that he was safe but would be a day late for work! He planned on taking the next helicopter out.

With Jari as guide we skied through the woods of Golden Valley below the ragged cliffs of Golden Mountain and then over the bumps—boulders in summer—of the Valley of the Rocks, with superb scenery all around. As we left the valley we saw that the whole slope to the north had avalanched. Fresh ski tracks cut across the base of the debris. We felt safer out in the center of the valley. The heat of the sun increased, but we were climbing and the snow stayed firm. We rounded a corner to view the magnificent soaring spire of 11,871-foot Mount Assiniboine, a classic mountain, a mountain of dreams, the perfect mountain of childhood memories. Assiniboine grew closer, towering over the lesser, splendid peaks on either side, as we skied gloriously past snow-covered Og Lake. By 4:00 P.M. we had reached Lake Magog at the foot of the peak, where there are a private lodge and some basic log cabins that are rented to skiers and backpackers by the park authorities. We were welcomed by the winter warden, Nena, with tea and firewood and were soon safely ensconced in one of the cabins and feeding the woodstove with logs. Firewood is provided for those, like us, who ski in under their own power. Those who come in by helicopter are expected to bring their own.

"Fleabane" was to be our home among the Naiset Cabins for four nights. With the woodstove roaring each evening it was a snug haven from the cold, and we were able to dry out wet gear every night. We abandoned the idea of skiing out of the area; all routes involved descending into the forest, and we knew too well how rotten the snow was lower down. Instead we decided on the decadent luxury of a helicopter escape. A ridge of high pressure crept in, so we had three days of hot sun and good skiing, during which we explored the area, climbing 9,300-foot Mount Cautley (with Jari before his flight out) and Nublet; visiting Wonder Pass, a magnificent viewpoint, and the cirques below the Assiniboine glaciers; and skating across Lake Magog. On one day we climbed into a cliff-rimmed cirque below Terrapin Mountain from where we watched and listened to the many spring avalanches thundering down the gullies on Wedgewood Peak. The whole area is strikingly beautiful, one of the most impressive mountain areas I have visited. The peaks, glaciers, lakes, and forests complement each other, making for a perfect symmetry far beyond any artistry human beings can achieve. By 2:00 P.M.

each day the snow was too soft to ski, so we spent the afternoons reading, sunbathing, and talking to the warden and her five-year-old daughter, Layla. Not many young children are lucky enough to spend their winters in a place like this.

The only upset to our idyll was the visit one night of a porcupine to our cabin. It wedged itself into the tunnel between the snow that had fallen from the roof and the cabin wall and proceeded to try to eat the cabin. The sound was marginally less abrasive than that of a chainsaw and nearly as loud. Initially, I had no idea what it was, but Todd muttered the word *porcupine,* leaped out of his sleeping bag, grabbed the hut broom, and went outside. The noise ceased immediately, and he was back inside within a few minutes.

Within a few minutes more the noise had begun again. "Someone else's turn," said Todd. Jari appeared to be asleep. Wearing just a sweater, underpants, and down bootees I ventured out into the snow clutching the broom. I then spent a good half hour running around in the middle of the night trying to get the porcupine to vamoose. I couldn't reach it when I poked the broom along the tunnel, and I wasn't going to crawl in too close to the beast's spines. I climbed onto the cabin's low roof and tried poking the porcupine with ski poles and broom handles from above, falling off the roof several times in the process. I finally managed to get the by now presumably terrified creature to leave the tunnel by lying down in the entrance and lobbing snowballs at it. When they hit, it fled out of the far end. Wanting to thoroughly discourage it from returning, I pursued it across the snow, yelling loudly, until it took refuge up a tree. Cold and exhausted, with grazed and bruised legs, I returned to the cabin and slid gratefully back into my sleeping bag. Todd and Jari thought the whole performance, heard from the warm depths of their sleeping bags, hilarious.

The lodge was built and the area opened up to skiers by a Norwegian named Erling Strom early this century, I learned from his autobiography *Pioneers on Skis,* which I borrowed from Nena. When a party led by Strom ascended the Columbia Icefield to climb Snow Dome in the 1930s, they ended up by mistake on a shoulder of Castleguard Mountain in a whiteout. I was pleased to learn that others had found navigating up there a little problematic!

An overnight low of +38°F during our last night marked the end of the season, so it was with only slight regret that we boarded the helicopter, the last of the winter, for the 20-minute flight back to Canmore and civilization. Just what level of civilization we could not have imagined—that evening we found ourselves disbelievingly lodged in the very grand and imposing Chateau Lake Louise, not the usual accommodations for a couple of impoverished skiers. The last night we had spent in town we had bivouacked in swampy woods near the bus station! The unexpected rise in our standard of living was courtesy of Jari, who met our helicopter in Canmore in his Mercedes. We knew him as a fellow wilderness skier. To guests of the chateau he was better known as the head chef. His hospitality and friendship ensured that the rest of our rather fragmented Rockies ski expedition would be spent in comfort and style. A superb meal of Rocky Mountain trout, specially prepared for us by Jari, made for a fine end to our Assiniboine trip.

With 10 more days and virtually no low-level snow left, Todd and I returned to the ice fields to ski the classic Wapta Traverse from Bow Lake to Wapta Lake, climbing some peaks along the way. On the first day of May we set off with heavy 10-day loads, wading through the knee-deep, slushy snow-ice along the edge of Bow Lake. We camped the first night on a bluff in the forest above the snowmelt-swollen Bow River, with views up to the permanent snows of Bow Glacier and, perched on a rock outcrop at the edge of the ice, Bow Hut, our destination the next day—just two miles away but much higher. Immediately above the camp towered the steep northern slopes of Crowfoot Mountain. They were almost snow-free, though we did see one big avalanche come crashing down. Having been warned by the Banff National Park ranger when we collected our wilderness permits that the first bears were out of hibernation and on the move, we cooked and ate a hundred yards from the tent and used the climbing rope to hang our food high in a tree. But it was noisy Clark's nut-crackers that tried to steal our food, rather than bears.

The summer trail, mostly snow-free, led on through the forest to a ford of the river, beyond which enough icy snow remained for us to start skiing again. The river was in full spate, powering down the gorge below in great surges of whitewater, so we stayed high up on the bank, crossing much avalanche debris in the gullies that split the mountainside. In places we had to remove our skis to negotiate large boulder fields. Slowly and with much hard work we progressed upward. Finally we climbed into a desolate snow- and moraine-dotted cirque backed by hanging glaciers that marked the edge of the Wapta Icefield. Much of the snow had gone from the lower moraines, leaving a mixture of soft mud and pebbles on the steep slopes above the cirque that led to Bow Glacier and Bow Hut. As we labored up, a huge avalanche poured down cliffs from the ice field above. (It looked oddly familiar. Back home I found a picture of an avalanche in exactly the same place adorning the front cover of Tony Daffern's *Avalanche Safety for Skiers and Climbers*.) Bow Hut appeared before us. The two-mile journey had taken four hours.

Three basic mountain refuges are spread out along the Wapta and Waputik ice fields, all on the 8,150-foot contour line, and we had booked into them, courtesy of Banff National Park, not fancying more nights spent cowering in a tiny storm-swept tent. Bow Hut, a large fiberglass construction resembling an upturned boat, was cold but roomy and windproof. This refuge was designed by a mountaineer-architect named Philip Delesable and built in a weekend in 1968 from prefabricated materials brought in by helicopter. The cost was met by Peter and Catherine Whyte, two local artists and mountaineers whose artwork can be seen in a gallery in Banff. The hut has tables, benches, and sleeping platforms for 18, complete with open-cell foam pads. There are no stoves for cooking or heating, though, so visitors must carry stoves and fuel plus warm clothes and sleeping bags. The hut is in a superb spot, with the soaring rock cone of St. Nicholas Peak rising above the white slopes of the ice field to the west and the peaks of the Front Ranges spreading out above dark, forested valleys to the east.

We were glad of the hut the first night as a bitter wind blew horizontal snow across the slopes outside. By dawn a few inches of fresh powder had fallen. By afternoon blue sky was appearing, and we made our first venture onto the ice field proper to view the magnificent circle of peaks ringing the white plateau.

A clear day following, we went north a few miles to the Peter and Catherine Whyte Hut so that we could turn around and ski the complete traverse. Below the hut lay an ice-covered pool at the foot of a glacier snout. We tramped down with the hut shovel and bucket and quickly dug through the slush to fresh water, saving us from having to melt snow.

The hut book registered a party of four that had passed through on one of the final days of a complete Jasper–Lake Louise high-level traverse on April 14, a day we had spent trapped in our tents on the Columbia. Three skiers from Banff arrived just before another storm blew in. It raged all afternoon, resulting in some immaculate powder on the slopes above the hut; we went out and skied in the whiteout that evening.

That storm was the last of the trip; there followed six days of perfect weather. Days of clear skies and hot sun were preceded by freezing, star-filled nights. Mount Rhondda was the start of this joyous finale to our skiing adventures, climbed as a diversion on our way back to Bow Hut. The tiny, shattered, cliff-rimmed summit gave magnificent and far-ranging views: nearby Mount Baker, the vast expanse of the Wapta Icefield, Mount Ayesha, Mount Collie, and more and more white peaks rippling into the horizon. Near the hut we met two skiers from Switzerland. They were on their honeymoon! They wanted to try telemarking, they said, and the Swiss Alps were too steep. By early afternoon the snow was too wet and soft for skiing, so we sat outside watching the mountains.

Next came 10,400-foot Mount Gordon, a two-hour climb from Bow Hut. Again superlative views, superlative skiing, and superlative weather. Moving on we crossed the St. Nicholas Peak–Mount Olive col and skied down Vulture Glacier to Balfour Hut, a wooden cabin situated on moraines between the Wapta and Waputik ice fields that provided tremendous views of 10,735-foot Mount Balfour, the highest peak in the area. To the west, Wave Creek led down to the deep cleft of the Yoho Valley.

By midafternoon the snow was too soft for skiing, so we walked over to the snout of one of the many icefalls that surround the hut and did a little basic ice climbing. Todd managed a fair height in his stiff boots and rigid crampons, but my articulated crampons kept falling off my more flexible boots, and I didn't get far. The icefall was a spectacular series of narrow crests and overhanging seracs shining green and blue in the sun. The ice was running with water, and by the time we coiled the rope and returned to the hut we were quite wet.

Visitors' sign-in books are always worth reading, but the one in Balfour proved more informative than usual. It contained a copy of an article from the *Canadian Alpine Journal* by Graeme Pole entitled "A Mountain Flooded with Ice: Mount Balfour." We learned that

Balfour was named after Scottish botanist John Hutton Balfour and that the peak forms a ridge running four miles along the Continental Divide between Balfour Pass and Lilliput Mountain. Geologically, wrote Pole, it is a "glacially sculpted shale pyramid atop stratified quartzite." Eight of the 10 principal glaciers of the Waputik Icefield rise on Balfour's slopes. W. D. Wilcox described Balfour as "a mountain flooded in ice" in 1896 in his book *Camping in the Rockies*. At that time the first ascent was a major mountaineering aim. It was achieved on November 11, 1898, by C. L. Noys, C. S. Thompson, and G. M. Weed via the southeast ridge and the Fairy Glacier. Balfour Pass was first crossed in a 12-hour expedition from the tongue of the Yoho Glacier to Lake Louise in 1901, while the first traverse of the mountain was done in 1933. Skis reached the summit two years later. The present hut, successor to many others, was built in 1971.

As the perfect weather continued, we spent an exhilarating day skiing the Diableret Glacier on the west side of Mount Balfour after meandering along the Diableret Spur overawed by the views. The ski down was so good that I climbed back up three more times just to enjoy it again, abandoning the fun only when the snow became so soft it was a struggle to regain the hut.

Continuing south meant climbing the steep, crevassed, and avalanche-prone Balfour Glacier, so we made a very early start after a night during which the wind howled around the hut, rattling the panels and windows and disturbing our sleep. The route lay below the massive walls of Balfour's east face, with much avalanche debris in evidence and a number of open crevasses to edge around. For the first and only time since we had left the Columbia we roped up. Once we reached 9,860-foot Balfour High Col we unroped to speed down the Waputik Icefield before traversing back up in the hot sun to the col with the Bath Glacier.

We had intended camping there but arrived so early that we continued on to the traverse of the long, thin Bath Glacier under the corniced cliffs of Mount Daly. Again, because of the narrowness of the glacier in places, we had to cross avalanche run-outs, and now it was later in the day and the hot sun had been blazing down for hours. There was an eerie, unsafe feeling, and we skied well apart. I arrived at one tiny col to hear Todd say, "Did you see that avalanche?" I hadn't. Thankfully. It had come down just behind me. We tiptoed on, at one point crossing a 200-foot-long creaking and soft steep slope above a steeper slope and then a sheer drop that, had it avalanched, would have precipitated us many hundreds of feet down into the forests beside Bath Creek. Eventually we reached safety and the last final steep slopes to the col with the cirque east of Paget Peak.

Cresting the ridge we looked down to the partially snow-free terrain leading down to the forests and the highway. A day later we were in a café beside the road. We had exorcised the Columbia with this very successful Wapta Traverse, and our tour was over. It had, in the end, been a great ski adventure.

Further Reading

Following is a selection of books on skiing, winter camping, and related subjects that I have found inspiring or informative.

Axcell, Claudia, Diana Cooke, and Vikki Kinmont. *Simple Foods for the Pack*. San Francisco: Sierra Club Books, 1986. Some good outdoor recipes.

Barnett, Steve. *The Best Ski Touring in America*. San Francisco: Sierra Club Books, 1987. A mouth-watering selection of tours.

Barnett, Steve. *Cross-Country Downhill and Other Nordic Mountain Skiing Techniques*. 3d ed. Old Saybrook, Connecticut: Globe Pequot Press, 1979. One of the first books to take the subject seriously.

Bein, Vic. *Mountain Skiing*. Seattle: The Mountaineers, 1982. Mainly nordic, though alpine is covered. Some useful information; some peculiar turns as well.

Brady, Michael. *Cross-Country Ski Gear*. 2d ed. Seattle: The Mountaineers, 1987. Ideal for those who want to understand ski construction or mount their own bindings.

Cinnamon, Jerry. *Climbing Rock and Ice: Learning the Vertical Dance*. Camden, Maine: Ragged Mountain Press, 1994. Technical climbing information.

Cliff, Peter. *Ski Mountaineering*. Old Saybrook, Connecticut: Globe Pequot Press, 1987. Aimed at the alpine ski tourer, but has some useful information and tempting routes for the nordic skier.

Daffern, Tony. *Avalanche Safety for Skiers and Climbers*. Seattle: Rocky Mountain Books, 1983. Readable and comprehensive. Worth careful study.

English, Brad. *Total Telemarking.* Crested Butte, Colorado: East River Publishing Company, 1984. A curious book mixing history with advice and stories of adventures.

Fredston, Jill A., and Doug Fesler. *Snow Sense: A Guide to Evaluating Snow Avalanche Hazard.* Rev. ed. Anchorage: Alaska Department of Natural Resources, 1985. Small pack-size booklet.

Gillette, Ned, and John Dostal. *Cross-Country Skiing.* 3d ed. Seattle: The Mountaineers, 1988. A good introduction to all aspects of nordic skiing technique. Entertaining and instructive.

Graydon, Don, ed. *Mountaineering: The Freedom of the Hills.* 5th ed. Seattle: The Mountaineers, 1992. Comprehensive and authoritative mountaineering handbook.

Gullion, Laurie. *Nordic Skiing: Steps to Success.* Champaign, Illinois: Human Kinetics Publishers, 1993. A progressive series of technique sequences for self-directed learning.

Hall, William. *Cross-Country Skiing Right.* San Francisco: Harper & Row, 1985. An instructor's manual with many useful exercises.

Ilg, Steve. *The Outdoor Athlete: Total Training for Outdoor Performance.* Evergreen, Colorado: Cordillera Press, 1989. Contains exercise programs for nordic skiing.

Kleppen, Halvor. *Telemark Skiing: Norway's Gift to the World.* Oslo: Det Norske Samlaget, 1986. An interesting history of telemark and cross-country skiing from a Norwegian perspective.

Kunelius, Rick, and Dave Biederman. *Ski Trails in the Canadian Rockies.* Banff: Summerthought, 1981. A good selection of routes from low-level cut tracks to glacier expeditions.

LaChapelle, E. R. *ABC of Avalanche Safety.* 2d ed. Seattle: The Mountaineers, 1985. Small enough for the pack or pocket.

Lennon, Peter. *Scandinavian Mountains.* Reading, England: West Col, 1987. A general guide to the area, with much useful information for the ski tourer.

Miller, Dorcas S. *Good Food for Camp and Trail. All-Natural Recipes for Delicious Meals Outdoors.* Boulder, Colorado: Pruett Publishing Company, 1993. Much useful information on nutrition and food types as well as details of freeze-dried meals and some tasty recipes.

Parker, Paul. *Free-Heel Skiing: The Secrets of Telemark and Parallel Techniques—In All Conditions.* Chelsea, Vermont: Chelsea Green

Publishing, 1988. The best book on nordic downhill techniques.

Patterson, R. M. *Dangerous River*. Chelsea, Vermont: Chelsea Green Publishing, 1992. Usually thought of as a canoeing book, but contains an exciting account of winter camping and sledging in the Mackenzie Mountains in the 1930s.

Prater, Gene. *Snowshoeing*. 3d ed. Seattle: The Mountaineers, 1988. *The* book on the alternative to skis.

Rowell, Galen. *High and Wild: Essays on Wilderness Adventure*. 2d ed. San Francisco: Lexikos, 1983. Contains stories of ski tours in the White Mountains, in the Ruby Mountains, around Denali, and in the Karakorum.

Selters, Andy. *Glacier Travel and Crevasse Rescue*. Seattle: The Mountaineers, 1990. Essential reading for glacier skiing.

Sheridan, Guy. *Tales of a Cross-Country Skier*. Sparkford, England: Oxford Illustrated Press, 1987. Stories of tours in the Himalayas, the Yukon, Iceland, and more.

Steele, Peter. *Medical Handbook for Mountaineers*. London: Constable, 1988. Useful reference work.

Steger, Will, with Paul Schurke. *North to the Pole*. New York: Ballantine Books, 1987. An exciting adventure story and much information on camping techniques in subzero temperatures.

Tejades-Flores, Lito. *Backcountry Skiing*. San Francisco: Sierra Club Books, 1981. Covers both alpine and nordic skiing.

Townsend, Chris. *The Backpacker's Handbook*. Camden, Maine: Ragged Mountain Press, 1993. Comprehensive guide to wilderness camping.

Watters, Ron. *Ski Camping*. San Francisco: Chronicle Books, 1979. Instructional book based on a trip through the Rocky Mountains in Idaho. Nice photographs.

Wilkerson, James A., ed. *Medicine for Mountaineering*. 4th ed. Seattle: The Mountaineers, 1985. Useful reference work.

Equipment Checklist

What gear you need for a specific tour obviously depends on the length of the tour, the nature of the terrain, the type of shelter you plan on using, the time of year, and other factors. Keeping gear to a minimum keeps the weight down, but there are always some items you can't do without (skis spring to mind!). The following is a comprehensive list of all the gear you might need at one time or another, though you would never carry it all on one tour. I use such a master list to make individual lists for each tour. That way I am unlikely to forget anything.

Packs and Sleds

Pack
Pulk
Hip pack

Ski Gear

Skis, bindings, and
   safety straps
Poles
Skins
Wax kit:
   grip waxes
   glide/paraffin wax
   cork
   plastic scraper
   thermometer

rag soaked in wax
   remover

Footwear

Ski boots
Gaiters
Insulated bootees
Hut shoes or slippers
Socks

Clothing

Lightweight base-layer
   top (synthetic,
   wool, or silk)
Lightweight base-layer
   bottoms (synthetic,

wool, or silk)
Medium or
   heavyweight base-
   layer top (synthetic,
   wool, or silk)
Medium or
   heavyweight base-
   layer bottoms
   (synthetic, wool, or
   silk)
Pile/fleece top or wool
   sweater
Trousers, knickers, or
   bibs
Down- or synthetic-
   filled top or
   windproof
   pile/fleece top
Vapor barrier suit

Windproof top
Rain jacket
Rain pants
Warm headwear (2)
Sun hat
Headover/neck gaiter
Liner gloves
Wool or pile gloves or
  mitts
Windproof overmitts
Insulated ski gloves
Bandanna

Shelter

Tent, with poles and
  stakes
Bivouac bag
Tarp
Sleeping bag
Vapor barrier liner
Insulating mat

Kitchen

Stove
Wind shield
Fuel
Fuel bottles or
  cartridges
Insulation pad for
  stove
Pans
Mug
Plate and bowl
Spoon
Pot lifter
Pot scrubber
Insulated flask
Collapsible water
  container—large
Water bottle(s)
Matches and lighter
Plastic bags
Food

Repair Kit

Needles and thread
Sticky-backed ripstop
  nylon sheets
Duct tape
Strong wire
Sheet metal for pole
  repair
Short length of wood
  for pole repair
Epoxy glue
Wire wool
Cross-head
  screwdriver
Vise-Grip
Plastic ski tip
Spare cable
Spare screws for
  bindings
Spare pole basket and
  tip
Sandpaper
Hose clamps
C-clamps
Stove maintenance
  kit and jet pricker
Self-inflating-mat
  repair kit
Swiss Army knife or
  Leatherman tool
Nylon cord

Light

Headlamp and spare
  bulb and batteries
Candles
Candle lantern
Gas lantern

Emergency and Safety

Snow shovel
Whistle
First-aid kit

Waterproof matches
Flares
Strobe flasher
Avalanche beacon
Snow saw
Ice ax
Crampons
Rope
Climbing harness
Slings and carabiners
Prussik loops/jumars
  (for crevasse
  rescues)
Navigation
Maps
Compass
Map case
Altimeter
Guidebook
Watch

Health and Hygiene

Sunglasses
Ski goggles
Sunscreen
Lip salve
Toilet paper, in plastic
  bag with matches
Wash kit

Keeping Records

Notebook, pens, and
  pencil
Camera, lenses, and
  film

Entertainment

Books
Cards
Games
Radio
Personal cassette
  player

Useful Addresses

Mail-Order Catalogs

Campmor, 810 Route 17 North, Paramus, NJ 07653-0999

Early Winters, P.O. Box 4333, Portland, OR 97208-4333

L. L. Bean, Freeport, ME 04033-0001

REI, P.O. Box 88125, Seattle, WA 98138-0125

Mail-Order Food

Alpineaire, P.O. Box 926, Nevada City, CA 95959. *Alpineaire lightweight dried meals are additive free and delicious, the best I've eaten.*

Bear Valley, Intermountain Trading Company, P.O. Box 6157, Albany, CA 94706-0157. *Makers of delicious high-calorie, nutritious, lightweight MealPack bars.*

Indiana Camp Supply, P.O. Box 2166, Loveland, CO 80539

Trail Foods, P.O. Box 9309-B, N. Hollywood, CA 91609-1309

The above two companies can supply a wide variety of foods.

Courses

American Mountain Guides Association, P.O. Box 2128, Estes Park, CO 80517. *Contact for details on guides and outdoor schools.*

SOLO, RFD 1, Box 163, Conway, NH 03818. *Runs wilderness first-aid courses.*

Wilderness Medical Associates, RFD 2, Box 890, Bryant Pond, ME 04219. *Runs wilderness first-aid courses.*

Wilderness Medicine Institute, P.O. Box 9, Pitkin, CO 81241. *Runs wilderness first-aid courses.*

Magazines

Backpacker, Rodale Press, 33 E. Minor St., Emmaus, PA 13098-0099. *Occasional coverage of wilderness skiing, good gear reviews.*

Couloir, Couloir Publications, 6438 Penn St., Suite A, Moorparle, CA 93210

Cross-Country Skier, P.O. Box 576, Mt. Morris, IL 61054. *The only nordic-ski magazine, covering everything from groomed-track skiing to backcountry. Good for information on the latest equipment.*

Explore, Suite 410, 310-14 St. N.W., Calgary, Alberta, T2N 2A1, Canada. *Occasional ski-touring features.*

Outside, 1165 N. Clark St., Chicago, IL 60610. *Occasional ski-touring features and gear reviews.*

Overseas Gear

Craghoppers, Bradford Road, Birstall, Batley, West Yorkshire, WF17 9DH, England. *Makers of superb liner-to-drop shell clothing, the best I have found for winter use.*

Hilleberg AB, S-840 43 Hackas, Sweden. *Makers of superb tunnel tents, designed for winter mountain use.*

Snowsled, Street Farm Workshops, Doughton, Tetbury, Gloucestershire, GL8 8TP, England. *Sleds and pulks of all sizes, including the lightweight Trail Pulk.*

Winter Photography

Since many ski tourers like to have a photographic record of their adventures, a few notes on winter photography may be useful.

Equipment needs to be robust and simple. Batteries don't last long in the cold, so if your camera is dependent on them, carry plenty of spares. You will often need to take photographs with gloves or mitts on, so cameras with large chunky controls are useful. Tiny buttons and dials can be very difficult to work with numb fingers and impossible with mitts on. I use Nikon cameras, which have easy-to-use controls. The manual Nikon FM2 uses batteries only for the exposure meter and is ideal for winter use. My other camera, a Nikon N8008, depends on batteries, but it has always worked fine in the cold, even in temperatures as low as –20°F. It does rocket through batteries, so if I carry only one camera, it is the FM2. In extreme cold I don't take my cameras out of their padded cases except when I am actually taking photographs.

Zoom lenses are useful when touring, both for their light weight and for composition. I carry 28–70 and 70–210 zooms plus a wide-angle 24mm lens for landscapes.

Keeping camera gear in the pack limits the number of photographs I take, so in all but the worst weather I keep a camera and lens slung across my body. To protect gear from blizzards, spindrift, and falls, I carry my cameras in padded pouches. There are many available, such as those made by Lowe, Tamrac, or Sundog. I use Camera Care Systems pouches and have never yet damaged a camera on a tour.

Beware of taking your camera out of its case inside a warm hut or tent; moisture vapor will condense on it if you do. External dampness can be wiped off, but it may also form inside the lens. If it does, removing the lens from the camera and holding it over (not too close!) a heat source such as a woodstove is the quickest way to dry it. Padded cases insulate your camera, so lenses will be fine as long as you don't open the case until it has been inside for a considerable time (overnight at least).

A few filters are useful. I always keep skylights on my lenses and carry a polarizer for darkening blue skies and enhancing colors, and an orange filter for bringing out clouds when using black-and-white film.

I handhold the camera for most skiing shots, but sometimes I carry a lightweight tripod for evening and early-morning pictures. I also have a tiny ballhead that can be clamped onto a ski pole for greater steadiness.

The light in winter is usually bright enough for slow and medium films. The pictures in this book were taken over a number of years and on different films; Kodachrome 64, Fujichrome 100 and 50, and my current favorite Fujichrome Velvia for color, and Ilford FP4+, Agfapan APX 100, and Fuji Neopan 400 for black and white. If a faster film is needed, films can be uprated. I spent one New Year far enough north in Norway for the sun never to climb above the trees. To enable me to take handheld pictures, I uprated Fujichrome 100 to ISO 200. The results were quite satisfactory, though on subsequent trips at that time of year I have carried a fast film, Ektachrome 400HC. Most print films have a greater latitude than slide films and can produce adequate results if underexposed.

The two biggest problems people seem to have with snow photography are making snow white rather than gray and avoiding turning people into silhouettes. Gray snow and black figures result when the exposure meter is fooled by the snow into "thinking" the whole scene is much brighter than it is. The solution is to take your meter reading not from the snow but directly from the subject, or else from the back of your hand held in the same light as is falling on your subject. An alternative is to let more light in by opening up a stop or so or by moving the exposure compensation dial, if your camera has one, to +1 or even +2. Some modern camera meters that average out tones are less prone to underexposing snow scenes than others. Overall, it is safer to take readings off your hand. And for important shots, bracket—take pictures at readings a stop above and a stop below the one you first use.

Glossary

Skiing and wilderness camping have distinct vocabularies for both technique and equipment. Mountain scenery has its own special terminology, too. Below you'll find brief definitions of common terms. Some are described in this book; others simply are terms you are likely to hear in conversations with other skiers or that may appear in other publications on cross-country skiing and wilderness camping.

ABS. Trade name for a strong plastic used in ski and binding construction.

Alpine Skiing. Downhill skiing with equipment that locks the heel down on the ski.

Altimeter. Instrument measuring barometric pressure that can be used for checking altitude or weather changes.

Angulation. Bending the body so that the legs and torso lean in different directions—used in downhill techniques.

Anticipation. Twisting the upper body in the direction of the next turn when linking downhill turns so that the legs follow the body, making starting the turn easier.

Arete. Narrow snow or rock ridge.

Aspect of Slope. The direction a slope faces; useful for navigation.

Avalanche. Snow or ice slide.

Backcountry Skiing. Skiing in undeveloped areas without prepared tracks or trails.

Bail. Adjustable clamp on three-pin binding that holds boot in place.

Balling Up. Buildup of snow under the ski or boot that impedes glide.

Banking. Leaning into a turn.

Base. 1: Part of ski in touch with the snow. 2: Part of snowpack next to the ground.

Base Preparation. Waxing and cleaning the ski base.

Base Wax. Wax used to keep base of ski in good condition.

Basic Stance. Standing with the knees flexed, hands slightly forward and weight over the balls of your feet.

Basket. Disc above point of ski pole to prevent pole from sinking into snow.

Bibs. Pants with high front and back, and shoulder straps.

Binding. Mechanical device mounted on ski for attaching boot.

Binding-flex. Boot-binding system in which binding flexes rather than boot.

Bivouac (Bivy). To spend a night out in the wilderness without a tent or snow shelter—may be planned or unintended.

Bivouac (Bivy) Bag. Waterproof cover for sleeping bag; used when bivouacking.

Boot-flex. Boot-binding system in which boot sole flexes rather than binding.

Box. Ski construction in which four load-bearing walls form a box enclosing the core.

Cable Binding. Binding in which an adjustable cable wraps round the lower boot—may be combined with a three-pin binding or a simple toe plate.

Calorie. Unit of heat output used as a measure of energy value of food and body energy expended.

Camber. The sprung curve of the ski base from tip to tail.

Camber Stiffness. Force needed to flatten ski onto snow.

Carabiner. Climbers' metal snap-link for attaching ropes to harnesses and slings.

Carbon Fiber. Strong, lightweight fiber used in ski poles, ski construction, and internal-frame packs.

Carving. Turning downhill on the edges of skis with minimal skidding.

Cemented Sole. Boot construction in which sole is glued and heat-bonded to uppers.

Chlorofiber. A PVC material used in base-layer clothing.

Christie. Abbreviation of Christiania, the former name of Norway's capital, Oslo, and an outdated name for parallel turns and stem turns (*stem christie*).

Classical. Traditional cross-country skiing style using the diagonal stride.

Col. A mountain pass.

Compression. Absorbing bumps by flexing the legs.

Conduction. Transfer of heat by direct contact.

Contact Length. Part of ski base touching snow when ski is unweighted.

Contour Line. Line on topographic map linking areas of equal height.

Convection. Transfer of heat by circulation of air.

Core. Center of ski.

Cork. Block of synthetic or natural material used for rubbing wax onto ski.

Corn. Snow with large, coarse grains formed after several freeze-thaw cycles and therefore common in spring.

Cornice. Wind-formed overhanging lip of snow on the lee side of ridges and cliffs. Dangerous as it may be invisible from above but can break off under weight of skier. Can also collapse and cause avalanche on slope below.

Counter. Stiff material inserted between outer and inner layer of the toe and heel of a boot; gives extra stiffness and support.

Counter-rotation. Pivoting the torso in opposite direction to legs in preparation for next turn when skiing downhill.

Crampons. A metal device with spikes that fits over a boot sole and provides grip when crossing ice or hard snow. Some crampons are rigid while others flex with the boot sole.

Crevasse. Split in a glacier; may be open (visible) or covered (invisible).

Crud. Difficult snow to ski, usually with a broken surface and a mixture of crust, ice, and soft snow.

Crust. Thin layer of crisp snow over softer snow that may or may not support your weight; caused by wind, freeze-thaw cycles, or sleet over snow.

Cup Crystals. Also called *depth hoar*; large crystals in the snowpack indicative of avalanche danger.

Damping. The degree to which a ski reduces vibrations.

Depth Hoar. Cup-shaped crystals created by recrystallization of water vapor that has risen through the snowpack after sublimation from crystals lower down. This process takes several weeks and requires a steep temperature gradient in the snowpack, so long cold spells are needed before depth hoar becomes a problem.

Diagonal Stride. The traditional way of skiing on the flat by sliding directly forward on one ski and then the other with alternate leg and arm movements.

Diagonal V. A skating technique for uphill skiing.

Direct Descent. Skiing straight down a slope with no turns.

Double Camber. A stiff camber found in classic cross-country skis; makes for good glide on the flat.

Double Poling. Using both arms to plant poles and propel skis that are kept parallel forward.

Downhill Turning. Skiing downhill while making turns across the fall line.

Down-unweighting. Compressing the legs and sinking down to unweight the skis so they can be turned.

Duvet Clothing. Down-filled clothing.

Ears. Side pieces of the toe piece of a binding.

Edge. Bottom outside edge of ski.

Edge Change. Tilting the skis from one set of edges to the other.

Edge Set. Braking quickly by putting the skis on their uphill edges when crossing the fall line.

Edging. Tipping the skis onto their edges to maintain stability on a slope.

Epoxy. A resin-based glue.

EVA (Ethyl Vinyl Acetate). Flexible synthetic material used for ski-pole baskets, foam mats, and shoe insoles.

Evaporation. Conversion of water to vapor by heat.

Exposure. Feeling of height; also an outdated name for hypothermia.

Extension. Straightening the legs and body.

Fall Line. The way a snowball would roll, straight down a slope.

Fishscale. Trademark name for base pattern of waxless ski.

Flat Ski. Ski held flat on the snow.

Fleece. Brushed synthetic fabric, usually polyester; used for warm clothing and boot linings.

Flex. How much a ski will bend.

Free Skating. A skating technique done without poles.

Gaiter. Lower-leg covering used to keep snow out of boots and to add insulation.

Garlands. A pattern of consecutive downhill turns to the hill in the same direction; used as a learning technique.

Glacier. Mass of snow and ice sliding slowly downhill.

Glide. Sliding of a ski on snow.

Glider. Wax used on tip and tail of ski base to aid glide.

Gore-Tex. Trademark for a waterproof "breathable" microporous membrane; used in shell clothing, bivy bags, tents, and boot linings.

Granular Snow. Snow with large, coarse crystals.

Graupel. Round ice crystals that can form an unstable layer in the snowpack, increasing avalanche danger.

Grip. 1: Ski pole handle. 2: How well a ski adheres to the snow.

Groove. 1: Long, shallow indentation in ski base that aids ski in following a track. 2: Slot in boot heel for holding a cable.

Hail. Precipitation in the form of small balls or lumps, usually consisting of concentric layers of clear ice and compact snow.

Half Plow. Sliding one ski out at an angle to act as a brake while keeping the other one pointing downhill.

Hanging Glacier. Small glacier in hanging valley that sits high on the side of a steep valley; stonefall and avalanches from these can be a danger to skiers below.

Hard Wax. Grip wax for cold weather.

Heel Plate. Small plate, usually with serrated upper edges, fitted to ski under boot heel; provided with bindings.

Herringbone. Method of climbing slopes with skis spread in a V; named for pattern this technique leaves in the snow.

Hickory. A type of wood used in ski construction.

Hockey Stop. Stopping quickly with an abrupt parallel turn across a hill.

Hydrophilic. Water attracting; hydrophilic coatings and membranes are waterproof because they are solid. They allow water vapor—body moisture—to pass through to the outside along chains of hydrophilic molecules, minimizing condensation.

Hypothermia. Life-threatening chilling of the body due to wind, cold, and wetness.

Icefall. Steep, potentially dangerous part of glacier with many crevasses and seracs.

Injection Molding. Method of attaching sole to boot without stitching.

Insole. Innermost sole in a boot.

Jump Turn. Jumping the skis out of the snow while you are supported by the poles and turning in the air; useful for skiing breakable crust.

Kick. Backward-thrust of toe to provide forward glide in diagonal striding.

Kicker. Grip wax applied to midsection of ski.

Kick and Glide. Alternative name for diagonal stride.

Kick Turn. Method of turning when stationary by lifting one ski and placing it in the opposite direction, then swinging the other ski around.

Klister. Extremely sticky grip wax for warm, wet, and old metamorphosed snow.

Klister Wax. Sticky wax—between klister and hard wax in consistency; used in temperatures around freezing.

Langlauf. German term for track skiing.

Light Touring. Skiing on easy terrain out of tracks.

Loipe. A set track.

Lycra. Trade name for stretchy fabric.

Marathon Skate. Skating technique for use in tracks.

Moguls. Bumps formed by skiers repeatedly turning on the same spot on a prepared downhill trail.

Moraine. Long heap of stones and gravel pushed out or left by a glacier.

Névé. Firm, well-consolidated snow.

New Nordic Norm Backcountry (NNNBC). Beefed-up version of Rottefella's flex binding system for touring.

Nonwax Ski. *See* Waxless Ski.

Offset Edges. Metal edges that protrude from the sides of a ski for ease of sharpening.

Open Turn. A parallel turn with a wide stance.

Outrigger. Extending one ski outward as a support while turning on the other ski.

Overturning. Turning too far into the slope so that momentum is lost.

Parallel Turn. Downhill turn made with the skis parallel throughout.

Pattern Base. Waxless ski base.

Pile. Synthetic, fuzzy fabric used for warm clothing and sleeping bags.

Pin Binding. Binding with three short protrusions in toe plate that mate with holes in sole of boot.

Piste. A prepared downhill ski run.

Pivot Point. Location on binding where binding or boot hinges to allow heel lift.

Pole Plant. Touching the snow with a pole to trigger a turn, or driving the pole into the snow to push forward.

Poling. Using poles to help propel oneself.

Polyester. Synthetic material used in combination with fiberglass in ski-pole shafts and pulks and as a fabric for base-layer garments and warmwear and, usually in combination with cotton, windproof outerwear.

Polypropylene. Synthetic material used for ski bases and "wicking" base-layer clothing.

Polyurethane (PU). Synthetic material used as a foam in boot soles and ski cores, and as a waterproof coating.

Polyvinyl Chloride (PVC). Synthetic material (sold under various names) used in base-layer clothing and as a foam core in skis.

Powder. Light, dry, uncompacted snow that falls in cold temperatures.

Pozi-Drive. Trade name for screwdrivers and screws used to mount bindings.

Pressure. Putting your weight onto a ski.

P-tex. Trade name for a type of ski-base material.

Pulk. Sledge that runs directly on snow without runners.

Radiation. Heat transfer (loss) between bodies through space. Radiated heat passes from one body to another through space without heating that space.

Railed. Ski base on which the edge is higher than the center.

Randonnee. French term for mountain ski touring on alpine skis.

Reverse Camber. The shape a ski forms when pressured strongly; the smoother the curve formed, the easier a ski will turn.

Rime. Frost feathers or snow crust built up on windward sides of objects such as boulders; formed by supercooled fog or cloud.

Rip-Stop. Thin nylon fabric with thicker threads at regular intervals that prevent tears from spreading; used for shell clothing, down-clothing outers, tent flysheets, and sleeping-bag outers.

Roller Blades. Skates with wheels instead of blades; used for training.

Roller Skis. Short boards with wheels underneath; used for training.

Salomon Nordic System (SNS). Flex binding system for racing and in-track skiing.

Sastrugi. Ridges of snow formed by the wind.

Schuss. Gliding straight down a slope with no turns.

Scraper. Flat plastic or metal tool the edge of which is used to remove old ski wax or ice buildup.

Self-arrest. Method of stopping a slide with an ice ax or a ski pole.

Serac. A large, usually unstable, tower or pillar of ice or snow found in icefalls.

Set Track. Machine-cut track.

Shank. Stiffening plate, usually metal, in boot sole.

Short-Swings. Short-radius parallel turns, useful for narrow gullies or very steep slopes, with focus on unweighting.

Shoulder. Widest part of ski.

Shovel. The section of the ski from the shoulder to the tip.

Side-cut. Curve on side of ski due to ski being wider at tip and tail than at waist; aids turning.

Sideslip. Controlled method of letting skis slip sideways down a slope, either directly or at an angle, by releasing edges.

Sidestepping. Moving uphill, downhill, or on the flat by stepping the skis sideways.

Side Walls. Sides of a ski.

Single Camber. A ski with an even flex from tip to tail.

Skate Turning. Using one or more skates to turn on the flat or downhill.

Skating. Moving on the flat with the skis in the form of a V—a technique akin to ice skating.

Skidding. Downward slipping of the skis during a turn.

Skins. Strips of synthetic material stuck to ski bases to give grip during ascents.

Sliding. Moving forward or backward without skidding.

Snow Bridge. Bridge of snow over a stream or crevasse.

Snowplow. Method of braking or controlling speed on descent by forming an inverted V with the skis.

Snowplow Turn. Turning while in the snowplow position by putting weight onto one ski.

Split Leather. Inside of cowhide split into sheets; used for boot uppers.

Star Turn. Turning full circle on the flat by linked step turns.

Steering. Using a twisting motion of the legs and feet to turn skis; an integral part of most downhill turns.

Stem Christie. A turn that begins as a stem turn but finishes in a parallel position (also see *Christie*).

Stem Turn. Downhill turn achieved by sliding—*stemming*—or stepping one ski out at an angle to the other so it points in the direction of the turn, then putting weight on it.

Step-Telemark. Lifting one ski out into the telemark position.

Step Turn. Method of turning on the flat or downhill by picking up—stepping—each ski in turn and placing it in the new direction.

Straight Run. Descending straight down a slope with no turns.

Stride. Gliding on a ski by sliding it forward and then weighting it.

Stride Length. The distance between one stride and the next.

Swing to the Hill. *See* Hockey Stop.

Swing Weight. Balance of ski pole.

Sympatex. Trade name for a waterproof, breathable, hydrophilic membrane used in shell clothing and boot linings.

Tacking. Climbing uphill in a series of traverses linked by half kick turns.

Tail. Rear end of a ski.

Telemark. A maneuver where both knees are bent and one ski is advanced; used for turning downhill and for fore-and-aft stability when skiing over bumpy terrain. Named after the region of Norway where it was invented.

Thinsulate. Trade name for polypropylene/polyester microfiber insulation used in clothing, gaiters, and boot linings.

Three-Pin Bindings. *See* Pin Bindings.

Tip. 1: Front of ski. 2: Spike of ski pole or ice ax.

Toe Binding. Binding that clamps boot welt to ski at the toe.

Toe Insert. Metal plate in toe of boot to reinforce flex point and pin holes.

Tongue. Leather strip under boot laces that keeps out snow and debris.

Top-Grain Leather. Outside of cowhide; the most waterproof and durable leather for boots.

Top Sheet. Upper surface of ski.

Torsional Stiffness. How well a ski resists twisting along its axis.

Track. Track made by skiers.

Tracking. Following a straight line.

Track Setter. Sledgelike machine, towed by a snowmobile, that cuts tracks.

Track Skis. Skis for use in cut tracks.

Transition Snow. Snow at a temperature around the freezing point.

Traversing. Skiing across a slope or up or down it at an angle to the fall line.

Tuck. Crouching low when downhill running to minimize wind resistance (and look good!).

Unweighting. Taking your weight off a ski.

Uphill Ski. The ski that is uphill during a traverse.

Uphill Turning. Turning away from the fall line and into a hill to decrease speed.

Up-unweighting. Rising up to unweight the skis before turning.

Verglas. Clear coating of ice on rocks and other objects, formed by water cooling rapidly; usually very slippery.

Vibram. Trade name for heavy-duty lugged sole commonly found on telemark/backcountry touring boots.

V1-V2. Types of skating techniques, the first combining double poling with every other skating step; the second, double poling with every skating step. Also known as two-skating and one-skating.

Waist. The narrowest part of a ski.

Waxable Skis. Skis with bases designed to be waxed for grip and glide.

Waxing Iron. Iron for melting wax onto skis and then smoothing it out.

Waxing Torch. Small blowtorch used for waxing.

Waxless Skis. Skis with pattern on base to provide grip and glide.

Wax Pocket. Midsection of stiff-cambered skis; designed to hold wax.

Wax Remover. Solvent for dissolving wax on ski base.

Wax Zone. Area in center of ski that should be grip-waxed.

Wedge. Another name for the snowplow position.

Weight Shift. Moving your body weight from one ski to the other;

also known as weight transfer.

Whiteout Conditions. Where wind-blown snow makes for poor visibility and difficulty distinguishing the ground from the sky.

Wicking. Transporting of moisture through a fabric away from the body; a required property of garments worn next to the skin.

Windchill. The cooling effect of wind on bare skin.

Windslab. Layer of snow formed by wind on lee side of slopes; a cause of avalanches.

XCD. Short for cross-country downhill skiing.

Index